Principles of Safety
in Physical Education and Sport

Neil J. Dougherty IV, Editor
Rutgers University

sponsored by the
National Association for
Sport and Physical Education

an association of the
American Alliance for Health, Physical
Education, Recreation, and Dance

Purposes of the American Alliance for Health, Physical Education, Recreation, and Dance

The American Alliance is an educational organization, structured for the purposes of supporting, encouraging, and providing assistance to member groups and their personnel throughout the nation as they seek to initiate, develop, and conduct programs in health, leisure, and movement-related activities for the enrichment of human life.

Alliance objectives include:

1. Professional growth and development—to support, encourage, and provide guidance in the development and conduct of programs in health, leisure, and movement-related activities which are based on the needs, interests, and inherent capacities of the individual in today's society.

2. Communication—to facilitate public and professional understanding and appreciation of the importance and value of health, leisure, and movement-related activities as they contribute toward human well-being.

3. Research—to encourage and facilitate research which will enrich the depth and scope of health, leisure, and movement-related activities; and to disseminate the findings to the profession and other interested and concerned publics.

4. Standards and guidelines—to further the continuous development and evaluation of standards within the profession for personnel and programs in health, leisure, and movement-related activities.

5. Public affairs—to coordinate and administer a planned program of professional, public, and governmental relations that will improve education in areas of health, leisure, and movement-related activities.

6. To conduct such other activities as shall be approved by the Board of Governors and the Alliance Assembly, provided that the Alliance shall not engage in any activity which would be inconsistent with the status of an educational and charitable organization as defined in Section 501 (c) (3) of the Internal Revenue Code of 1954 or any successor provision thereto, and none of the said purposes shall at any time be deemed or construed to be purposes other than the public benefit purposes and objectives consistent with such educational and charitable status.

Bylaws, Article III

Table of Contents

Preface

In 1983 the National Association for Sport and Physical Education published *Physical Education and Sport for the Secondary School Student*. This completely updated and revised edition of the earlier *Physical Education for High School Students* met with immediate and continued success. Although designed primarily for use as a student textbook, the quality and accuracy of the content as well as the clear and direct application of teaching and learning progressions has led to its widespread acceptance as a teaching guide as well.

The same quality of authorship and validity of content which led to the broad acceptance of *Physical Education and Sport for the Secondary School Student* has led to another use which although not planned for, probably could have been anticipated. It is frequently introduced as evidence either supporting or condemning the actions of a teacher who is being sued for an accidental injury which arose in his/her class. The everpresent threat of litigation in connection with student injuries; the inescapable fact that the guidelines and recommendations of the Association are frequently considered in assessing potential liability and; most importantly, the desire to promote the safest programs possible have, therefore, precipitated the development of *Principles of Safety in Physical Education and Sport*.

This text is designed to provide the professional with a straightforward and complete resource of those factors which must be considered in the provision of safe units of instruction in the commonly taught sports and activities. Using a format which relies heavily on checklists and outlines, the authors have provided the essential information in a manner which facilitates its use in the development of detailed unit and lesson plans as well as for quick pre-class safety checks.

It is the intention of the National Association for Sport and Physical Education that this book, like *Physical Education and Sport for the Secondary School Student*, will assist the teacher in the development and implementation of a safe and well balanced program of activities from which today's youth can benefit throughout their lifetime.

Neil J. Dougherty IV
Editor

Authors

The Injury Problem
David A. Feigley
Rutgers University
New Brunswick, NJ

Legal Responsibility for Safety
Neil J. Dougherty
Rutgers University
New Brunswick, NJ

Administration of Safety
Patricia E. Barry
Montgomery County Public Schools
Rockville, MD

First Aid and Sport Safety Policies
Phil Hostler
East Brunswick High School
East Brunswick, NJ

Archery
Claire Chamberlain
University of Lowell
Lowell, MA

Basketball
James Bryant
San Jose State University
San Jose, CA

Coed Flag Football
Maryann Domitrovitz
Pennsylvania State University
University Park, PA

Dance
Lynne Fitzgerald
Morehead State University
Morehead, KY

Field Hockey
Barbara Belt
John F. Kennedy High School
Silver Spring, MD

Fitness/Weight Training
Clair Jennett
San Jose State University
San Jose, CA

Golf
DeDe Owens
University of Virginia
Charlottesville, VA

Orienteering
Arthur Hugglestone
Smith Environmental Education Center
Rockville, MD

Racquet Sports
John P. Smyth
The Citadel
Charleston, SC

Self-Defense
Kenneth Tillman
Trenton State College
Trenton, NJ

Soccer
John F. Fellenbaum, Jr.
McCaskey High School
Lancaster, PA

Softball
Diane Bonanno
Rutgers University
New Brunswick, NJ

Sonia Regalado & Patricia Peters
East Brunswick High School
East Brunswick, NJ

Swimming
Ralph Johnson
Indiana University
Indiana, PA

Track and Field
LeRoy T. Walker
North Carolina Central University
Durham, NC

Tumbling
Diane Bonanno
Rutgers University
New Brunswick, NJ

Volleyball
Barbara Viera
University of Delaware
Newark, DE

Wrestling
Douglas Parker
Springfield College
Springfield, MA

CHAPTER 1

The Injury Problem

DAVID A. FEIGLEY

Rutgers University
New Brunswick, NJ

Accidents just happen. Or do they? While accidents and the injuries resulting from them, by definition[1], are not caused by someone's purposeful actions, a moment's reflection will indicate that most accidents have a clear cause-and-effect relationship between some preceding event, action, or circumstance and the accident itself. Systematic recordkeeping has frequently shown that accidents occur more regularly in some circumstances than others. Unfortunately, those causal relationships often become obvious only after the fact.

SCOPE OF THE PROBLEM

Sports injuries are only a small part of the national statistics describing preventable illness and injury. According to the National Safety Council (1984), more than 100,000 accidental deaths and approximately 9 million disabling injuries are reported annually. At an April 2, 1986 news conference, Alvin R. Tarlov, president of the Henry J. Kaiser Family Foundation, stated that, "Preventable illness and injuries claim nearly 1.3 million American lives and cost the nation more than $300 billion each year." Table 1 compares the relative rank of accidents with other major causes of death in the United States.

While sports injuries represent only a small portion of these deaths, the fact that sports fatalities are likely to occur early in the potential life span of the victim magnifies their impact on the lives of the victims and their families. Table 2 presents data from the National Electronic Injury Surveillance System (NEISS) representing reported deaths in 15 sports totaled from 1973 to 1980.

Comparisons of injury or fatality rates for the general population versus the rates for athletes are difficult to make because of the lack of information and because the data that is available has been collected using different criteria. According to the National Safety Council (1984), approximately 100,000 accidental deaths of all types are reported annually in the United States (an average of one death every five minutes!). Using an estimated population of 226.5 million (1980 census estimate), the fatality rate indicates that 441.5 people per

TABLE 1
Relative Frequency of Accidents and Other Causes of Death in the United States

Rank	Cause of Death
1	Heart Disease
2	Cancer
3	Stroke
4	Accidents
	Motor Vehicle
	Falls
	Drowning
	Fires, Burns
	Suffocation—Ingest Object
	Poisoning by solids and liquids
	Firearms
	Poisoning by gases and vapors
5	Pneumonia
6	Diabetes Mellitus
7	Chronic Liver Disease, Cirrhosis
8	Atherosclerosis
9	Suicide
10	Homicide
11	Certain Conditions Originating in Perinatal Period
12	Nephritis and nephrosis

Source: National Safety Council, *Accident Facts*, 1984, p. 8.

million die each year from accidents of all types. In baseball and softball combined, an estimated 11.5 to 13.6 million players between the ages of 5 and 14 years participate in the U.S. each year (U.S. Consumer Product Safety Commission, 1984). The National Electronic Injury Surveillance System recorded 51 total deaths between 1973 and 1983, for an average of 6.4 deaths per year in baseball and softball combined. Thus,

---

[1] Once intentional harm is assumed, the incident can no longer be defined as an accident but rather becomes classified as a crime.

TABLE 2
Sports Related Fatalities to Persons 5–14 Years of Age January 1973–December 1980

Sport	Fatalities
Baseball	40
Football	19
Golf	13
Ball Sports[a]	7
Basketball	6
Soccer	6
Trampoline	6
Wrestling	2
Ice Hockey	2
Track and Field	2
Racquet Sports	1
Tetherball	1
Lacrosse	0
Volleyball	0
Gymnastics	0
Total	105

[a]Sports for which the specific activity was not specified.
Source: U.S. Consumer Product Safety Commission/Epidemiology, Division of Hazard Analysis, 1981

TABLE 3
Estimated, Sports-Related, Medically Attended Injuries to Persons 5–14 Years of Age During the Calendar Year 1980

Sport	Medically Attended Injuries
Football	499,400
Baseball	359,400
Basketball	295,300
Gymnastics	209,200
Ball Sports	133,200
Soccer	107,400
Wrestling	55,100
Volleyball	46,500
Ice Hockey	28,900
Track and Field	22,600
Racquet Sports	17,100
Golf	11,600
Trampoline	7,200
Tetherball	5,500
Lacrosse	2,100
Total	1,800,500

[a]Sports for which the specific activity was not specified.
Source: U.S. Consumer Product Safety Commission/Epidemiology, Division of Hazard Analysis, 1981

the rate of fatalities in baseball and softball ranges from .5 to .6 deaths per million participants. While this comparison is clearly limited by the fact that the recording systems were different and the rates were compared across different age ranges (all ages for national rate vs. 5- and 14-year-olds in baseball/softball), the magnitude of the rate differences is so great that there is almost certainly a dramatically lower fatality rate for the sports of baseball and softball than for the national average. Since baseball is the most dangerous sport in terms of fatalities (See Table 2), the conclusion appears warranted that sports have a relatively low fatality rate compared to the national general population average.

Nonetheless, according to experts in epidemiology and public health, nearly two-thirds of all illnesses and injuries could be prevented. Nowhere is this fact more relevant than with sports injuries. While many assume that most sports injuries are the result of "accidents," these accidents are frequently the result of factors which lead predictably to injuries. For example, different sports have different frequencies of injury (see Table 3). Often these accidents and injuries can be traced directly to social, environmental, and behavioral factors which, if regulated, would result in dramatic reductions in deaths and injuries. The fact that injuries are often considered "accidental" or as part of the inherent risk of sports is one of the major reasons why these social, environmental, and behavioral factors remain uncontrolled and, thus, why accidents and injuries continue to occur. If such accidents and injuries were perceived as predictable results of the lack of public health and accident control policies, actions would likely be taken to reduce "accidents" in terms of both frequency and severity.

DEFINING AN ACCIDENT

All of us have undoubtedly experienced "accidents" at times throughout our lives and have a general understanding of the term. When attempts are made to measure and understand accidents within the context of the study of safety, however, the need for a specific definition becomes obvious. Definitions serve two functions: first, they provide a specific *focus* as to what is to be studied; second, they provide peripheral *boundaries* concerning what to include and what to exclude from the topic to be analyzed.

Agencies which collect data on sports injuries have a variety of definitions of sports injuries resulting partially from the fact that different agencies have different purposes for such data (e.g., knowing what injuries require treatment vs. determining the cause of such injuries) and because agencies differ in their organizational responsibility to the participating athlete (national survey systems vs. the local coaching staff).

The two major defining characteristics of accidents are that they have *unintended causes* and *undesirable effects* (Thygerson, 1986). For example, the National Safety Council defines an accident as "that occurrence in a sequence of events which usually produces unintended injury, death, or property damage" (*Accident Facts*, 1984). Thygerson (1986) points out that two frequently included subfactors defining an accident are that: a) the event is *relatively sudden* (measured in seconds or minutes); and that b) the *damage results from a form of physical energy* (e.g., mechanical, thermal, chemical). The former characteristic distinguishes accidents from chronic overuse injuries while the latter distinguishes between accidental injuries and illness and disease.

DEFINING AN INJURY

The term injury is often defined independently of accident. Haddon (1980) defined injury as "damage or trauma to the body caused by exchanges with environmental energy that are beyond the body's resilience" (page 1). Two practical considerations are often part of injury definitions. First, an injury is deemed to have occurred if the victim loses time from an activity such as work, school, or play. For example, the National Athletic Injury/Illness Reporting System (NAIRS) defines a reportable injury as "any injury/illness which causes the cessation of an athlete's customary participation throughout the *participation-day following day of onset*." Thus, time lost from practice is often used as the threshold to determine whether damage sustained by an athlete is considered severe enough to be classified as an injury. The second practical consideration is the referral to a medical professional such as a trainer, nurse, physician, or emergency staffer. Bumps, bruises, and chronic stiffness which do not necessitate a visit for medical treatment are rarely counted in injury statistics. Only if their severity prompts a formal visit to a medical professional do they typically become classified as an injury.

Within the context of sports, distinctions are often made between injuries *directly* or *indirectly* attributable to participation in a sport. Damage sustained from mechanical energy tends to be more commonly associated with injuries resulting from accidents termed "directly attributable" to sport than to other forms of energies. For example, an accident caused by being hit by a ball or bat is likely to be seen as directly attributable to sport while heat stroke caused by a lack of water while training in hot, humid conditions is more likely to be classified as an indirect sports injury.

ACCIDENTS VERSUS INJURIES

These distinctions in definitions are more than simply semantics. Safety experts, for example, often distinguish between *accident prevention* and *injury prevention*. Injury is viewed as only one of many possible outcomes of an accident. Efforts toward accident prevention are focused on education, prohibitions, and regulation while efforts toward injury control focus on the lessening of injury and a prevention of death by using rescue, safety belts, emergency medical care, helmets, and similar techniques.

DEFINING SAFETY

While the term "safety" is generally understood, its scientific meaning is often quite vague. According to Lowrance (1976), an activity is safe if its risks are deemed acceptable; and acceptability is a matter of personal and societal value judgements. Thus, what is judged "safe" varies from time to time and from situation to situation. Furthermore, Lowrance argues that what is typically measured scientifically is not safety but degree of risk. An activity is judged safe if the risks associated with that activity are judged acceptable. Stated differently, risk involves the calculation of the probability of harm—a scientific measurement. Safety involves the judgement of the acceptability of those risks—a value judgement. Thus, *risks* are something we *measure* while *safety* is something we must *judge*.

DEFINING RISK

Thygerson (1986) defines "risk" as "possible loss or the chance of a loss" (page 39). Theoretically, measuring risks is quite straightforward. Taking into consideration the population data, the exposure data, and the injury data, the calculations for determining risk are quite simple. From a practical standpoint, measuring such risks is rarely carried out because gathering the appropriate data is often quite a substantial task. There are three general methods of measuring risk: (1) relative risk methods; (2) probability of occurrence methods; and (3) relative exposure rate methods.

1. Relative risk methods. An activity or hazard is rated according to a standard which can be ranked along a dimension of more or less. For example, a boxing glove with nine ounces of padding is considered to be more risky than a glove with twelve ounces of padding. Sometimes a rating scale is adopted to reflect the approximate degree of risk. For example, in women's artistic gymnastics, athletes select skills rated from level "a" (easy) to level "d" (extremely risky).

2. Probability of occurrence. The likelihood of future injuries can be accurately estimated if records have been kept over reasonable periods of time for sizable populations which will continue the activity under similar conditions. Just as the National Safety Council can predict the number of fatalities for a given holiday period, the American Football Coaches Association Committee on Football Injuries can predict the number of football related fatalities for the upcoming season. Both groups have compiled a long history of fatality statistics which permit such prediction. If the future circumstances were changed from the situation upon which the original data were based, the estimates would differ from the actual observed fatalities. For example, if the weather changed (e.g., it rained) or a rule change were implemented (e.g., spearing was eliminated in football), the actual number of deaths or injuries would change. Table 4 reports the number of deaths directly attributable to participation for high school and collegiate football across a 25-year period. While it is clear that fatalities were already on the

TABLE 4
Direct Football Fatalities from High School and Collegiate Programs 1961–1985

5-Year Block	High School	College
1961–65	75	12
1966–70	103	12
1971–75	61	7
1976–80	44	2
1981–85	24	4

Source: *National Federation News*, National Federation of State High School Associations, June, 1986

decline, there was a decided additional drop in fatalities during the period after the 1976 rule change which eliminated spearing (i.e., making initial contact with the head).

3. *Relative exposure.* Risks may be portrayed in terms of exposure rates in order to compare different risks. For example, during the five-year period between 1959 and 1963, 820,000 youths played football and 86 deaths were recorded. During the period from 1971 to 1975, 77 deaths were reported but the exposure rate rose substantially to 1,275,000 players (Torg, 1982). Thus, the actual risk appeared to have decreased during the early 1970s (1.0×10^{-4} vs. 6.0×10^{-5} respectively for the two 5-year periods). Exposure rates can take into consideration not only the number of participants, but also the number of practices, number of hours per practice, and the number of actual sporting attempts, depending on the degree of sophistication of the measurement of exposure. An advantage of this technique of expressing risk is that different sports or different dimensions can be compared on a rate basis. For example, Reif (1981) estimates that, while the risk of death in collegiate football is one in 33,000 exposures, the risk of injury or long-term disability is as high as 1 in 18 exposures[2].

OVERUSE SYNDROME INJURIES

A relatively new category of pediatric injuries specific to organized sports programs for preadolescent and adolescent athletes has developed recently. These injuries are called overuse injuries and are the result of purposeful, repetitive training. They are clearly injuries although they are not accidental. In fact, they are clearly predictable and often endured specifically in the quest for higher levels of performance from physically immature athletes. Previously,

overuse injuries were restricted to adult activities, often in the form of bursitis and tendonitis afflicting the construction worker or the weekend tennis player. Now, they are seen with increasing regularity in highly trained children.

According to Micheli (1986), children are particularly susceptibile to these types of injuries for two reasons. First, the growing cartilage of the joint surfaces may be more susceptible to stress, especially shear stresses both in terms of single impact trauma (e.g., growth plate fractures) and repetitive microtrauma (e.g., Osgood Schlatters disease, patellofemoral stress syndrome). Second, the process of growth itself renders children more susceptible to certain injuries. As growth occurs in the bones, the muscle-tendon unit spanning the bones and the joints becomes progressively tighter with growth, particularly during growth spurts. This reduced flexibility heightens the child's chances of both single impact injuries and repetitive microtrauma because of the increased tension across the joints and growing surfaces.

UNDERSTANDING THE INJURY PROBLEM

Effective understanding and control of the injury problem in physical education and sport requires a multistep approach. Figure 1 describes a possible model for analyzing injuries in sport.

DEFINE EXISTING PROGRAMS

First, the specific programs to be analyzed must be designated. While, at first glance, this step may seem obvious, on closer inspection, a variety of complicating factors become evident. If, for example, you wish to analyze football in terms of injury occurrence, you must decide what constitutes "football." Does your study include only organized programs, or any game, formal or informal, in which the participants play football? The problems associated with collecting data from organized programs

---

[2] Exposures were based on a per year basis in which 25 days of participation per year were assumed.

are likely to differ from those encountered while collecting data from parks, playgrounds, and "sandlot" football. In addition, you must decide if you are interested in injuries both directly and indirectly attributable to the activity or sport. For example, an injury resulting from tackling is likely to be directly the result of playing football, while a stroke occurring to an athlete on the sidelines may be unrelated to the individual's participation in sport. Other injuries may be caused by a combination of factors, some direct and some indirect. Heat exhaustion may be both attributable to weather conditions and to the wearing of heavy uniforms and intense training regimens during high heat/humidity conditions.

MONITORING AND DATA COLLECTION

Once the conditions defining the sport have been specified, an analysis of injury patterns requires an accurate monitoring of the frequency, type, and severity of injuries as well as the circumstances under which they occur. Here again, the problem of definition arises. What constitutes an accident or an injury? Depending on the purpose of the monitoring institution, the definitions of injuries may differ dramatically. A coach concerned about the welfare of young athletes may define an injury as a bruise which creates discomfort. An organization concerned about medical treatment may define injury as any physical problem which requires medical treatment. A league concerned about the severity of accidental injury may define an injury as any physical problem which requires the athlete to miss a day or more of training or competition. The data collected under each of these examples may be quite different and reflect decidedly different patterns.

The collection of accident and/or injury statistics appears deceptively simple. Even assuming that clear and adequate definitions of accident and injury have been established, the substantial prob-

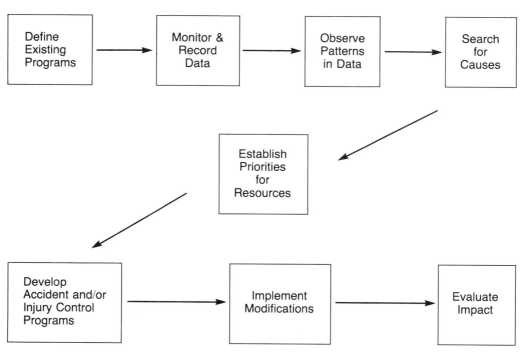

Fig. 1. Injury analysis and control model.

lems of collecting, storing, and retrieving data remain. Not only must data forms be developed and provided, but the responsibility for reporting the data must be assigned to specific individuals who have the authority to obtain the appropriate descriptive data. Data collection requires many costs in terms of time, effort, and material supplies, not to mention time away from other tasks often thought to be more pressing.

Subtle and not-so-subtle distortions of injury data are quite common. Coaches and administrators often feel pressure to portray their programs in as positive a light as possible. Documenting injuries often appears to be self-defeating to people held responsible for safety. An administrator who introduces an effective injury reporting system should be prepared to explain to superiors why a dramatic increase in injuries is now being recorded! Even the athletes themselves often minimize the reporting of injuries in order to avoid playing restrictions. Failure to complain and direct avoidance of reporting injuries is a major factor distorting accurate injury surveillance data.

PATTERN ANALYSIS

An examination of the data often reflects patterns which are not obvious to the casual participant because these patterns occur over long periods of time or across large populations of athletes. For example, Sands (1984) found that women collegiate gymnasts were significantly more likely to be injured in November and January than in any other months of the season and that the most common types of injuries occurred from the knee down. Further, heavier, taller gymnasts were more prone to injury than lighter, shorter gymnasts. Some of these findings are obvious. Few coaches would be surprised to find that heavier gymnasts are more prone to injury. Other findings are not so obvious or easily interpreted. The answer to why injuries occur more often in November and January requires further information and analysis. Klafs and Arnheim

(1981) concluded that injuries in high school sports were more likely to occur during the first 3 to 4 weeks of practice because athletes frequently lack flexibility, are overweight, or have little cardiovascular conditioning when they first report to practice. The Little League's analyses of injury patterns in organized youth baseball have revealed a number of obvious and non-obvious factors contributing to injury. "The result has been the elimination of steel spikes and the on-deck-circle, screening dugouts, mandating the use of face and head protectors for the batters, and installing breakaway bases, all of which have resulted in a decrease in injuries" (Klafs & Arnheim, 1981, p. 9). One of the most startling injury findings in recent years has been the observation that baseball and softball have the highest incidence of fatalities in youth sports, predominantly due to young children being struck in the chest by a baseball and suffering cardiac arrest (U.S. Consumer Product Safety Commission, 1984).

DETERMINE CAUSES

Once the descriptive data have indicated certain patterns, the cause of the patterns must be determined. Why do injuries typically occur during the third and fourth week of training? One possible explanation might be that this is the period during which athletes are shifting their training emphasis from conditioning to sport specific game skills. An equally plausible explanation might be that during the fall sports season, the third and fourth weeks are a period during which the athletes are more tired and distractible; they have switched from a summer schedule to a winter schedule in which they are attending academic classes as well as training on the athletic field. In fact, both of these reasons, in combination with others, might be causing the increased rates of injuries. Multiple causation of a class of injuries is more often the case than not. Attributing the "cause" of injuries to a single, antecedent event is often incomplete, if not directly misleading.

Some safety experts believe that the human element is the fundamental cause of virtually all accidents. Such a belief focuses on controlling human behavior as the main basis for reducing accidents and injuries. Safety education programs, reward and punishment contingencies for safe and unsafe behaviors respectively, and the identification of accident prone individuals are all safety approaches which rely on the assumption that human frailties create accidents and injuries. Clearly, there are circumstances in which human error leads to increased accident and injury rates. Individuals who lack knowledge of accepted safety practices may be more prone to injury. For example, athletes who have not been taught the fundamentals of falling safely appear to be at a higher risk than athletes who possess such skills. Nonetheless, the assumption that teaching falling automatically leads to reduced risk is unwarranted. Athletes who feel in control of the risk because they believe their skill at falling protects them may actually attempt more risky maneuvers and thereby increase their exposure to risk. The fact that as many accomplished swimmers as nonswimmers drown each year suggests that increased skill does not guarantee a reduced accident rate.

Furthermore, unsafe behavior may occur even though the individuals possess an awareness of what constitutes safe behavior. When safe behavior is inconvenient, uncomfortable, "unheroic," or reduces one's effectiveness at the sport, unsafe behavior becomes predictable. Often the value of behaving safely is less prominent than the value of the unsafe behavior. For example, the absence of injury is more difficult for a soccer player to observe than the fact that he or she can run faster without shin guards. In such cases, coaches and administrators must arrange the circumstances so that the athlete realizes that safety is important. For example, a rule which bars any soccer player from playing unless proper equipment is worn will demonstrate the need to wear shin guards.

While careless human behavior may often be the culprit in creating accidents and injuries, perceptive analyzers of safety should also be alert to opposing points of view. Robertson (1983) points out that although many "experts" insist that the injury problem is essentially a human behavioral problem, some of these opinions may be deliberately self-serving. That is, such opinions are offered by those who manufacture or provide the hazardous equipment and/or activity and, thus, who may wish to avoid regulation and being held responsible. Such biased perspectives may also come from the "human services" sectors such as educators, behavioral scientists, police, and others who benefit from labor-intensive behavior-change programs.

As Robertson states:

The wide-spread acceptance of the premise of correctable human error cannot be entirely attributed to brainwashing by those with obvious self-interests, however. The assumption that human beings are for the most part rational actors in complete control of their actions is imbedded in our mores and laws. To question the assumption is to question both a cultural theme and a basis for self-esteem. It is true that in many contexts this cultural myth is harmless. Where split-second decisions mean the difference between life and death or health and disability, however, as is frequently the case in handling highly concentrated energy, reliance on the myth of the rational, fully informed, constantly alert, lightning quick human being is, paradoxically, an irrational act. (Robertson, 1983, p. 65–66).

ESTABLISH PRIORITIES

Clearly, some types of injuries warrant more concern than others. Fatalities need to be dealt with at a higher priority than minor cuts and abrasions. Some injury prevention is also more feasible and/or requires less investment of resources. Providing access to water during training in order to reduce heat stroke requires less of a resource investment than building a foam pit for safe landings in high-risk gymnastic skills. While the arguments over the value of a human life have both philosophic and practical overtones, the issue is one which goes beyond the scope of this chapter. (The interested reader is referred to Thygerson, 1986, Chapter 6.) Any reader who feels that practical value considerations are not a current issue is invited to sit in on a jury trial in civil litigation following an accidental death.

DEVELOP EFFECTIVE PREVENTION PROGRAMS

Haddon (1980) outlined ten strategies for controlling injuries once the causes of those injuries have been determined. Those who use this list to analyze injury control options should realize that effective analysis requires that all options be initially considered. While some options are already in use or can be easily applied, others appear difficult, if not impossible to implement and are often casually dismissed during the initial stages of injury-control analysis. The practical aspects of implementation should be set aside until after all possibilities have been outlined.

1. *Eliminate the hazard.* Sports injuries can certainly be reduced by eliminating the sports or activities which cause injuries. While few would advocate the wholesale elimination of sport, there are a variety of examples where steps have been taken to eliminate specific sports. In 1977, the American Academy of Pediatrics advocated that trampolines be banned from instructional programs and eliminated as a competitive sport. Periodic cries for the elimination of boxing (usually prompted by a death) are relatively commonplace. The swinging rings in gymanstics have been eliminated both in physical education classes and in competition. In a different venue, commercial motels and hotels throughout the United States have virtually eliminated diving boards from their recreation swimming pools.

2. *Reduce the amount of the hazard.* Often, sports have been modified to reduce the amount or degree of risk incurred by the participant, especially younger, less experienced participants. Young platform tower divers train and compete on 5, 6, and 7 meter platforms rather than the 10 meter tower required by international rules. A "softer" ball has been introduced into age group baseball as a result of the knowledge that being hit in the chest with a hard ball is a major cause of death. Limiting the degree of vertical drop on novice ski trails to intentionally curtail the speeds which beginner skiers can attain reduces the amount of hazard. Similarly, shortened playing periods, age categories, and weight classes for young, less experienced players provides a degree of hazard reduction.

3. *Prevent or reduce the likelihood of the release of already existing hazards.* Coefficients of friction which create injuries can be improved. Baseball bases which slide instead of creating barriers which "snap" ankles and the use of magnesium carbonate ("chalk" or "mag") by gymnasts to reduce the likelihood of slipping are two examples.

4. *Modify the rate or spatial distribution of the release of the hazard from its source.* The use of seat belts in midget racing cars and the rapid release bindings on skis are examples.

5. *Separate, in time or space, the hazard and the participant.* Providing bicycle and jogging paths which are isolated from streets and highways separates the hazards (faster vehicles) from the participants (cyclist and joggers). The separation of spectators, benches for nonplaying athletes, and equipment storage area from the playing field also reduces the likelihood of injuries caused by colliding with other players or objects after running out of bounds. Likewise, isolating playing fields from such potential hazards as streams, roads, and con-

struction sites reduces the potential for accidents and injuries.

6. *Interpositioning of material protective barriers.* The use of football and lacrosse helmets, gymnastics mats, chest protectors in baseball and fencing, protective eye glasses in racquetball and squash, and mouth guards in contact sports are prime examples of the use of such a strategy.

7. *Modify the basic relevant qualities of the hazard.* The surfaces of playgrounds and playing fields can be covered with materials which are softer than asphalt, concrete or crushed stone. The use of breakaway goalposts or foam yard markers in football illustrate protective changes introduced into the basic characteristics of the hazard.

8. *Make what is to be protected more resistant to damage.* Conditioning athletes to be stronger and more flexible decreases their susceptibility to certain types of injuries. Providing unlimited access to water and gradually increasing workout intensity during periods of high temperatures allows the athletes to become acclimated and more resistent to heat disorders.

9. *Counter damage already done.* Emergency first aid training to stop bleeding and CPR training to restore heart function and breathing are fundamental to effective sports medicine programs. Recognizing potential spinal injuries and knowing that immobilization of such injured athletes is essential to prevent further injury is a prime example of preventing further damage resulting from a sports injury. Well situated, well-trained and well-equipped professionals ready to respond quickly can make substantial differences in the fatality rate and the severity of damage occurring from traumatic injuries.

10. *Stabilize, repair, and rehabilitate the damage.* Rehabilitative physical therapy programs, reconstructive surgery, and the use of knee and ankle braces to facilitate recovery from sprains and strains illustrate this approach.

IMPLEMENT SAFETY MODIFICATIONS

Knowing the cause of a type of injury may suggest a variety of prevention techniques, not all of which are equally effective. Knowing, for example, that being hit in the chest with a baseball or softball is the major cause of death among baseball/softball players suggests that chest protectors may be warranted. Getting players to actually wear such protective devices is yet another matter. Implementing programs often requires much lead-time and substantial resources. Resistance to change also impedes the effectiveness of prevention programs. While the use of helmets is now accepted in ice hockey, during the early stages of its implementation it was resisted by players and coaches alike. Paradoxically, the implementation of effective injury reduction programs is most difficult in areas in which the individual participant carries the most responsibility for his or her own safety.

ASSESS THE INFLUENCE OF PREVENTION PROGRAMS

Again, the monitoring of ongoing programs is required in order to assess the effectiveness of prevention programs. Often, the frequency of injury experienced by an individual instructor, participant, or program is so small that patterns are difficult to detect without a recordkeeping system which extends over a period of years and across many similar programs.

Researchers at the University of North Carolina have compiled statistics of football fatalities annually since 1931. Table 4 describes the pattern of injuries in high school football programs plotted in 5-year blocks since 1961. There has been a steady decrease in the number of fatalities directly related to football since the peak observed between 1961 and 1965. A similar decline has occurred in indirect fatalities during this same period. While a variety of factors have contributed to this steady decline, a significant rule change was implemented in

1976. Initial contact with the head while blocking and tackling (spearing) was ruled illegal. This rule change was introduced because of an awareness, not only of fatalities in football, but because statistics revealed that the vast majority of fatalities since 1960 were due to injuries to the head and neck. This information led to the development of a prevention program involving protecting this area of the body via improved equipment and rule changes to eliminate the use of the head as a tackling technique. Continued monitoring of injury frequencies indicated that such programs have achieved the desired effect of reducing injuries and fatalities. Penalties for spearing and rigid enforcement of those penalties plus an increased awareness on the part of coaches and athletes regarding the nature and severity of injuries produced by spearing have all contributed heavily to the reduction of fatalities resulting from head and neck injuries. Data continue to indicate that deaths in football are still primarily caused by head and neck injuries. Efforts continue to develop even more effective prevention of such injuries.

A PRACTITIONER'S ANALYSIS

The professional in sport and physical education can gain an understanding of the factors which should be controlled by using a simple, yet effective approach to analyzing the safety requirements of the program. While the number of specific concerns to which attention must be focused can be overwhelming, virtually all can be subsumed under the following classification plan. When analyzing a specific program, ask the following three questions:

1. *Are the athletes prepared for the activity?* Have they been properly conditioned for the demands of the sport? Have they been taught the appropriate prerequisite skills? Have they been taught to appreciate the risks inherent

in their particular sport? Have the basic safety regulations been taught to them in terms they can understand? Has the instructor/coach clarified exactly what is expected of the athlete during the learning and/or performance stages?

2. *Is the instructor prepared to teach the skill and supervise the activity?* Does the instructor have the prerequisite knowledge of the biomechanical and teaching progressions of the skill? Is the instructor capable of individualizing the learning sequence and teaching progressions to accommodate the needs of the athlete, both real and imagined? Is the instructor aware of the common errors made by beginners and the likely hazards to be confronted by both the student and the instructor during the learning of the skills? Is the instructor familiar with the level of mental and physical preparation of the athlete and can the instructor modify the learning progressions to match the learner's preparation with the difficulty of the task?

3. *Is the environment adequately prepared for the performance of the skill?* Is the protective equipment available and properly positioned? Is the apparatus and/or protective equipment properly adjusted for the athlete? Has the activity been properly designed for the space, lighting, facilities and number of athletes available? Have the athletes been properly matched for size, skill and maturity? Have activity areas been clearly defined and separated from traffic lanes, resting stations and teaching stations?

Clearly, the number and type of questions which one can ask under each heading has not been exhausted. They depend on the specifics of the activity taught and the degree of risk associated with that activity. This strategy does, however, provide direction in terms of systematically examining the three primary areas in which teachers and administrators are responsible for providing adequate care and supervision for their students.

REFERENCES

Clarke, K. S. (1982). An epidemiologic view. In J. S. Torg (Ed.), *Athletic injuries to the head, neck, and face* (pp. 15–22). Philadelphia: Lea & Febiger.

Football injury survey: Number of deaths in high school football hits all-time low with only five fatalities. (1986). *National Federation News, 3*, 6–9. (Available from the National Federation of State High School Associations, Kansas City, Missouri)

Hadden, W. Jr., (1980). The basic strategies for reducing damage from hazards of all kinds. *Hazard Prevention, 16*, 1.

Hadden, W. Jr., (1980). Advances in the epidemiology of injuries as a basis for public policy. *Public Health Reports, 95*, 411–421.

Klafs, C. E., & Arnheim, D. D. (1981). *Modern principles of athletic training* (5th ed.). St. Louis: C. V. Mosby.

Micheli, L. J. (1986). Pediatric and adolescent sports injuries: Recent trends. In K. B. Pandolf (Ed.), *Exercise and sport sciences reviews*. New York: Macmillan.

Morris, A. E. (1984). *Sports medicine: Prevention of athletic injuries*. Dubuque, IA: Wm. C. Brown.

National Safety Council. (1984). *Accident Facts*. Chicago: Author.

Reif, A. E. (1981). Risks and gains. In P. F. Vinger & E. F. Hoerner (Eds.), *Sports injuries: The unthwarted epidemic* (pp. 56–64). Littleton, MA: PSG Publishing.

Robertson, L. S. (1983). *Injuries: Causes, control strategies, and public policy*. Lexington, MA: Lexington Books.

Rutherford, G. W., Kennedy, J., & McGhee, L. (1984). *Baseball and softball related injuries to children 5–14 years of age*. Washington, DC: U.S. Consumer Product Safety Commission.

Rutherford, G. W., Miles, R. B., Brown, V. R., & MacDonald, B. (1981). *Overview of sports-related injuries to persons 5–14 years of age*. Washington, DC: U.S. Consumer Product Safety Commission.

Sands, B. (1984). Injury data NCAA female gymnasts 1983–84: Data reveals potential patterns. *Technique: The Official Publication of the United States Gymnastics Association, 4*, 7.

Thygerson, A. L. (1986). *Safety* (2nd ed.). Englewood Cliffs, NJ: Prentice Hall.

Torg, J. S. (1982). Problems and prevention. In J. S. Torg (Ed.), *Athletic injuries to the head, neck, and face* (pp. 3–13). Philadelphia: Lea & Febiger.

CHAPTER 2

Legal Responsibility for Safety in Physical Education and Sport

NEIL J. DOUGHERTY IV

Rutgers University
New Brunswick, NJ

photo by Jim Kirby

The number of lawsuits brought against physical educators and coaches has reached an unprecedented high point and, from all indications, will continue to rise in the foreseeable future. Consider the following reasons why this may be the case:

- The overwhelming majority of all school-related injuries occur in conjunction with physical education and sport.
- A tort is a legal wrong for which one may seek recompense through legal action.
- Under the civil laws of the United States, it is possible for practically any person to sue any other person at any time for any reason. While the outcome of the suit is, by no means, guaranteed, the right to initiate it is virtually unquestioned.
- The overwhelming majority of all negligence suits are settled prior to the completion of the trial process.
- Both the number of lawsuits and the size of the settlements or awards has increased drastically in the last five to ten years. This has, of course, been reflected in the cost and availability of liability insurance as well as the nature and continuation of many programs.

The field of physical education and sport unquestionably carries with it a higher risk of injury than most other areas of the curriculum. The relative ease with which one can institute a lawsuit and the high likelihood of some form of settlement, regardless of the strength of the case, has led to an increasing level of professional concern over issues related to risk management and liability.

While there are many negative aspects to the liability problem, such as spiralling insurance costs and the loss of some programs and activities, the increased concern over liability has also resulted in safer programs and has been used by knowledgeable teachers and administrators as a highly persuasive argument for program and facility improvements. Further, although no amount of planning or preparation can guarantee freedom from injuries and subsequent lawsuits, a thorough understanding of the legal process and the elements of risk management can greatly increase one's chances of success when such a situation arises. This chapter will, therefore, examine the fundamentals of the legal process as they relate to physical education and sport. Those factors which most commonly give rise to lawsuits will be discussed in an attempt to lay a foundation for the sport specific safety principles dealt with in the remainder of the text.

THE LEGAL PROCESS

Tort claims in physical education and sport are primarily the result of personal injuries caused by the alleged negligence of the teacher or the coach. In order for the plaintiff or injured party to prevail in such a suit, several elements must be proved by the greater weight of evidence.

Duty. The defendant must be shown to have had a responsibility to provide for the safety and welfare of the plaintiff. If the injured party was a student in the defendant's class, or a player on his/her team, then the duty is virtually assured.

Breach of Duty. It must be shown that the defendant failed to provide the standard of care which could reasonably be expected of a professional under the same or similar circumstances. A duty can be breached either by omission or by commission. That is, the defendant either failed to do something that he/she should have done, or did something he/she should not have done.

Damage. In order to institute a tort claim, the plaintiff must have suffered an actual loss to his person, property, or interest.

Foreseeability. It must be shown that the defendant should have been able to predict the likelihood of an accident or injury arising out of the specific circumstances in question.

Proximate cause. The mere presence of an act of negligence is not sufficient grounds to allow the plaintiff to prevail.

It must be shown, further, that the injury for which recompense is sought was actually caused or aggravated by the specific act of negligence in question.

A key point in this entire process is the establishment of the standard of care required of the defendant. In this regard, the prudent person principal is most commonly employed. We are obligated to perform as would a reasonably prudent individual under the same or similar circumstances. While this statement is essentially correct, remember that it is also very superficial. The yardstick by which professional conduct will be measured in court is the established standards and practices of the profession as applied and explained by a prudent professional . . . an expert. It is essential, therefore, that we take every reasonable precaution to guarantee that our teaching and coaching behavior always meets or exceeds the currently accepted practices and procedures of the profession.

LEGAL AND QUASI-LEGAL DEFENSES

There are several legal arguments and professional procedures which can help to form the basis of a defense in the event of a lawsuit. While these are useful tools in the litigation process, they are even more valuable as indices of administrative and supervisory responsibilities with regard to risk management.

Contributory/comparative negligence. In states which adhere to the principle of contributory negligence, the plaintiff is barred from recovery if it is proved that his/her own negligence helped to cause or aggravate the injury. In the majority of states, however, the doctrine of comparative negligence is now applied. In such a situation, the jury will be asked to apportion a relative percentage of responsibility to the plaintiff and to the defendant(s). The size of the award which the plaintiff could receive would then be diminished by his/her percentage of responsibility. If, for instance,

Mary Addams was seeking $250,000 damages for an injury sustained in a soccer class, and if the jury found her to have been comparatively negligent in the amount of 45%, then the maximum award she could receive would be 55% of $250,000, or $137,500. Obviously the amount of responsibility which a student can assume for his/her own welfare is a function of age, intelligence, skill, and background in the activity. In general, the more thorough the instruction, the more explicit the warnings, and the more consistent the feedback, the more the students will be expected to assume some reasonable share of the responsibility for their own safety.

Assumption of risk. It is often argued that an individual who takes part in certain types of vigorous physical activities must assume the risk of accident or injury which is normally associated with that activity. Assumption of risk, however, is a technical term which many feel has no validity as a separate defense.[1] Reduced to simplest terms, no one can be expected to assume a risk of which he/she is unaware. If the teacher fails to warn the student of the dangers involved in the activity and/or fails to guarantee the level of instruction, skill, and feedback necessary for the student to reasonably protect him/herself from those dangers, then the teacher may very possibly have been negligent in the fulfillment of his/her duties and the student cannot be held to have assumed any risk or responsibility. If, on the other hand, the student was properly instructed, warned, and provided with reasonable feedback regarding his/her performance, and despite this, acted in a manner which increased the likelihood of his/her own injury, then there may be grounds for a valid claim of contributory or comparative negligence. In either case, however, the assumption of risk terminology is merely excess verbal baggage which has no real place as a separate defense in today's law.

Informed consent. While written docu-

[1] *Meistrich v. Casino Arena Attractions, Inc.,* 31, NJ, 44 (1959).

ments such as waivers and permission slips cannot provide absolute legal protection from our own acts of negligence, they can, when properly understood and executed, be very useful tools in the reduction of liability.

For our purposes as physical education teachers and coaches, the most commonly used informed consent documents can be grouped into two major categories: release forms, often called waivers, and participation agreements, which include permission slips.

A *release* or waiver is a contract, signed by the participant and/or his/her parents, which purports to absolve the teacher or coach from liability in the event that an accident or injury arises from some specifically named activity. Waivers have very little absolute legal value for several reasons: (a) the courts are reluctant to allow one to be contractually protected from the consequences of his/her own negligent actions; (b) since no person can legally waive the rights of another, parental waivers executed on behalf of a minor child cannot be held valid; and (c) the requirement of a release prior to participation in a public program is frequently held to be a violation of public policy and, therefore, invalid.

A *participation agreement* is of particular value in circumstances where a release or waiver cannot apply. It is, in essence, a signed statement indicating that the participant and/or his/her parents understand the dangers which are inherent in the activity, know the rules and procedures and the importance of following them, fully appreciate the possible consequences (i.e. specific types of injuries or even death) of the dangers involved and, knowing all this, requests to participate in the activity. Van der Smissen has indicated that, in order to be effective, participation agreements should meet the following criteria:

1. They must be explicitly worded.
2. If there are rules that must be followed, it is preferable that the rules be listed in the agreement or listed on the reverse side of the paper.

3. The possible dangers inherent in the activities must be spelled out in detail, along with the consequences of possible accidents to the participants.

4. The participant must sign after a statement expressly assuming the risks of the participation.[2]

While a participation agreement will not prevent a lawsuit or absolve the teacher or coach of the responsibility for his/her negligence, it clearly establishes the awareness level of the participant and his/her willingness to assume reasonable responsibility for his/her own welfare and compliance with appropriate rules and procedures. It can, therefore, be a very valuable tool in the establishment of a contributory or comparative negligence defense.

RISK MANAGEMENT

The best possible means of avoiding costly liability claims and judgements is by recognizing those circumstances in which injuries are most likely to occur and by taking appropriate steps to eliminate or minimize the chances of their occurrence—that is, through a carefully applied process of risk management.

Most activity-related lawsuits allege that the teacher or coach was negligent in the fulfillment of his/her professional responsibilities with regard to one or more of the following areas: supervision, selection and conduct of the activity, and environmental conditions. This is not surprising since it is possible, through careful analysis of these areas, to identify virtually all controllable injury causing factors within an activity. For this reason, the areas of supervision, selection and conduct of the activity, and environmental conditions provide an excellent organizational focus for a general program of risk management and prevention as well as for identifying specific safety principles within individual activities.

---

[2] Betty van der Smissen (1985, March). Releases, waivers, and agreements to participate. *National Safety Network Newsletter, 1* (4), 2.

Supervision. The structure of the educational environment and the nature of the students dictate the absolute necessity for effective supervision. A skilled supervisor (teacher, coach, group leader, etc.) can, in the normal course of his/her duties, prevent many needless accidents. Effective supervision is, therefore, recognized as an essential element in the delivery of safe and successful programs of physical activity and is called into question virtually every time a negligence suit is instituted. In developing educational programs, therefore, it is necessary to provide a sufficient number of supervisory personnel to manage the group in question, and to insure that the supervisory personnel employed possess the necessary knowledge and skills to fulfill their responsibilities.

The individual teacher or coach is responsible for the provision of both general and specific supervision. The broad overall supervision of a class or team is referred to as general supervision. In providing effective general supervision, one is expected to maintain visual contact with the entire group, to be immediately accessible to them, and to apply a high level of professional skill in the detection and remediation of deviations from safe and prescribed procedures. Specific supervision, on the other hand, refers to situations of direct interaction between the teacher and one or more students. Direct supervision might be required in order to correct some noted deviation from safe practices or procedures, to provide individual feedback, or to lend direct assistance when a student is about to attempt a new or particularly dangerous skill. The intensity and specificity of the supervision is inversely proportional to the ability of the student to understand and appreciate the dangers of the activity, to assess his/her performance and skill level, and to adhere to required safety procedures. Generally speaking, therefore, as the age and ability of the students decreases, the need for specific supervision can be expected to increase and the advisability of allowing extended periods of time with only general supervision can be expected to decrease.

Decisions regarding the relative proportion of general to specific supervision are, of course, dependent upon the particular group and situation in question. It should be remembered, however, that the need to provide specific supervision to one or more individuals does not remove the need to provide general supervision for the remainder of the group. The teacher cannot, therefore, become so engrossed in providing individual feedback to students in the northeast corner of the gym that he/she fails to detect and correct the hazardous situation which may be occurring in the southeast corner.

The following general guidelines should prove helpful as you seek to provide effective supervision for all activities:

1. Take whatever steps may be necessary to guarantee your own competence in the activity being taught. You must be the expert!

2. Establish general safety rules for the gymnasium, locker rooms, etc. Rules should be explained to the students, posted, reinforced, and consistently enforced.

3. Develop the habit of writing detailed lesson or practice plans. The act of planning will help to identify and correct many potential hazards. Moreover, the plans themselves can serve as valuable legal evidence of your preparation and knowledge with regard to the subject matter as well as the preparation of your students.

4. Never leave your class or team unsupervised. A quick phone call in the office, or a brief stop in the equipment room to retrieve some forgotten item presents a period of supervisory absence and, thus, is a potential source of negligence. In such a case, if it is determined that the presence of the teacher would have resulted in the correction or the prevention of the injury causing behavior, then the injury sustained by the student can be proximately related to the negligence of the absent teacher.

5. Take care to arrange your classes so that the entire group is within your field of vision. Move about the area in a manner which maximizes student contact and minimizes the length of time during which your back may be turned to any portion of the group.

6. Be sure to secure the facilities and equipment when they are not in use. If facilities are left open and equipment is left out, it is reasonable to expect people to use them. Unplanned and unsupervised activities of this nature frequently lead to injuries and lawsuits.

7. In the event of an emergency, you will be expected to render necessary first aid until appropriate emergency personnel (trainer, nurse, doctor) arrive. Be sure that you are adequately prepared to do so.

8. Establish a list of emergency procedures to be followed in all accident cases. This will prevent student confusion, unnecessary delays in treatment, and supervisory breakdowns. Who goes for help? Who supervises the class? How is he/she contacted? What do the unaffected students do?

9. The actions of one or more students should never be allowed to endanger the safety or interfere with the learning of others.

Selection and conduct of the activity. As professionals we are expected to select activities which are appropriate for the age and ability levels of our students. Having selected an appropriate activity, we are further expected to provide instruction which is factually accurate and which is presented in a manner which maximizes the likelihood of student success. This instruction should be supplemented by warnings with regard to any potentially hazardous conditions involved in the activity, the provision of appropriate safety devices and protective measures, and the provision of feedback through which the student can gauge and modify his/her performance.

The courts have been relatively consistent in their recognition of the fact that very few activities are inherently unsafe. The issue in question, therefore, should an injury occur, is whether the injured student was physically capable of successful participation and was properly prepared and instructed. While certain risks may be deemed necessary in the interests of good programming and total student development, such risks must be well thought out and justified, and the potential for student injury must be minimized. The following guidelines should be considered when selecting and developing any activity.

1. Always select activities which are within the reasonable ability limits of the students.

2. Readiness is an individual matter. Pre-testing and screening, careful record keeping, and the development of individualized progressions are, therefore, essential to safety and success.

3. The development and maintenance of comprehensive lesson plans and curriculum guides is essential both to instructional success and to a sound legal defense in the event of a lawsuit. They provide evidence regarding the nature and organization of the instruction as well as previous student experiences and background.

4. Always have planned rainy day activities to correspond to planned outdoor activities. It is both difficult and embarrassing to try to justify an injury which occurred in an ad libbed activity which had to be pulled together because an outdoor lesson was rained out.

5. All activities should be justifiable within the context of the educational objectives of the school. Too frequently, activities selected solely on the basis of expressed student enjoyment are not particularly enjoyed by all and result in needless injuries. Such injuries are very difficult to justify.

6. Procedures should be developed for the acceptance of medical excuses and for return to activity after serious injury or illness. Never allow an injured or ill student to participate without a medical clearance.

7. Do not attempt to coerce students to perform when they are, by their own admission, fearful or unequal to the task. Such action is almost impossible to justify when it results in an injury.

8. Provide all necessary protective

measures and devices, and require their use.

9. If adequate protective measures cannot be provided, then the activity, itself, should be modified.

10. Be sure that all instruction is consistent with the most professionally accepted information and procedures and includes warnings regarding the dangers involved and the manner in which they can be avoided or minimized.

11. Take whatever steps may be necessary in order to avoid mismatch situations in activities where there is a strong likelihood of physical contact. It should be remembered, however, that a mismatch is a function of size, strength, skill, and experience. The sex of the participant is not a controlling factor.

12. Above all, remember that the focus of the educational process is the student, not the activity. Our responsibility, therefore, is to tailor the activity according to the skills of our students in order to provide the safest and most productive learning experience for all.

Environmental conditions. In addition to providing a safe activity under competent professional supervision, one must also take appropriate measures to provide for the safety of the facilities and equipment used. Before allowing students to use an instructional area or a piece of equipment, it should be carefully inspected for safety and proper function. Such things as debris or potholes on playing fields or loose racquet heads can lead to participant injuries. When this occurs, the teacher/coach will, almost invariably, be called upon to explain the procedures he/she followed in order to prevent injuries due to unsafe environmental conditions.

While obvious hazards such as water on a court surface or a cracked bat usually result in immediate remediation, many teachers unknowingly create environmental hazards by the manner in which they use an otherwise safe facility. Instructing students to run across the gym, tag the far wall and return, for instance, is simply inviting an injury due to a collision with the wall. This is not the fault of the facility. It is a function of the manner in which

the facility was used. Similar situations can be seen where one fails to provide a sufficient buffer area around a playing field or court. Participants must be expected to run out of bounds and beyond finish lines. A sufficient buffer zone is, therefore, essential to safe play. Other teacher imposed and easily corrected environmental hazards include: relays where the turning directions and running lanes have not been clearly specified; the use of improper substitute equipment such as candy wrappers for bases; or the use of equipment which requires a level of skill beyond that of the participants. An example of the latter circumstance would be the use of fixed post bases with unskilled participants where sliding is allowed. While these bases offer distinct advantages with skilled sliders who recognize their unyielding characteristics, they are unsafe for those who lack such skill and knowledge. If, therefore, they were to be used with an unskilled group, sliding should be disallowed in the interest of safety.

The following general guidelines should prove helpful in reducing the number of injuries due to hazards within the environment.

1. Start every day with an inspection of the facilities which your classes will be using. Note any hazards such as broken glass, slippery surface, loose fittings, etc., and take steps to eliminate them.

2. Make appropriate planning modifications to keep students away from hazardous areas until repairs can be completed. If a problem is located in a general use area, consider some form of marking as a warning to others.

3. All equipment in use should be inspected daily.

4. Teach students to inspect equipment and require them to do so each time it is issued. This double check system virtually eliminates the possibility of teacher negligence associated with equipment failure.

5. Under no circumstances should students be allowed to use equipment which is in a state of disrepair.

6. Be sure all facilities and equipment

meet or exceed recommended size and safety specifications, e.g. thickness of mats, free area around courts, and landing pits.

7. Do not hold running activities on an uneven or slippery surface.

8. Provide and require the use of appropriate safety equipment. Post signs and reminders to keep the importance of this issue clearly in the minds of the students.

We are living in an age of litigation. Disputes and losses, whether real or imagined, are commonly brought before the courts for adjudication. It is not surprising, therefore, that in a profession such as physical education and sport, where the possibility of participant injury is present, there should be a great concern for matters of legal liability. To the degree that this concern manifests itself in careful attention to standards of safety and professionalism and thoughtful program planning,

it is healthy and should be cultivated. Care must be taken, however, to prevent overreaction. It is one thing to eliminate unnecessary risks; it is quite another to eliminate programs or activities entirely because some risk happens to be involved. Risk is an unavoidable component of sport. It cannot be eliminated, but it must be controlled. The task of the teacher is to eliminate all unnecessary risks, and to reduce as much as possible those that remain. If, after doing this, the educational value of the activity can be shown to substantially outweigh the risks, then the activity has a valid place in the curriculum and should be retained. If, however, the potential risks cannot be justified in this manner or if all reasonable steps have not been taken to guarantee the safety of the participants, then program modifications must be implemented in order to prevent needless injuries and costly lawsuits.

CHAPTER 3

Administration of Safety in Physical Education and Sports

PATRICIA E. BARRY

Montgomery County Public Schools
Rockville, MD

The administration of safety in physical education and sport cannot be a fragmented effort. It must be part of a total school safety program with the full participation of the district administration and the local school. A safety program must be designed which is in concert with all aspects of the philosophy, administration, and management of the entire organization.

Regardless of the organization, an effective safety program must encompass:

1. Maximum production.
2. Maximum cost effectiveness.
3. General efficiency.
4. Safety for all involved (this includes students, employees, and other persons and patrons who are involved in the activities of the institution).

Within the educational setting, generally accepted ingredients of a safety program include:

1. Policy development.
2. Safety committee (a physical education teacher or physical education and sport administrator should serve on this committee).
3. Accident reporting and investigation.
4. Safety inspections.

ROLE OF THE ADMINISTRATOR

The physical education and/or athletic administrator serves primarily as a facilitator of the official safety policies of the school or school district by insuring that proper communication channels to each employee, student, and patron are constantly open and operating.

Responsibility for the overall safety of the organization resides in the hands of the institution's chief administrator who appoints general and specific safety coordinators and committees. Specific areas of responsibility must be identified. Physical education and sport are, of course, two very important aspects of the total safety structure and should be delegated to a specific individual who has the training and expertise necessary to succeed at the task.

The primary administrative responsibilities for physical education and/or athletics may be accomplished by several persons or, in fact, may be the task of one person in a small school district.

Regardless of the size or type of education institution, several areas *must* be addressed by those professionally trained in the field of physical education and sport. Some things to keep in mind are the following:

- Physical educators and coaches should not become overly concerned about legal issues. Rather, they should take positive measures to prevent accidents. The goal is to minimize the frequency and severity of injuries.
- Accidents will never be eliminated. The term "safety measures" in physical education should not necessarily signal elimination of an activity. Taking actions to enhance activity, health, adventure, and fun should be the primary goal. Activity elimination as a means of accident prevention is a negative and often counterproductive approach.
- Recommendations for the purchase of equipment and supplies designed and constructed for optimal safety in the particular situation must be made by trained physical educators or by the athletic administrator.
- Proper maintenance and reconditioning of physical education and athletic equipment and supplies must be regularly completed in compliance with the manufacturer's specifications.
- Regardless of the activity, careful and constant supervision of students in physical education and athletics is a must.
- General supervision is also important and this responsibility may fall upon all professionals regardless of their specific assignments. Locker room coverage, for example, is often shared by teachers and coaches.
- Skill classification and proper assignment of the individual physical education student and athlete are very important. Assigning of students to specific positions or modifying the rules

are two methods of managing this responsibility.

- Class size is of major importance in physical education. Both the activity and the facility are influencing factors. In general, physical education class size should match that of other subjects, as approved by the school or system.
- Budget constraints can never be justified as reasons for not providing recommended protective equipment. When protective equipment is available, teachers must require its use.

ACCIDENT REPORTING

We live in a data-oriented society. The accessibility of today's computers has created the demand for detailed reporting and analyzing of all aspects of health and safety. Completion of accident reports is necessary in order to properly interpret information and to eliminate avoidable accidents. The purpose, however, is *not* to eliminate the activity or to reduce the resultant health benefits and fun. Figures 1 and 2 are examples of effective forms for reporting student or employee injuries.

ROUTINE MAINTENANCE

Routine preventative and emergency maintenance requests with safety implications should be submitted as soon as they are identified. Copies of these requests should be sent to all appropriate persons and kept on file by the departmental chairperson/teacher or coach.

BUDGET IMPLICATIONS

Budget planning is necessary for the successful maintenance and renovation of existing facilities. Safety projections for new facilities must be made in advance. These "capital budget" requests can usually be projected several years in advance. At the same time, accurate justification for need must be documented.

There are a number of publications which can be helpful in this area. One

such source is *Planning Facilities for Athletics, Physical Education and Recreation* (Flynn, 1985).

SAFETY AWARENESS AND FORESEEABILITY

Although the ultimate responsibility for the safety of students, employees, and patrons lies within these groups themselves, the search for existing and potential safety hazards is a continuous process in which all physical educators and coaches must constantly participate. Everyone must be encouraged to carry an awareness and foresight of safety issues into every aspect of their lives, whether at home, in the classroom, at work, at the beach, in the mountains, or on the highway.

Professional safety awareness and foreseeability are not limited to seeing the broken glass on the playing field. Safety begins much earlier with someone picking up the unbroken glass bottle which may have been littering the field for days. It includes insuring that there are trash receptacles in appropriate locations and that the receptacles are serviced regularly. If littering is a severe and a constant problem, then there is a need to ask for cooperation from the local school and nearby commercial establishments that serve as vendors of bottled beverages. Consideration could even be given to limiting beverage sales to cans and paper cups.

Investigating the cause of problems and providing measures for the prevention of future ones are far more important steps than trying to determine whose responsibility it is to remove the broken glass from the field after the fact. The broken glass must be removed; however, the glass is only a symptom of a greater problem that needs to be solved with a more long term solution.

SUPPORT MATERIALS

A number of reference publications are available to assist the concerned administrator. The National Safety Council and the Association of School

_____OSHA Case Number (School Number plus additional digit for number in calendar year)

Division of Insurance and Retirement MONTGOMERY COUNTY PUBLIC SCHOOLS 850 Hungerford Drive Rockville, Maryland 20850	EMPLOYEE ACCIDENT REPORT

INSTRUCTIONS: Refer to special instructions on the reverse side before completing the form. Send original and one copy to the Division of Insurance and Retirement, Educational Services Center, one copy to your area office, and retain one copy in the school.

TIME AND PLACE

1. Location of school or place where accident or exposure occurred _____ Code 1

   Employer's premises _____ Yes _____ No

2. Date of injury or initial diagnosis of occupational illness _____ M M D D Y Y   day of week _____

   Hour of day _____ AM _____ PM   3. Date disability began _____ 19 ___ _____ AM _____ PM

4. Was injured paid in full for day of injury? _____ Yes _____ No. 5. When did you or your supervisor first know of injury? _____

6. Name of immediate supervisor _____

INJURED PERSON

7. Name of injured _____   Social Security Number
   (Type or Print)   First   Middle   Last

8. Address _____
   No. and Street   City or Town   State   Zip Code

9. Check (✔) _____ Married _____ Single _____ Widowed _____ Widower _____ Divorced _____ Male _____ Female   10. Age _____

11. Occupation when injured _____   Code 2   Was this his/her regular occupation? _____ Yes _____ No

    If not, state regular occupation _____ 12. How long employed _____ Wage per hour _____

    Wage per day _____ Average weekly earnings _____ No. hours worked per day _____ No. hours worked

    per week _____. If board, lodging, fuel, or other advantages were furnished in addition to wages, give estimate of value per day, week

    or month _____

CAUSE OF INJURY

13. Machine, tool or substance causing injury _____   14. Was safety appliance or regulation

    provided? [ ] Yes [ ] No. Was it in use at time? [ ] Yes [ ] No.   Code 3   15. What was employee doing when injured?

    Be specific. If he was using tools or equipment or handling material, name them and tell what he was doing with them. _____

17. Did disability arise out of and in the course of claimant's last employment? _____ Yes _____ No

NATURE OF INJURY

18. Nature of injury or occupational disease _____   Code 4

    Part of Body _____ Code 5   Type of injury _____ Code 6

19. Probable number of work days away from work _____. 20. Has injured returned to work? _____ Yes _____ No.

    If so, date and hour _____. At what wage? _____. At what occupation? _____

    _____ Part-time _____ Full-time _____ Light Duty _____ Temporary Reassignment

21. Name and address of physician _____

    Name and address of hospital _____
    _____ Inpatient _____ Outpatient

WITNESSES

Witnesses to accident _____   Phone or Address
    Name

_____   Phone or Address
    Name

MOTOR VEHICLES

23. If motor vehicles are involved, give name and address of insurance carriers _____

PERSONAL PROPERTY LOSS

24. Clothing or other personal property damage as the result of enforcement of school regulations. If so describe _____

    (Proof of loss must accompany this form)

25. Has injured died? [ ] Yes [ ] No

26. Date of this report _____ 27. School or Department _____

    Signed by _____   Title _____
    Principal/Department Director

MCPS Form 285-1, Revised May 1980

Fig. 1. Employee accident report. From *Safety Handbook,* Montgomery County Public Schools, Rockville, Maryland (1985).

COMPLETE ENTIRE FORM PROVIDING ALL APPROPRIATE INFORMATION. THE ITEMS BLOCKED MUST BE COMPLETED FOR COMPUTER PROCESSING. FORM WILL BE RETURNED TO ORIGINATOR IF NOT CORRECTLY PREPARED AND CODED.

ITEM 1 — Enter name and four-digit code assigned to the department or school where the injury occurred.

ITEM 2 — Hour of day: 12 noon will be entered as 1200 AM; 12 midnight will be entered as 1200 PM.

ITEM 11 — Enter occupation and use the MCPS Personnel Position Class code assigned to the occupation of the injured employee. If the injured person is a volunteer worker, enter 'VOLU' for this code.

ITEM 13 — Enter agency of injury and appropriate code from list below.

ITEM 18 — Enter nature of injury, part of body, type of injury and appropriate code for each from list below.

CODE 3 – AGENCY OF INJURY
MACHINERY

BUFFER	001
GRINDER	002
JOINTER	003
LATHE	004
LAWN MOWER	005
PLANER	006
SAW, BAND	007
SAW, CIRCULAR	008
SAW, JIG	009
SEWING MACHINE	010
VISE	011
PAPER CUTTER	012
METAL SHEARS	013
DRILL PRESS	014
WELDER	015
PRINT PRESS	016
SAW, RADIAL	017
OTHER	099

HANDTOOL

AXE	100
CHISEL	101
DRILL HAND	102
FILE	103
HAMMER	104
KNIFE	105
NEEDLES	106
PAPER CUTTER	107
SAW HAND	108
SCISSORS	109
SCREWDRIVER	110
WRENCH	111
OTHER	199

WALKING/WORKING SURFACES

INTERIOR FLOOR (NEC)	201
EXTERIOR GROUNDS	206
INTERIOR STAIRS	207
EXTERIOR STEPS	212
SCAFFOLDING	214
LADDER	220
OTHER	299

MATERIALS/EQUIPMENT

ATHLETIC EQUIPMENT, NEC	301
BASEBALLS, FOOTBALLS, VOLLEYBALLS AND THE LIKE	302
BIOLOGICAL SUBSTANCE	303
BOXES	328
CEMENT, CONCRETE	326
CHEMICAL SUBSTANCES INCLUDING POISONS	304
CORDS	323
FENCES AND WALLS	305
FLAMMABLES, SUCH AS MATCHES, GAS	307
FURNITURE, SUCH AS DESKS, CHAIRS	308
GLASS AND GLASSWARE	309
HOT LIQUIDS, SUBSTANCES	310

CODE 3, CONTINUED
MATERIALS/EQUIPMENT, CONTINUED

KITCHEN EQUIPMENT, STOVES, OVENS	311
KITCHEN FOODS	312
KILNS, OVENS	313
LOCKERS	330
MEDIA EQUIPMENT	327
PROTECTIVE EQUIPMENT	315
PROTECTIVE CLOTHING	316
POLES, RODS	317
PAINTS, LACQUERS AND SPRAYS	318
WINDOW, DOORS	319
WOOD, LUMBER	320
METAL	321
PENS, PENCILS	322
STEEL WOOL	325
TRASH CANS	324
VENETIAN BLINDS	329
OTHER	399

PLAYGROUND APPARATUS	400

VEHICLES

AUTO	500
BICYCLE	501
BUS SCHOOL	502
MOTOR BIKE	503
MOTORCYCLE, MOTOR SCOOTER, SCHOOL OWNED OR LEASED	504
PUBLIC CARRIER	508
TRUCK	509
OTHER	599

MISCELLANEOUS

PERSON INVOLVED	601
OTHER PERSON OR PERSONS	602
SKATEBOARDS	603
SCOOTERS	604
TOYS, OTHER	605
ANIMALS, INSECT BITES	607
TREES, SHRUBS	608
OTHER, NEC	699

CODE 4 – NATURE OF INJURY

ABRASION/BRUISE	01
AMPUTATION	02
ASPHYXIATION	03
BITE	04
BURNS/SCALDS	05
CONCUSSION	06
CUTS/LACERATION	07
DISLOCATION	08
DROWNING	09
ELECTRICAL SHOCK	10
FOREIGN BODY IMBEDDED	11
FRACTURE	12
POISONING	13
PUNCTURE	14
SPRAIN/STRAIN	15
TEETH DAMAGED	16
INTERNAL INJURIES	17

CODE 4 – NATURE OF INJURY,
CONTINUED

MULTIPLE	18
UNKNOWN	98
OTHER	99

CODE 5 – PART OF BODY INJURED

ABDOMEN	01
ANKLE	02
ARM	03
BACK	04
CHEST/RIBS	06
EAR	07
EYE	09
FACE	10
FINGERS/THUMB	11
FOOT	12
HAND	14
KNEE	16
LEG	17
MOUTH, LIPS, TONGUE	18
NECK, THROAT	19
SHOULDER/COLLAR BONE	31
SKULL SCALP, BRAIN	32
TEETH	33
WRIST	35
TOES	34
MULTIPLE	36
INTERNAL ORGANS	98
UNKNOWN	99
SPINE, HIPS	38
GROIN	39

CODE 6 – TYPE OF INJURY

FALL FROM ELEVATION	101
FALL ON SAME LEVEL	102
STRUCK AGAINST	103
STRUCK BY	104
CAUGHT IN, UNDER, BETWEEN	105
OVER EXERTION/STRAIN	106
CONTACT w/ELEC. CURRENT	107
CONTACT w/EXTREME TEMP.	108
MOTOR VEHICLE ACCIDENT	109
ASSAULT	110
ANIMAL, INSECT BITE	111
OCCUPATIONAL SKIN DISEASE	210
DUST DISEASE OF LUNGS	220
RESPIRATORY CONDITION DUE TO TOXIC AGENTS	230
POISONING/SYSTEMATIC EFFECTS OF TOXIC MATERIALS	240
DISORDERS DUE TO PHY. AGENTS	250
DISORDERS ASSOC. WITH REPEATED TRAUMAS	260
ALL OTHER OCCUPATIONAL ILLNESS	290

Fig. 1 (continued). Employee accident report. From *Safety Handbook,* Montgomery County Public Schools, Rockville, Maryland (1985).

Division of Insurance and Retirement MONTGOMERY COUNTY PUBLIC SCHOOLS Rockville, Maryland	STUDENT ACCIDENT REPORT

Please read the instructions on the back of the Goldenrod copy before completing the following:

SECTION A

(1) Name of Injured _____
      Last Name   First Name   Middle Name

(2) Home Address _____
      Street   City   State   Zip Code

(3) School Name _____ (4) School Number ☐☐☐

(5) Grade ☐☐   (6) Age ☐☐   (7) Sex ☐

(8) Date Occurred ____ / ____ / ____   (9) Time Occurred ____ : ____ ☐ AM ☐ PM
      Month   Day   Year

(10) Date Accident Reported ____ / ____ / ____   (11) Type of Activity ☐☐
      Month   Day   Year

(12) Specific Activity ☐☐☐   (13) Location of Accident ☐☐☐

(14) Description of Accident _____
_____
_____

(15) Was an adult present at scene of accident?   ☐ Yes   ☐ No

(16) Name of Individual _____

SECTION B

(1) Nature of Injury ☐☐ , ☐☐ , ☐☐   (2) Part of Body ☐☐ , ☐☐ , ☐☐

Immediate Action Taken:

(3) First Aid ☐ Yes ☐ No, By _____

(4) Sent to Health Room   ☐ Yes ☐ No, By _____

(5) Sent to Doctor ☐ Yes ☐ No, By _____ Name of Doctor _____

(6) Sent back to Class   ☐ Yes ☐ No, By _____

(7) Sent to Hospital ☐ Yes ☐ No, By _____

Name of Hospital _____

(8) Was Parent, Guardian, or Neighbor Notified   ☐ Yes ☐ No, Date Notified ____ / ____ / ____
      Month   Day   Year

How Notified _____ Time Notified ____ : ____ ☐ AM ☐ PM

By Whom _____

(9) Total Number of Days lost from School ☐☐☐ ☐

(10) Student has Accident Insurance   ☐ Yes ☐ No

AUTHORIZATION

_____   _____
Principal's Signature   Date

MCPS Form 525-2, Revised September 1975   Distribution: White/Canary/Pink to the Division of Insurance and Retirement
                                                             Goldenrod — File

Fig. 2. Student Accident Report. From *Safety Handbook,* Montgomery County Public Schools, Rockville, Maryland (1985).

INSTRUCTIONS FOR COMPLETING THE STUDENT ACCIDENT REPORT FORM

GENERAL:

Complete *all* of the questions and the authorization section. If not complete the form will be returned. Send the White/Canary/Pink copies within two (2) weeks to "The Division of Insurance and Retirement" — Washington Center. Keep the Goldenrod copy for your files. Examples of reportable accident reports are: All injuries to the head, eye, neck or spine; any bone or joint injury that results in swelling; any puncture wound, burn or laceration that looks as though it may require sutures; injestion of any drug, chemical or foreign materials and other such accidents.

SECTION A

ITEMS 1 THRU 4 — Must be completed as indicated. **ITEM 5** — Indicate the grade level such as 01, 02, 03 ···12 for Grade one (1) thru twelve (12), Head Start should be shown as "24", Kindergarten as "25", Special Education as "26", and Ungraded as "27". **ITEM 6** — **AGE** — State age of student on last birthday. **ITEM 7** — **SEX** — Indicate "M" for male and "F" for female. **ITEM 8** — **DATE OCCURRED** — Indicate date per example: 06/10/71 = June 10, 1971. **ITEM 9** — **TIME OCCURRED** — Indicate the exact time the accident occurred per example: 02:10 = Ten minutes past two O'clock. Check whether AM (Morning) or PM (Afternoon). **ITEM 10** — **DATE ACCIDENT REPORTED** — Indicate per example: 06/21/71 = June 21, 1971.

ITEM 11 — **TYPE OF ACTIVITY** — Indicate using one (1) of the following codes:

01 Elem. Physical Educ.	03 Elem. Non-Phys. Educ. & Non-Noon Recess	05 Secondary Non-Phys. Educ.
02 Elem. Noon Recess	04 Secondary Physical Educ.	06 Varsity & Jr. Varsity

ITEM 12 — **SPECIFIC ACTIVITY** — Indicate using one (1) of the following codes:

101 Archery	109 Fencing	117 Parallel Bars/Horizontal	125 Tennis
102 Badminton	110 Field Hockey	118 Physical Fitness/Calisthenics	126 Track and Field
103 Balance Beam	111 Football	119 Rings/Ropes	127 Trampoline/Mini Tramp.
104 Baseball	112 Games	120 Slides/See Saw	128 Tumbling
105 Basketball	113 Golf	121 Snow and Ice Sports (Skiing)	129 Vaulting Box
106 Cheer Leader	114 Jungle Gym	122 Soccer/Field Ball	130 Volley Ball
107 Dance	115 Kickball	123 Softball	131 Weight Lifting and Training
108 Dodge Ball	116 Muscleman	124 Swings	132 Wrestling/Self Defense

ITEM 13 — **LOCATION OF ACCIDENT** — INDICATE BY USING ONE (1) OF THE FOLLOWING CODES:

201 All Purpose Room	207 Corridor	213 Lavatories	219 Pedestrian
202 Athletic Field	208 Grounds/Non Playground	214 Library	220 Playground
203 Auditorium, Stage	209 Gymnasium and Auxiliary Gym	215 Locker Room	221 School Bus Passenger
204 Bicycle	210 Home Arts	216 Motor Vehicle Passenger	222 Special Activities (Field Trips, Clubs, Class Trips, etc.)
205 Cafeteria	211 Industrial Education shops	217 Music and Band Room	223 Stairs
206 Classroom	212 Laboratories	218 Outdoor Education Site	224 Conference Room
			225 Career Programs/ Off Campus

ITEM 14 — **DESCRIPTION OF ACCIDENT** — Briefly describe how the accident occurred.

ITEM 15 — **WAS AN ADULT PRESENT AT SCENE OF ACCIDENT** — Check Yes or No.

ITEM 16 — **NAME OF INDIVIDUAL** — Print the individual's full name.

SECTION B

ITEM 1 — **NATURE OF INJURY** — Indicate using one (1) and not more than three (3) of the following codes that best describe(s) the injury(ies).

37 Abrasion/Bruise	24 Concussion	31 Foreign Body Imbedded/Loose	35 Object in Mouth/Poisoning
23 Amputation	21 Death	26 Fracture/Chipped	30 Puncture
25 Asphyxiation	28 Dental	22 Internal Injuries	36 Sprain/Strain/Pulled Muscle/ Torn Ligament
38 Bite	27 Dislocation	29 Laceration/Cuts	
32 Burns/Scalds/Chemical	33 Electrical Shock	34 Object in Eye	

ITEM 2 — **PART OF BODY** — Indicate using one (1) and not more than three (3) of the following codes. If more than 3 parts of the body have been injured, indicate the most serious.

69 Ankle	68 Elbow	62 Genital Area	66 Knee	64 Shoulders/Collar Bone
65 Arm	53 Eye	72 Hand	67 Leg	61 Stomach
55 Back	56 Face	52 Head	58 Mouth/Lips/Tongue	73 Teeth
60 Chest/Ribs	75 Fingers/Thumb	63 Hip	54 Neck/Throat	74 Toes
57 Ear	71 Foot	51 Internal Organs	59 Nose	70 Wrist

ITEM 3 — **FIRST AID** — Check Yes or No. If Yes is checked, indicate who gave the student First Aid (Nurse, Secretary, etc.)

ITEM 4 — **SENT TO HEALTH ROOM** — Check Yes or No. If Yes is checked, indicate who sent the student to the Health Room (Secretary, Teacher, etc.)

ITEM 5 — **SENT TO DOCTOR** — Check Yes or No. If Yes is checked, indicate who sent the student to the Doctor (Secretary, Teacher, Nurse, etc.) Print the Doctor's name.

ITEM 6 — **SENT BACK TO CLASS** — Check Yes or No. If Yes is checked, indicate by whom.

ITEM 7 — **SENT TO HOSPITAL** — Check Yes or No. If Yes is checked, indicate who sent the student to the Hospital (Nurse, Teacher, etc.). Print the Hospital's name.

ITEM 8 — **WAS PARENT, GUARDIAN, OR NEIGHBOR NOTIFIED** — Check Yes or No. **DATE NOTIFIED** — Indicate date per example: 05/21/71 = May 21, 1971. **HOW NOTIFIED** — By telephone, etc. **TIME NOTIFIED** — Indicate the exact time per example: 10:50 = 10 Minutes before 11 O'Clock. Check whether AM (Morning) or PM (Afternoon). **BY WHOM** — Print full name of person who notified the parent or guardian.

ITEM 9 — **TOTAL NUMBER OF DAYS LOST FROM SCHOOL** — Indicate per following examples:

000.5 = ½ day	001.0 = 1 day	100.0 = 100 days	023.5 = 23½ days

ITEM 10 — **STUDENT HAS ACCIDENT INSURANCE** — Check Yes or No.

AUTHORIZATION

This form must be signed by the Principal, also indicate the date this report was signed.

Fig. 2 (continued). Student Accident Report. From *Safety Handbook,* Montgomery County Public Schools, Rockville, Maryland (1985).

Business Officials of the United States and Canada have published the *School Safety Handbook* (Haering, 1986). It provides, perhaps, more detailed information than the typical physical education and sport administrator may need on a daily basis. However, it encompasses all aspects of school safety programs. For example, a few categories of specific information of interest to the physical educator, sport administrator, teacher, and coach are:

- accident reporting/record keeping
- emergency action guides including many disasters, severe weather, lighting conditions, and evacuation plans
- physical education facilities
- physical education apparatus
- tumbling, track and field, trampoline
- eye protection
- showers
- rifle club
- football insurance
- seasonal safety

LOCAL SAFETY HANDBOOKS AND POLICIES

Each school district should have an official collection of its school safety policies and regulations. Further, each local school should have a safety committee and specific procedures for handling its needs.

Within the overall safety plan for the district are such general categories as:

- safety education and accident prevention
- risk management
- traffic and bus safety
- fire safety
- plant and eyeglass safety
- emergency and disaster preparedness
- health
- instructional and special activities area (It is in this section that safety in physical education and athletics is generally addressed.)

Local school system handbooks generally quote school board and official institutional regulations. Some that might be of particular interest to physical educators would pertain to:

- student accident reports
- employee accident reports
- reporting student accidents
- fire safety for schools
- emergency and disaster procedures
- health care for allergic children
- emergency care for pupils subject to anaphylactic reaction to an insect sting or ingestion
- emergency first aid
- reporting and caring for an animal bite
- dogs on school grounds

Other general administrative policies and regulations of the school system to be considered in the local manual might include:

- administration of interscholastic athletic programs
- interscholastic athletics in the state (state regulation)
- extracurricular activities
- policies with regard to showering
- pupils excused from physical education classes
- student accident and football insurance
- policies with regard to equipment
- use of trampolines in physical education classes
- rifle club activities and control of rifle ranges

The following excerpts (see Figure 3) typify elements of a local safety handbook (Montgomery County Public Schools, 1985).

WHERE TO START

If your school does not have a formal safety handbook, several established references exist which can be helpful in developing a schematic plan to be completed as your local situation dictates. The entire physical education and athletic staff should work together on this project in order to guarantee the best and most useful handbook possible.

The following general questions for physical education teachers and coaches should be considered in the development of the handbook:

1. Does your school district, institution, or school have an overall safety

8-61   SAFETY IN PHYSICAL EDUCATION

A. Administrative Responsibility for Safety in Physical Education

Safety must play an integral part in physical education instruction. There are certain controls that will aid in eliminating or minimizing accidents.

B. Orientation

Making teachers aware of established rules, regulations, and procedures contained in the Physical Education courses of study, in the Montgomery County Public Schools *Policies and Regulations Handbook*, and in this handbook.

C. Unique Situations

Policies should be formulated to cover variations in physical layout.

D. Rules and Regulations

All rules and regulations pertaining to the use of facilities and equipment should be brought to the attention of the staff.

E. Periodic Inspection

All physical education facilities, equipment, and grounds should be checked periodically to eliminate hidden hazards or unsafe conditions.

8-62   INSTALLATION AND MAINTENANCE OF PHYSICAL EDUCATION FACILITIES

A. There shall be continuous evaluation and research on the safety aspects of facilities, equipment, and supplies.

B. Only approved equipment shall be installed on playgrounds or gymnasiums.

C. The school administration shall confer with the physical education supervisor regarding the location of physical education equipment and apparatus before installation.

D. All relocation of equipment must be approved by the school administration, supervisor of physical education, and director of the Division of Maintenance.

E. All physical education equipment shall be installed according to the standard specification for that equipment or grade level.

F. Playing surfaces should be free of obstructions, uneven surfaces, and slick spots and should be on level ground when possible.

G. Equipment found to be faulty should be labeled with a red tag and immediately withdrawn from use.

8-63   SAFETY INSTRUCTION IN PHYSICAL EDUCATION

Adequate instruction relative to the many facets of physical education activities will eliminate many needless accidents. Instruction should be provided in proper skills and attitudes while in the locker room, gym, shower room, etc. Definite procedures should be set up to cover before-class activities and supervision of those arriving early. Activities should be organized so that skills will be progressive. Care should be taken not to place students in activities or situations for which they are not structurally or functionally prepared. Certain activities require large and more secluded areas for safe execution; these areas include archery, golf, etc.

Fig. 3. Excerpted from *Safety Handbook,* Montgomery County Public Schools, Rockville, Maryland (1985).

8-64   APPARATUS, STUNTS, AND TUMBLING

A. Instruct students in:

    1. The safe use of equipment.

    2. The dangers inherent in each stunt.

    3. The proper mechanics of each stunt.

B. Condition the student in advance of each apparatus stunt.

C. Present a good demonstration either by teacher or capable student.

D. Provide sequential instruction allowing for mastery of fundamentals before attempting more complex moves.

E. Make sure that students have a clear understanding of what they are attempting.

F. Remember that the proper uniform is an important aspect of safe, pleasurable gymnastics.

    1. Remove all jewelry, bracelets, pencils, pens, etc.

    2. Use sneakers or gymnastic shoes.

G. Insist upon proper warm-up period before any stunt is attempted.

H. Magnesium carbonate should be available and used.

8-65   SHOWERS

A. Shower rooms shall be used under strict supervision of a teacher.

B. Running or playing in the shower room is prohibited.

C. Standing on locker room benches is prohibited.

D. Snapping of towels at other students is prohibited.

E. Use of the master shower control is the responsibility of the teacher. Students shall not be assigned this responsibility.

F. Swinging or chinning from bars or pipes in the locker room is prohibited.

G. Benches should be inspected frequently for splinters, protruding nails, sharp corners, etc.

8-66   SAFETY GUIDELINES FOR INDOOR TRACK PRACTICE

A. Teams will not use corridors as practice areas until 45 minues after the end of the school day.

B. Teams will practice outside when weather permits.

C. Signs will be posted stating when and where teams will be practicing.

D. Monitors should be stationed at all corners and intersections to warn persons who may be in the halls while students are running.

E. Announcements will be made over the public address system making faculty and students aware that practice has begun.

F. Teams that have safe areas may practice earlier than the 45-minute limit.

Fig. 3 (continued). Excerpted from *Safety Handbook,* Montgomery County Public Schools, Rockville, Maryland (1985).

program with an assigned supervisor? Do you know who that person is?

2. Are safety policies and practices dynamic and changing as facilities, curricula, and other factors change?

3. Does your institution provide teachers with written updates, workshops, and in-service programs in the areas of general and specific safety concerns?

4. Does your local school have specific safety guidelines and a safety committee? Is a physical educator on that committee?

5. Are emergency first aid procedures known by all staff members in the school?

6. Are there regular documented inspections of all physical education and athletic facilities?

7. Is your maintenance department or system responsive to safety concerns?

8. Is documented accident reporting (for students and employees) completed in a timely fashion?

9. Are all students and employees informed about student insurance and workman's compensation policies and procedures for reporting accidents?

10. Does the school physical education and athletic administration insist that all students be properly supervised not only in the actual teaching of the activity but also in the locker room prior to and following class?

11. Are all federal, state, and local laws, codes, and ordinances followed?

12. Are the sport-related safety regulations required in the "official" rulebooks used by the school enforced? (Examples: National Operational Committee on Standards for Athletic Equipment warning labels, padded volleyball standards).

13. Does the climate in your area warrant cold or hot weather procedures to be followed for specific activities?

14. Do you know who is directly in charge of overall general safety in:
   a. your school district?
   b. your school?
   c. your physical education program?
   d. your athletic program?

15. How are injuries reported?
   a. Is a written report made?
   b. What information is included?
   c. Are reports reviewed and analyzed regularly?
   d. Are recommendations made based on the reports?

16. Has your school developed a working relationship with:
   a. local fire and rescue squad?
   b. local hospitals, clinics and/or physicians?

17. Does your school maintain up-to-date health records on staff and students?
   a. Are these records for people with special needs specially coded?
   b. Are the physical examinations filed for athletes?
   c. How does important health-related data get to physical education teachers and coaches?

SAFETY CHECKLISTS

Checklists are of use to teachers and coaches if they are directed to specific areas. Individual teachers and workers should add to the checklists as appropriate. The following are suggested areas of concern in the development of individual safety checklists:

- security and stability of hanging apparatus
- bleachers (indoors and outdoors)
- showers and locker areas
- floor surfaces—clean, nonslipping
- field conditions (free from rocks and glass, adequate turf)
- tennis court surfaces
- fire exits
- fire drill procedures for classes and athletic events
- general maintenance (preventative and necessary) regularly documented
- proper indoor and outdoor lighting as needed
- proper security—gym, locker rooms, outdoor facilities

Safety and Locker Room Standards
For Students in Physical Education

In physical education, students participate in a regular program of vigorous exercises and activities which require that consideration be given to attire, personal hygiene, and locker room procedures. The following standards are recommended to protect each student and enable him/her to obtain the maximum benefit from the program:

1. Students will have a complete change of clothing for physical education. A T-shirt and shorts or a school physical education uniform are appropriate for most classes. Sweat suits are recommended for outdoor classes conducted during cool weather.

2. Appropriate athletic shoes will be worn to class. This is important for the safety of the student and for the protection of various surfaces. The shoes should have flat soles (not elevated in any way) and should be properly laced or fastened.

3. All personal belongings are to be locked up during class time. Gym clothing is to be locked in the assigned short locker at the end of class. Locks left on long lockers will be removed.

4. Students are to limit their use of the locker room to physical education class time and as appropriate for athletic teams.

5. Students are expected to arrive and depart from the locker room at the appropriate time.

6. All injuries are to be promptly reported to the teacher. The nurse will be notified as required.

7. To prevent loss, damage, or personal injury, students should not wear jewelry during physical education class.

8. Safety glasses with elastic head strap or other eye protection are recommended when wearing prescription glasses or contact lenses.

9. Students are to remain off the bleachers, stage, and equipment unless otherwise directed by the teacher.

10. Food, gum, beverages, and glass are to be kept out of the entire physical education area. Please do not litter.

Fig. 4. From *Safety Handbook,* Montgomery County Public Schools, Rockville, Maryland (1985).

- windows secure and unbroken
- proper ventilation
- appropriate safety padding
- weight training and gymnastics equipment regularly checked and repaired as needed
- all National Operational Committee on Standards for Athletic Equipment requirements met
- all appropriate rule books used for specific sports adhered to in the areas of safety equipment
- appropriate information given to substitute teachers not familiar with either the school, subjected area, or activity being taught.

HAZARDOUS MATERIALS

A number of federal and state ordinances have strict guidelines which require manufacturers of any potentially caustic or toxic materials to provide the consumer with a Material Safety Data Sheet. It is most important to have this information on all materials used within the physical education and athletic programs which may have hazardous potential.

Hazardous materials may frequently be found in physical education and athletic areas. Some of them may be:
- swimming pool chemicals
- training room and first aid room supplies
- field paints
- mat and ball cleaning agents
- gym floor cleaners and sealers

Administrators, coaches, and teachers should be aware of all hazardous and toxic substances used. A list of these materials should be developed and a safety data sheet on each item should be requested from the manufacturer. Some state laws require that this information be maintained on file.

POSTING SIGNS AND WARNING LABELS

The posting of signs and decals certainly does not remove the possibility of

DO NOT SIT OR STAND ON BLEACHERS WHEN THEY ARE CLOSED

Fig. 5. From *Safety Handbook*, Montgomery County Public Schools, Rockville, Maryland (1985).

accidents. It can, however, serve as an everpresent reminder that precautions need to be taken in a particular area or activity.

Signs may be professionally produced. However, with the advent of inexpensive and creative graphics software programs for personal computers, signs can also be easily made at the local level and be very specific to the situation.

Some manufacturers of equipment are now voluntarily providing warning labels which must be placed on equipment and supplies. These labels are generally inexpensive or free. Administrators should provide teachers with such materials, and if no administrator for safety in physical education and athletics exists, the teacher and coach should assume this responsibility.

Figures 4-9 are examples of both locally produced signs and manufacturers' warning labels.

USE OF THIS EQUIPMENT IS RESTRICTED TO STUDENTS ACCOMPANIED BY A TEACHER.

THIS LOCKER ROOM IS FOR THE USE OF PHYSICAL EDUCATION STUDENTS AND TEAM MEMBERS DURING THEIR ASSIGNED PERIODS EXCLUSIVELY.

Fig. 6. From *Safety Handbook,* Montgomery County Public Schools, Rockville, Maryland (1985).

WARNING

Participation in gymnastic activities involves motion, rotation, and height in an unique environment and as such, carries with it a reasonable assumption of risk.

This equipment is intended for use ONLY by properly trained and qualified participants under supervised conditions. Use without proper supervision could be DANGEROUS and should NOT be undertaken or permitted.

WARNING

Catastrophic injury, paralysis, or even death can result from improper conduct of the activity.

GERSTUNG/GYM-THING, INC.

Fig. 7. Gymnastics warning label. From Gerstung/Gymthing, Baltimore, Maryland.

WARNING

Do not strike an opponent with any part of this helmet or face mask. This is a violation of football rules and may cause you to suffer severe brain or neck injury, including paralysis or death.
   Severe brain or neck injury may also occur accidentally while playing football.

NO HELMET CAN PREVENT ALL SUCH INJURIES — USE THIS HELMET AT YOUR OWN RISK

WARNING

Do not use this helmet if the shell is cracked or deformed of if interior padding is deteriorated. Do not clean or shine with any agent except plain soap and water. The prolonged use of other chemicals may cause serious shell degradation.

THIS BATTERS HELMET CANNOT PREVENT ALL HEAD INJURIES IN BASEBALL OR SOFTBALL

Fig. 8. Helmet warning labels.

WARNING

Any activity involving motion or height creates the possibility of serious injury, including permanent paralysis and even death from landing or falling on the head or neck.

You assume a risk of serious injury in the use of this equipment, but this risk can be significantly reduced by always following these simple rules:

1) Use ONLY under the supervision of a trained and qualified instructor. We recommend instructors certified by the United States Gymnastics Association or United States Gymnastics Federation.

2) KNOW YOUR OWN LIMITATIONS. Follow USGSA or USGF progressive learning techniques. Always consult instructor.

3) The equipment MUST be used with proper mats, spotting equipment, and qualified spotters SUITABLE to the activity or skill. Always consult instructor.

4) Always INSPECT for loose fittings, damage, and proper positioning before each use.

5) TEST STABILITY before each use.

EN 9837   97520

WARNING

1. Misuse and abuse of this trampoline is dangerous and can cause serious injuries.
2. Read instructions before using this trampoline.
3. Inspect before using and replace any worn, defective, or missing parts.

Fig. 9. Your gymnasium mats, apparatus, trampolines, and high jump/pole vault landing pits should bear current warning labels. Please inspect your equipment. These are sample labels available from Nissen, Inc., Cedar Rapids, Iowa.

REFERENCES

Flynn, Richard B., editor and contributing author. (1985). *Planning facilities for athletics, physical education and recreation.* North Palm Beach, FL: The Athletic Institute; and Reston, VA: American Alliance for Health, Physical Education, Recreation and Dance.

Haering, Franklin C., project chairman and principal author. (1986). *School safety handbook.* Reston, VA: Association of School Business Officials in cooperation with National Safety Council.

Safety handbook. (1985). Rockville, MD: Montgomery County Public Schools.

CHAPTER 4

First Aid and Sport Safety Policies

PHIL HOSSLER
East Brunswick High School
East Brunswick, NJ

photo by Jim Kirby

The field of first aid in physical education and sport is a vast one that encompasses many general and specific concerns. Entire books and courses of study have been devoted to this subject. This chapter deals with the basic administrative and procedural concerns in the implementation of emergency care and prevention of injuries in physical education classes and sporting activities.

There is no other field where the adage, "an ounce of prevention is worth a pound of cure" carries greater weight than in medicine and related medical fields. The health care afforded physical education classes and athletic teams has become as much a concern of the legal profession as the education profession. The provision of adequate, systematically reviewed, and continually updated health care for physically active youth is clearly an area in which the physical education and athletic departments must do their homework. An effective sports medicine program educates as well as alerts coaches and teachers to the relevance of proper training, prevention, and handling of activity injuries.

According to the American Association for Health, Physical Education and Recreation, "The extent to which society views an event as serious and unexpected determines whether it will call that event an accident. What one group calls an accident may not be regarded as such by another group." (*Sports Safety*, 1977) Being injured, therefore, may be different than being in an accident. The difference is based on causal factors in the setting, possibilities for prevention, and the seriousness of the harm.

An injury may occur at any time and in any location. There is *no* sport or physical education activity which is immune from injury 100% of the time. Steps can be taken, however, to deal with any injury which may occur and to ensure as adequate and proper care as is possible in any given situation.

Reasonable and prudent forethought will enable one to produce a predetermined master plan for dealing with this possibility of injury. Although many injuries can be prevented, others cannot be foreseen, therefore, it behooves each department, department head, and all persons responsible for governing the physical activities of youth to remember the infamous Murphy's Law which states "anything that can go wrong, will go wrong."

The following items should be addressed in an emergency medical system master plan:

- proper supervision of activities
- adequate medical preparation and supplies
- adequate training in injury recognition and first aid treatment by staff
- frequent appraisal of facilities and equipment

SUPERVISION OF ACTIVITIES

The best method of handling injuries in physical education classes and athletic teams is to *anticipate* and *prevent* their occurrence. Supervision is more than just a visual surveillance of the activity, it involves vocal clues to hazardous situations. Students and athletes should be reminded of, and if necessary reprimanded for, actions which produce a hazardous situation for themselves or others. Prior to each activity or new skill, the instructor should indicate the desired objectives as well as the possible detrimental results and dangerous behavior patterns inherent in the activity.

It is assumed, and it should be required, that any coach or instructor who is introducing, conducting, or merely overseeing an athletic or physical activity is knowledgeable in that area. Physical educators are often schooled in the correct manner to teach skills, but too often are not schooled in the myriad of ways in which students can be injured. Athletic coaches should make certain that they study not only their "game plan" for success but also the possibility of a "lame plan" for injury.

There is no substitute for experience. Coaches and teachers who have been practicing their craft for years have learned how to anticipate and prevent many accidents. The "volunteer" or "walk-on" coaches or the novice teacher, however, often are not experienced and may fall prey to enthusiastic "short vision." Some basic guidelines for supervision to prevent injuries would include:

1. *Never leave the site where the activity is being conducted.* Rapid response to severe bleeding and head injuries may be the difference between life and death.

2. *Be in a position to supervise.* This may require some adjustments in activities such as cross country and fitness trails.

3. *Anticipate problems.* As a professional you are expected to identify potential dangers and take precautions against them. Included here are such concerns as:

   a. defective equipment such as fencing foils with no protective tips, bats which are cracked or have slippery grips, and mats which are worn or thin
   b. lack of safety measures such as water on the gym floor, improperly secured nets and debris on the playing field
   c. equipment/clothing which is poorly-fitted or defective
   d. activities which are inappropriate for the capabilities or conditioning level of the participants.

4. *Never permit horseplay.*

5. *Never knowingly permit rules, regulations, or safety procedures to be violated* (Continuing Responsibility of Instructors for Student Injuries, 1984).

MEDICAL PREPARATION AND SUPPLIES

There is a difference between the handling of injuries during the school day and those that occur during after school athletics. For this reason, they will be addressed separately within this section.

ATHLETIC MEDICAL PREPARATION AND SUPPLIES

Both the physical education department and the athletic program must demonstrate forethought in their preparation for athletic injuries. The following criteria may be used to determine the degree of thoroughness shown in anticipation of both life threatening and non-life threatening situations. This list is not complete in all aspects for every situation, but rather is a guideline for the development of one which is specific to the individual situation.

1. Employ an athletic trainer certified by the National Athletic Trainers Association. A certified athletic trainer can provide not only quality injury care, but can also provide the athletic department with better evaluation and disposition of injured athletes, and in-house treatment and therapy for injured athletes under the direction of a physician. A certified trainer is a valuable resource in the prevention of possible injurious situations.

2. Provide each team with a first aid kit (including a separate kit for junior varsity and varsity teams). These kits should be checked periodically and supplies replaced as needed.

3. Place in each first aid kit an emergency contact card (see Figure 1) for each athlete and manager associated with the team.

4. Place in each team's first aid kit a list of those team members who have allergies, special conditions, or any other noteworthy medical condition. This information can be obtained from the athletes' medical histories or from the nurse's office.

5. Provide each member of the coaching staff and place in each first aid kit a card containing important emergency phone numbers such as first aid, police, and hospital.

6. The use of ice in first aid is of the utmost importance. Every athletic team should have the capability of carrying ice in some form with them to all games, both home and away, and to practices. Every school should have enough ice

ATHLETIC EMERGENCY CONTACT

NAME _____ DATE OF BIRTH _____ AGE _____
        LAST   FIRST

PARENT NAME _____ PHONE _____ _____
            MOTHER   AT HOME   AT WORK

           _____ PHONE _____ _____
            FATHER   AT HOME   AT WORK

If you cannot be reached, is there someone you wish to be responsible for your child?

NAME _____ PHONE _____

FAMILY PHYSICIAN _____ PHONE _____

INSURANCE COMPANY _____ POLICY NUMBER _____

KNOWN ALLERGIES TO MEDICATIONS _____

Fig. 1. Emergency contact card.

for first aid for all teams as well as ice for the team's drinking purposes. Even a minor injury, if allowed to go unattended, may delay the athlete's return to activity. The application of a cold modality (ice bags, ice towels, chemical cold packs) is accepted as essential initial first aid for virtually every athletic injury. Nurses, coaches, physical education teachers, and athletic trainers should instill in their student-athletes the practice of "when in doubt, apply ice." Generally ice is applied for 20–30 minutes and then removed for 30–60 minutes; this process is repeated several times daily. The techniques for the use of ice in the first aid treatment of injuries should be known by all coaches, athletes and parents.

7. It is essential to provide water for those teams practicing indoors as well as outdoors. Heat related disorders may be precipitated in a poorly ventilated, humid gymnasium or wrestling room just as easily as those which occur outdoors in the heat of August.

8. All injuries should be properly and promptly reported. In the absence of an athletic trainer, the coach must record the details of the injury and report them to the proper authority. This will greatly help the attending physician as well as avoid entanglements and delays with the insurance companies.

9. It is desirable to obtain a system of communication by which those teams practicing on fields which are an appreciable distance from the training room or nurse's office may be in instant communication with the proper person. Walkie-talkies may be carried in each team's first aid kit and a base station kept in the training room, nurse's office or main office. In the event of a serious injury, the time saved could be crucial. In some situations, it may be more practical to provide telephones which are connected to a main switchboard. Regardless of the method used, it is important that needless loss of time be avoided when dealing with a serious and/or possibly life threatening injury.

10. There are special items which may be deemed advisable to obtain, however, these require special training to use and should not be used by untrained personnel. Oxygen cylinders are beneficial in certain emergency situations which might occur in an athletic

setting. Their use should be confined to only those persons who have been instructed by medical personnel since, ". . . oxygen is a medication. This means that you will have to decide if it is needed, how much to provide, what results are expected, and what harm may be done. The use of oxygen is a special responsibility that can be given only to someone of professional status." (*Oxygen*, 1980)

Splints have long been a mainstay of first aid procedures. Their use has diminished over the past years due to three reasons: first; a decreased number of coaches who have training in their application; second, the increased availability of first aid and rescue squads; and third, fear of possible legal ramifications due to improper application and transportation of the injured. Splints have value in the athletic setting, and their use should not be overlooked. Their application is best left to persons who have been properly trained.

The following flowchart (see Figure 2) demonstrates a typical manner in which a physical education or athletic department may handle an injury. In the flowchart, the words "coach" and "trainer" may be interchanged with "teacher" and "nurse" respectively. The Emergency Medical System includes injury recognition, first aid procedures, cardiopulmonary resuscitation, and proper disposal of the victim. This disposal may be to the parents, the nurse, the first aid squad, or the physician. It is paramount that each physical education and athletic department develop an emergency medical system such as this one and ensure that all necessary persons are aware of the system.

PHYSICAL EDUCATION MEDICAL PREPARATION AND SUPPLIES

In most school systems the preparation demonstrated by the physical education department to handle injuries during classes might be characterized by the phrase, "Go see the nurse." In the majority of cases this may suffice, however, failure to prepare for those instances when such a disposal of an injury would not suffice is inexcusable and negligent. Remembering that "anything that might go wrong, will go wrong" should encourage departments of physical education to make preparations to prevent and handle activity injuries.

Most physical education teachers have had minor injuries in their classes sometime during their professional lives. Most of these are easily handled by sending the student to the nurse's office and later signing the accident report. But what about that time when the student walks into the swinging bat of another student, or when the student steps in a hole and cannot bear any weight on an ankle, or when a fight occurs and one of the combatants is bleeding profusely? What forethought was given to communications, transportation, and preparation by the physical education department? What preparations were made for that one time when the life of the student may actually be endangered?

Each physical education department must take steps to ensure adequate preparation to prevent and handle an injury that may occur.

1. Provide all staff members with in-service opportunities to obtain and/or renew basic first aid and CPR certification. It is vital that all teachers take steps via courses, in-service clinics, membership in professional organizations, etc., to remain current in their knowledge and ability.

2. Project the attitude that hazardous situations *should* be reported and that steps *will* be taken to eliminate them as quickly as possible. It is very discouraging for teachers to report areas of concern and then have the reports ignored.

3. The school system should work in cooperation with the school physician(s) to assess the existing capabilities of the physical education department, nurse's office, and building administration to handle both minor and major injury situations. This assessment should be periodically reviewed and updated.

LIFE THREATENING SITUATIONS

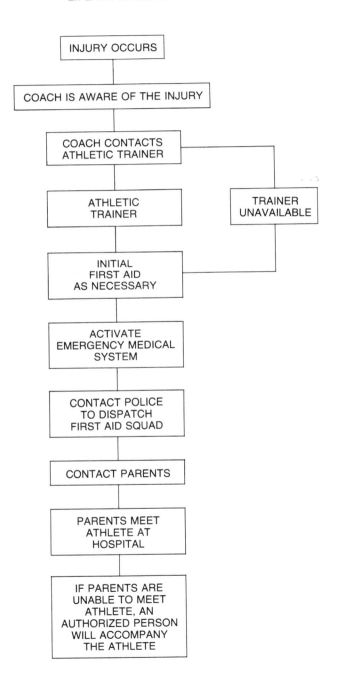

Fig. 2. Emergency medical procedures

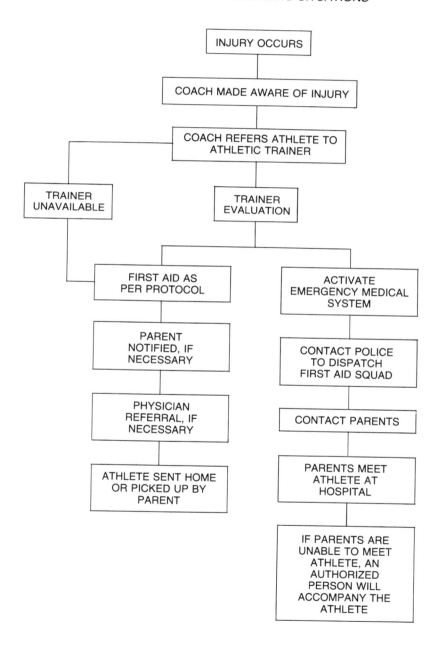

NON-LIFE THREATENING SITUATIONS

INJURY OCCURS

COACH MADE AWARE OF INJURY

COACH REFERS ATHLETE TO ATHLETIC TRAINER

TRAINER UNAVAILABLE

TRAINER EVALUATION

FIRST AID AS PER PROTOCOL

ACTIVATE EMERGENCY MEDICAL SYSTEM

PARENT NOTIFIED, IF NECESSARY

CONTACT POLICE TO DISPATCH FIRST AID SQUAD

PHYSICIAN REFERRAL, IF NECESSARY

CONTACT PARENTS

ATHLETE SENT HOME OR PICKED UP BY PARENT

PARENTS MEET ATHLETE AT HOSPITAL

IF PARENTS ARE UNABLE TO MEET ATHLETE, AN AUTHORIZED PERSON WILL ACCOMPANY THE ATHLETE

Fig. 2. Emergency medical procedures (continued)

4. The money spent to purchase a system of small walkie-talkies would be well worth the expense if the time saved was responsible for the saving of only one student's life.

WHAT WOULD YOU DO IF. . . .

Your class is outdoors playing softball. You are more than ¼ mile from the building. One of the students hits the ball and releases the bat by throwing it over his shoulder. (You have warned the students against this practice, but it happened anyway.) The bat strikes the next batter across the bridge of the nose. The student immediately falls to the ground bleeding profusely from the nose and upper lip. When you reach him he is conscious but in great pain. What do you do?

There are several options and decisions to be made, but they can be grouped into two general categories:

Solution #1-Oops!

1. Try to stop the bleeding with the palm of your hand.
2. Send a student to the nurse's office.
3. Do you know CPR if the student should need it?
4. How is the nurse going to get to you?
5. Does the nurse know if you need an ambulance?
6. What do you do with the rest of the class?
7. How much time is all this taking?

Solution #2-Planned!

1. Using the cleanest material available, e.g. a white T-shirt, try to stop the bleeding with direct pressure.
2. While another student holds the bandage in place, you communicate with the nurse's office via your walkie-talkie.
3. You inform the nurse what has happened, that the student is conscious and cognizant but that a first aid squad will most likely be needed.
4. The nurse telephones for an ambulance.

5. The nurse telephones the parents telling them what has occurred; the parents will meet the first aid squad at the school or the hospital.
6. The student is positioned to treat for possible shock.
7. The class is instructed to join the adjacent class under the supervision of another teacher.
8. A vehicle such as the athletic department's golf cart is used to transport the nurse to the scene to await the ambulance.
9. The student is transported by the first aid squad.
10. You fill out the necessary forms as soon as reasonably possible making certain to include statements by students in the class that indicate that you did indeed instruct them in proper safety procedures.

Which of these two reactions would make the parents feel better about the care afforded their child? Which of these two reactions would stand up better in a court? Is it necessary to go to the extreme in all situations? Probably not, but it is impossible to know beforehand which situations will be routine and which will be life-threatening. It is vital that preparations be made to ensure the highest degree and greatest amount of quality care in *all* situations.

INJURY RECOGNITION AND FIRST AID

One should not be fooled into believing that the hiring of a certified athletic trainer should relieve the coaches of all first aid responsibilities. There will be times when the athletic trainer will not be available, for example, during away games. Therefore, every member of the coaching staff should have a minimum of advanced first aid and cardiopulmonary resuscitation certification. It is recommended that the athletic department, in cooperation with the health classes or local first aid squads, provide in-service opportunities for all coaches in the district to obtain and/or renew their certifications. The athletic trainer can provide in-service education on injury recognition for the coaching staffs.

The Committee on the Medical Aspects of Sports of the American Medical Association recommends that in order to protect the athlete at times of injury, the following steps for aid should be followed:

1. *Stop* play immediately at first indication of possible injury or illness.

2. *Look* for obvious deformity or other deviation from the athlete's normal structure or motion.

3. *Listen* to the athlete's description of his complaint and how the injury occurred.

4. *Act*, but move the athlete only after serious injury is ruled out (The Professionally Responsible Coach, 1982).

It is important to remember that first aid is the immediate and temporary care given to someone until the services of advanced medical care can be obtained. One of the cardinal rules of activity injury care is characterized by the acronyms ICE, PIE, RICE, and ICES. The common members of all these neumonic devices are the letter "I" which stands for ice and the letter "E" which stands for elevation. The letters "C," "P," and "S" represent similar ideas of compression, pressure and support respectively. The "R" denotes rest. These simple words represent the proper method of dealing on a same day basis with athletic injuries.

If the teacher, coach or trainer did not actually see the injury occur, it is important to obtain an accurate description of the mechanism of injury either from the victim or a witness. It is also crucial to determine the exact location of the injury, usually by asking the victim to touch the location. Using these two parameters, mechanism and exact location of the injury, the medical personnel are better able to assess the nature and severity of the injury. For example, if an athletic steps in a hole while running, it is important to assess the speed that the athlete was running, the depth of the hole, the weight of the athlete, the location of the injury, a previous history of injury to this joint, any signs of deformi-

ty, and the degree of normal function that the joint possesses. It is often difficult, if not impossible, to categorically determine the exact nature of an injury. For example, if a student forces a finger into hyperextension when hitting a volleyball, it would be impossible to determine the presence or absence of a fracture. General rules of thumb which apply to such injuries would include:

1. Asking the athlete if he/she can move the finger is not a valid question to assess the presence of a fracture. It is possible to move and bear weight on fractured bones.

2. Check for obvious deformity and loss of function.

3. Tapping the end of the finger may produce a dull "thud" in an intact finger and a feeling of "pins and needles" in a broken finger.

4. The degree of stiffness and swelling is not directly proportional to the severity of the injury.

5. If there is any doubt as to the nature, severity or the athlete's ability to function, the services of a physician should be obtained.

Table 1 lists several mechanisms of injury which may occur in physical education or athletic settings. Note that the care listed for each injury is of a first aid nature; follow-up care and treatment should be left to those individuals who are trained in athletic therapy.

APPRAISAL OF EQUIPMENT AND FACILITIES

Physical education classes have an advantage over athletic teams in terms of appraising the condition of the equipment since the equipment is used as often as eight to ten times each day by different instructors. A variety of supervisors will enhance the chances of defective equipment being fixed or replaced before it might be used and result in possible injury. Once a defective piece of equipment is located, it is important that it be reported and removed from use. This extends beyond pieces of equipment which are handheld; it in-

TABLE 1
First Aid and Emergency Procedures

Bones and Joints

Dislocation—Support joint. Apply ice bag or cold cloths to reduce swelling, and refer to physician at once.

Bone Bruise—Apply ice bag or cold cloths and protect from further injury. If severe, refer to physician.

Broken Nose—Apply cold cloths and refer to physician.

Heat Illnesses

Heat Stroke—Collapse WITH DRY WARM SKIN indicates sweating mechanism failure and rising body temperature.

THIS IS AN EMERGENCY: DELAY COULD BE FATAL

Immediately cool athlete by the most expedient means (immersion in cool water is best method). Obtain medical care at once.

Heat Exhaustion—Weakness WITH PROFUSE SWEATING indicates state of shock due to depletion of salt and water. Place in shade with head level or lower than body. Give sips of dilute salt water, if conscious. Obtain medical care at once.

Sunburn—If severe, apply sterile gauze dressing; refer to physician.

Impact Blows

Head—If any period of dizziness, headache, uncoordination, or unconsciousness occurs, disallow any further activity and obtain medical care at once. Keep athlete lying down; if unconscious, give nothing by mouth.

Teeth—Save teeth if completely removed from socket. If loosened, do not disturb; cover with sterile gauze and refer to dentist at once.

Celiac Plexus—Rest athlete on back and moisten face with cool water. Loosen clothing around waist and chest. Do nothing else except obtain medical care if needed.

Testicle—Rest athlete on back and apply ice bag or cold cloths. Obtain medical care if pain persists.

Eye—If vision is impaired, refer to physician at once. With soft tissue injury, apply ice bag or cold cloths to reduce swelling.

Muscles and Ligaments

Bruise—Apply ice bag or cold cloths and rest injured muscle. Protect from further aggravation. If severe, refer to physician.

Strain and Sprain—Elevate injured part and apply ice bag or cold cloths. Apply pressure bandage to reduce swelling. Avoid weight bearing and obtain medical care.

Open Wounds

Heavy Bleeding—Apply sterile pressure bandage using hand pressure if necessary. Refer to physician at once.

Cut and abrasion—Hold briefly under cold water. Then cleanse with mild soap and water. Apply sterile pad firmly until bleeding stops, then protect with more loosely applied sterile bandage. If extensive, refer to physician.

Other Concerns

Blister—Keep clean with mild soap and water and protect from aggravation. If already broken, trim ragged edges with sterilized equipment. If extensive or infected, refer to physician.

Foreign Body in Eye—Do not rub. Gently touch particle with point of clean, moist cloth and wash with cold water. If unsuccessful or if pain persists, refer to physician.

Source: Prepared by the AMA Committee on the Medical Aspects of Sports in cooperation with the National Athletic Trainers Association and the National Federation of State High School Athletic Associations.

cludes larger pieces such as wire back-stops, surfaces on floors and tracks, fields, and other activity areas.

Surfaces that are hazardous include fields with extremely uneven terrain, and smooth surfaces such as tracks or blacktop which become covered with a layer of water or sand. Some floor surfaces, in the presence of high humidity and/or air conditioning, fail to provide normal traction and can become hazardous.

Athletic coaches often are able to purchase equipment of the highest quality due to greater availability of funds and/or to the increased demands placed on the equipment in a competitive situation. The coach, athletic trainer, equipment manager, athletic director, and athlete should work cooperatively to ensure that all pieces of equipment:

- are maintained according to manufacturer's instructions
- are properly fitted to the individual
- are periodically checked for defects
- that are required by national or local rules to be worn during participation are worn by all athletes
- that are subject to recertification by the National Operating Committee on Standards for Athletic Equipment (NOCSAE) are recertified annually

The first aid kit provided for each athletic team is a piece of equipment that should be periodically checked and updated as needed. Although there are some sports which require specialty items in their first aid kit, the following items should be included in all first aid kits:

- adhesive tape
- tape adherent
- underwrap
- ace bandages (4-inch is the most versatile size)
- band-aids
- extra large band-aids
- lubricant (e.g. vaseline)
- analgesic cream (heat cream)
- tongue depressors
- pieces of foam rubber with varying thicknesses
- sterile gauze pads

- triangular bandage
- emergency contact cards for all athletes and managers
- money for pay phones
- paper and pencil

CONCLUSIONS

During any athletic activity there is the possibility of an injury occurring. It is the responsibility of those persons charged with the governing and implementation of the activity, whether it is interscholastic, intercollegiate, Pop Warner, Little League, recreational, or physical education, to try to prevent injuries through (a) proper conditioning, (b) observation of rules, (c) proper use of equipment, and (d) elimination of hazardous practices and situations. Supervisors, coaches, and teachers also have the responsibility of knowing what to do when an injury occurs. This does not imply that everyone involved in the activity must know how to treat some of the more serious injuries, but it does mean that everyone should know how to activate an effective emergency medical plan.

All activity injuries, regardless of severity, are best handled by preventing their occurrence. Prevention requires forethought and planning. Within the organizational structure of the school system, there should be input from physicians, nurses, athletic trainers, teachers, coaches, first aid personnel, and administrators to ensure a properly planned and adequate system for handling both minor and serious injuries. The emergency medical system must take into consideration the respective first aid training and competencies of those persons working within it and must include considerations for proximity of medical personnel within the system and those individuals outside the immediate system. Communication and transportation limitations must be considered and steps made to correct areas of weakness.

REFERENCES

Continuing responsibility of instructors for student injuries. (1984). Phoenix, AZ: Universal Dimensions, Inc.

Oxygen. (1980). (Vol. G-4). Arlington, VA: The Compressed Gas Association, Inc.

Sports safety. (1977). Washington, DC: American Association for Health, Physical Education and Recreation.

The professionally responsible coach: a seminar on the liability of coaches and the safety of athletes. (1982). Phoenix, Arizona: Athletic Institute of Continuing Education.

CHAPTER 5

Archery

CLAIRE CHAMBERLAIN

The University of Lowell
Lowell, MA

Archery is an exciting, challenging sport. Because of the equipment used, however, it can also be a dangerous and potentially lethal activity. For this reason, it is imperative that both the supervisor and the participant know and appreciate the risks. Simple carelessness with a bow and arrow can result in serious injury. Safety, then, must become a stringent habit for all concerned.

The recent rise of lawsuits due to negligence has focused the public's attention on the need for qualified supervision, appropriate emergency procedures, proper equipment and facilities, and attention to detail. It is the teacher's responsibility to provide a safe environment in which archery can be taught. Not only must the student understand what to do and why, but also what not to do and why not. Failure to explain the dangers involved could result in a lawsuit. A person who has "failed to warn" adequately can be held liable for resultant injuries.

Archery is a rewarding activity. Infuse respect for safety in your students, and you will have a safe, enjoyable program.

SUPERVISION: CHECKLIST

1. Only qualified people should supervise archery.

2. Keep the class size small. Have no more than four people shoot per target. A partner system can work well, and classes may shoot in flights.

3. Never instruct from in front of the line when arrows are nocked.

4. If correcting someone, do not put your hand or arm in between their bowstring and bow. They may release the arrow, and you may get hit by the string.

5. Emergencies.
   a. School, club, or camp emergency procedures should be delineated well in advance and posted.
   b. Know the location of the nearest telephone. If it is a pay telephone, have the appropriate change available as well as telephone numbers needed.
   c. If you are outside, consider bringing a first aid kit with you. If the target range is a considerable distance from any phone, perhaps you could obtain a walkie-talkie to call for assistance.
   d. Have current first aid certification.

6. Establish clear directions, either by voice or by whistle, to begin shooting, to cease fire, and to retrieve arrows.

7. Emphasize that each participant shares the responsibility for safe conduct of him/herself and of others. The warning cry is "hold your arrows!" Teach it and practice it so that there is instantaneous response.

8. If you wish to have several archers shooting at different distances at the same time, always move the targets, never the people. Never have more than one shooting line at any given time.

9. Assign specific equipment to each student after checking it carefully, particularly arrow length. It is helpful to post the student's names and which equipment has been assigned for their future reference.

10. Keep all unused tackle locked up.

INDOOR RANGE: CHECKLIST

1. Locate the range away from other simultaneous activities.

2. Have easy visibility within and around the area.

3. Any doors to the target range should be closed during class. Post signs "Archery in progress." It is helpful if the locks on the doors permit people to leave the area but not to enter it. Unsuspecting people may wander into the area and unknowingly become a target. If possible, have entries limited to behind the shooting line.

4. Put up an appropriate backdrop to catch those arrows which miss the target. It can be a specialized archery backdrop curtain or bales of hay.

5. Have clearly marked shooting lines. The archers will straddle the line while shooting. A good set-up is to have one shooting line with targets placed at different distances.

6. Any obstacles or other activity equipment should be removed from the area.

7. Targets should be mounted securely. If target mats are placed on roll-a-way stands, archers should check their sturdiness after each end. An unbalanced target of any type could pitch forward and injure participants and/or arrows in the target.

8. Post safety rules.

OUTDOOR RANGE: CHECKLIST

1. Use natural terrain when possible. Having a grassy hill behind your targets eases the task of looking for arrows.

2. As much as possible, choose an area free of obstacles: trees, telephone wires, rocks, goalposts, and the like. A considerable area behind the targets should also be cleared.

3. Mark the target area well. Rope it off and post signs. Access to the range should be limited to participants.

4. Have clearly marked shooting lines.

5. Targets should be secured.

6. Keep grass mowed well. Long grass hinders the archer from locating missing arrows.

7. Post safety rules.

EQUIPMENT SAFETY

If the archery equipment is kept in good condition, then chances for accidents and injuries lessen, and learning is enhanced. Poorly-maintained equipment represents an accident waiting to happen. Equipment failure can be due to a manufacturing flaw, abuse, aging, or just plain neglect. It is imperative that equipment be inspected when purchased, before and after each season, and, in some cases, before each end shot. Share this responsibility with the archers, and the job can be done quickly and efficiently.

ARROWS: CHECKLIST

1. Any arrow that has a split, crack, or a deep puncture should be destroyed and discarded to prevent its use. Do not shoot damaged arrows.

2. Before each end, check carefully to see if any arrow that missed the target was hit by another arrow. Look for a puncture mark and test the arrow's rigidity. If the hole is too deep, and the arrow begins to crack, destroy the arrow.

3. Tips and nocks should be whole. If not, some can be removed and replaced with glue.

4. Blunt tips should be sharpened—check with your maintenance department. Arrows hitting hard objects can cause the tip to be driven into the shaft. If there are any resultant splintering on the arrow shaft, sand off those splinters.

5. The fletching (feathers) should be whole and secured. If they are not, it can cause the feathers to penetrate the bow hand when shot.

6. Students must shoot with the proper length arrow. Too short an arrow can be overdrawn which is extremely dangerous. Either the arrow could be shot into the bow hand or, if drawn far enough, could hit the inside of the bow and shatter in the archer's face. It is better to shoot with an arrow that is a bit too long than one that is too short.

7. Excess dried glue around the feathers should be sanded to avoid any abrasion (feather cuts) on the bow hand as the arrow is released.

BOW SAFETY: CHECKLIST

1. Limber up each bow gradually, if it has not been used for several days, with gentle quarter or half draws. This reduces the chances of the bow breaking due to too much stress too soon.

2. Bows are designed to bend in a certain direction and on a particular plane. When stringing, brace the bows carefully on the desired plane to avoid damaging or breaking the bow. Make sure bows are not strung inside out.

3. Before bracing, make sure the string is secured in the bottom notch. Inspect the bow for splits, tears, cracks, or any suspicious damage. Stress marks in fiberglass bows appear white in color. Stringing a damaged bow can cause the bow to break.

4. As you brace the bow, use sufficient pressure on the bow to bend it so that you have enough room to move the

string up the bow and not get your fingers caught. Secure the loop into the upper notch. If the string goes beyond the bow and comes off, the bow may rebound into the archer's face.

5. Check the strings for undue wear and tear. Replace them immediately with strings of proper length that match the poundage of the bow.

6. Apply bee's wax to any strings which are separated. (Rub with a towel to create heat. Do not put bee's wax on the serving; use paraffin, if needed.)

7. All bows must be strung to their proper fistmele, or distance between bow and string. Too little can cause a severe wrist slap; too much may result in a broken bow.

8. Do not go into full draw position and release without an arrow on the string. Either the bow or string might break.

CLASS ORGANIZATION: CHECKLIST

1. Wear simple, comfortable clothing. Secure long hair away from the bowstring. Remove bracelets, necklaces, watches. Bulky articles in shirt pockets such as pens, pencils, and eyeglasses should be removed before shooting. Sleeves, sweaters or jackets which are pushed up at the bowarm elbow should be smoothed out. The released bowstring could be caught and impeded by any of the above.

2. Flat, rubber-soled shoes are best for indoor shooting, not only to protect the floor, but also to assure a constant height when shooting. Appropriate footwear is important when shooting outdoors. When on a club range, archery golf course, or when hunting, more sturdy shoes are advisable for sure footing and for protection from thorns, underbrush, and poison ivy.

3. Watch students brace their bows. Be sure they do it correctly. Have them check that the bow is not strung inside-out.

4. All arrows must be checked for safety. (See previous section.)

5. Assign no more than four stu-

dents per target. Check to see that the bows are right-side up.

6. Shooters will straddle the clearly defined shooting line and will wait for the signal to begin shooting. Review, also, the warning cry of "Hold Your Arrows!" (In field archery, cry "Timber" before shooting.)

7. When finished, all shooters will step back from the shooting line and wait until the command to retrieve arrows has been given. All arrows are retrieved at the same time.

8. Beginning students will tend to support their arrow with their bowhand index finger. Instruct them to wrap that finger around the grip before releasing the string; otherwise, they will experience a feather cut and impede arrow flight.

9. Beginning students will tend to extend or to hyperextend their bow arm elbow. Unless they turn that elbow slightly out, the string will slap the elbow and/or get caught on the top of the arm guard.

10. All shooters should wear arm guards and finger tabs or gloves to protect them from string slap or string abrasion. Check to see that they are on the correct arms and hands.

11. Avoid using high-poundage bows at short distances, as the arrows will tend to go through the target, causing damage to the arrow and to the target.

12. Never point an arrow at anyone. Nock and draw arrow only in the direction of the target.

13. Should an arrow fall from the bow in front of the shooting line, the archer may attempt to retrieve it with the bow. If he/she cannot reach it, it is considered a shot. Shooters may never step in front of the shooting line to retrieve any arrow unless the command to retrieve has been given.

14. If an arrow is hanging from the target, cease fire. Have the student insert the arrow properly into the target. Should it be left hanging, it becomes a target itself and could become damaged.

15. Inexperienced shooters tend to overdraw. Bows are designed to be pulled a certain distance. If they are overdrawn, injury could result: the bow can break; the arrow can break against the belly of the bow; or the arrow can be shot into the bow hand. Emphasize the correct anchor point.

16. All students must shoot from the same line. If you wish different distances, move the targets, not the people.

17. Bow hands too high on the grip can be too close to the arrow rest. When the arrow is released, feather cuts can result.

18. Remind students of the shared responsibility for safety. If they see anything unusual they should call out "Hold Your Arrows!" immediately. Once the situation is corrected, the signal to resume firing may be given by the instructor.

RETRIEVAL: CHECKLIST

1. No one will retrieve his/her arrows until the command is given.

2. One person, the target captain, should remove the arrows carefully. All others should stand away to avoid being poked by the withdrawn arrow.

3. Arrows driven into the target so that the feathers are wholly or partially covered should be retrieved by pulling from behind the target. Those buried in grass should be pulled from the tip end to avoid further feather damage.

4. Control arrows by holding the tips down. Fan out the arrows slightly to prevent feather damage.

5. Do not run with any archery tackle.

6. No one should return from his/her target until all arrows at that target have been located. This is both for safety and for courtesy.

7. Looking for lost arrows outside in the grass can be difficult, particularly if they are buried. Advise students to keep track of approximate locations of missed arrows.

8. Back at the shooting line, have the students check all their arrows for splits, cracks, blunt tips, splinters, punctures, missing nocks. Replace those arrows immediately. If outside, wipe moisture and dirt from arrows before shooting again.

9. Count your shooters. Make sure all have returned before firing again. If alone on the range, lean your bow against the front of the target as a signal you are up there looking for arrows.

10. Never stand and instruct from in front of the shooting line when students have arrows nocked.

11. Allow no horseplay, running, or loud noises on an archery range. Shooting safety is serious business.

EQUIPMENT CARE: CHECKLIST

1. Hang bows up, unstrung, when not in use or place in bow cases. It is helpful to group bows by poundage.

2. Arrows should be stored vertically and separately, to prevent warping or damage to feathers. Store arrows by length for easy reference.

3. Keep all tackle in a cool, dry place.

4. Periodically, wax the string with bee's wax and the serving with paraffin.

5. Wooden bows and arrows can be cleaned with Butcher's wax. Fiberglass equipment needs to be wiped with a clean, damp cloth and then wiped dry.

6. Treat leather tackle with any standard leather cleaner/preservative.

7. Keep all tackle locked up when not in use.

8. Dry the matts before storing.

REFERENCES

Klann, Margaret L. (1970). *Target archery.* Reading, MA: Addison-Wesley Publishing Company.

McKinney, Wayne C. (1985). *Archery.* Dubuque, IA: William C. Brown Publishers.

Niemeyer, Roy K. (1967). *Beginning archery, 2nd edition.* Belmont, CA: Wadsworth Publishing Company.

Pszcola, Lorraine. (1984). *Archery.* New York: Saunders College Publishing.

Rowe, Ruth E. and Bowers, Julia H. (1983). Archery. In N.J. Dougherty (Ed.), *Physical education and sport for the secondary school student* (pp. 35–44). Reston, VA: The American Alliance for Health, Physical Education, Recreation and Dance.

CHAPTER 6

Basketball

JAMES E. BRYANT
San Jose State University
San Jose, CA

photo by Jim Kirby

Basketball is an American game, and as such, has earned a reputation as an easy, safe game that *everybody* knows how to play. In reality, there are countless students who really don't know how to play the game skillfully and safely, and that situation creates potential problems.

Basketball requires physical stamina, speed, strength, explosive leg power, agility, and gracefulness. It is a non-contact sport with the potential for extensive physical contact. Playing on a hard surface in a confined space always involves a certain degree of risk. The extent of that risk is determined in part, however, by the instructor's skill in the supervision of students as they engage in the basketball activity. The ability of the instructor to select appropriate skill experiences for the student is essential. A logical class lesson with learning progressions must be developed and implemented. Finally, the environmental conditions must be controlled to minimize risk.

It is imperative that the physical education instructor has both a knowledge of the mechanics of basketball and an appreciation of the risks associated with the activity. The instructor must be in a position to anticipate safety problems and to plan strategies that will eliminate or reduce potentially serious situations.

SUPERVISION

A typical basketball class will consist of 25 to 40 students in a gymnasium facility that includes a 50' × 84' basketball floor. The facility can be further divided to accommodate game play by using the width of the court rather than the length, yielding a court size of 42' × 50'. The role of the instructor is to provide safe supervision for each student in that confined space. Strategies associated with the quality of supervision, the form of organization and control required, and effective planning are identified below.

QUALITY OF SUPERVISION

The quality of supervision of a basketball class requires that the instructor have a knowledge of the following.

1. *The mechanics of basketball.* It is important that the instructor understand how correct execution maintains a safe participation experience for all students.

2. *Skill progression.* The instructor must be knowledgeable enough to place skill acquisition experiences in perspective through a well designed and thought out progression.

3. *Student readiness.* The instructor must comprehend the wide variety of readiness levels of students and be capable of placing each student in a safe environment.

4. *Student capabilities.* The instructor must understand the student from a physiological, psychological and psychomotor perspective.

5. *Student behavior.* The instructor must encourage behavior that will enable the class to operate in a safe and efficient manner.

6. *Injuries associated with basketball.* The instructor should have a background that permits recognition and first aid treatment of injuries, as well as an understanding of their causes and their seriousness. This background should include the following common problem areas:

- blisters and the treatment and prevention of blisters
- calluses and the treatment of the callus
- sprains and the treatment and prevention of a sprain
- eye injuries
- finger injuries (e.g. jammed fingers)
- trauma injuries

Quality supervision also requires that the instructor sense the "messages of the gym." An example of this would be recognizing the potential for altercations between students, due to frustration, the physical contact that occurs in basketball or their general behavior. The instructor must create, enforce, and modify rules based on the physical, psychological, and emotional readiness of the students.

ORGANIZATION AND CONTROL

The organization and control of a basketball class also centers on the skills of the instructor. Following are requirements for maintaining this aspect of supervision.

1. The instructor must always maintain a visual and physical presence with each student. It is not acceptable to simply be in the area. There must be interaction with the students in the class, and the instructor must establish a position in the basketball area so that the total class can be observed even when he/she is working with a single student or a small group.

2. The instructor must develop a set of safety rules to be distributed to students and posted. In addition, these safety rules must be conveyed verbally to students on a regular basis. These rules should include:

- no one may engage in a basketball activity unless the instructor is present
- all basketballs are to be removed from the playing court area and placed on the ball racks unless being used by a student
- basketball shoes are to be worn during class
- abusive use of elbows and other forms of illegal contact are not permitted by basketball rules and will not be tolerated in class

PLANNING

Planning of a basketball class is crucial to the safety of all students. Planning should include the following.

1. *A detailed lesson plan* must be developed for each instructional class. The plan should relate directly to the day's class and specify safety strategies related to that class period.

2. *A lesson plan* should reflect an effort to provide a well supervised situation that would include the identification of:

- organized teaching stations that provide supervision and assistance for students practicing skills.
- logical progression. As an example, blocking out when rebounding should precede simply going to the basket and attempting to jump up and rebound the ball.
- proper warm up and cool down activities based on the most recent applied exercise physiology research.
- organized drills that are designed for the particular age and skill level of the class. These drills should reflect the elimination of situations that would create a frustration level leading to physical altercations.
- an instructional experience designed to enhance learning without fear of injury. Elimination of drills which place students in jeopardy (e.g. loose ball drills have a potential for injury beyond the norm, and should be controlled or eliminated. Rebound drills have risks, and playing five-on-five half-court basketball also has a greater potential for injury than a reduced number).
- specific instructions on the execution of a drill or the play situation. A good example would be the need for definitive directions to describe the path players should run during a drill in order to avoid collisions (e.g. running a fast break drill down court and then returning to the start in an organized fashion by running on the outside of the sidelines).

SELECTION AND CONDUCT OF THE ACTIVITY

The instructor's ability to select the proper class content and develop the safest possible experience for the student is dependent on several variables. These variables are based on the student's maturation level, ability level, and readiness.

Maturation level is of extreme importance in a basketball class environment. In a class with a variety of physical sizes (i.e. height, weight, and age) the potential for injury increases. Following are some examples of how to reduce the potential for injury through grouping.

1. *Group based on height, weight and age.* One method of grouping requires the establishment of a component system that assigns a point value to each size factor which then provides a balance for any learning experience the student may be involved in during class (e.g. all students with a component value of 20–24 are placed in a grouping, 25–29 in another grouping, etc.).

2. *Select instructional experiences that meet the maturation level of the student.* Using a drill that requires a student to exceed his or her physical capabilities can result in injury (e.g. a 5'2" student placed in a rebound drill with a 6'1" student places both students in jeopardy).

The ability level of a student is also of importance and needs to be considered when planning a basketball class. Mixing highly skilled students with less skilled students can create a safety problem. Again, grouping is needed, particularly if a class with mixed ability levels is assigned, rather than designated classes of beginning basketball, intermediate basketball, and advanced basketball. Two methods of reducing safety problems associated with ability levels are:

- ability group by balancing the skill level of each group during drills or play situations

- ability group by separating skill levels of each group (i.e. highest skill level in one group, next highest skill level in another group, etc.).

Within any ability grouping the instructor needs to instill in the students an attitude of responsibility for one another. Highly skilled players need to be aware of their peers who are less skilled, and learn to serve as a mentor during instruction rather than attempt to dominate a learning situation. This can lead to a reduction of injuries.

Student readiness is also of importance. A basketball class may have students not only with a variety of skill levels, but also various levels of motor readiness, interest, and motivation. Safety concerns associated with motor readiness include the following.

1. *Stressing of body awareness.* Basketball requires extensive jumping and movement skills. Students must often be taught how to be aware of what they are capable of doing. They need to be aware of their surroundings: where they are on the floor, how close they are to other players, and where they are supposed to be during a given circumstance.

2. *Stressing of how to fall properly.* For example, if the student is knocked down when rebounding under the basket or falls while dribbling the ball down the court, the student needs to be at an appropriate readiness level to avoid most injuries in those situations.

3. *Awareness of the physical fitness level of students* and the selection of appropriate skill experiences that match fitness levels.

Safety concerns related to student interest or motivation also must be considered when teaching basketball. These considerations include the following.

1. *Assisting students on how to deal with fears* associated with basketball. Those fears include fear of failure, resulting in tentativeness on the court which can contribute to injury, not only to the student with the fear but other students as well.

2. *Reduction of the pressures.* The pressure of performing and possibly failing in a game situation is severe and should be controlled. Remember, that "everyone is supposed to know how to play basketball" and it is embarrassing not to perform well. Another example of pressure reduction is the elimination of the need to excel on a skill test as the requisite for a "good grade."

ENVIRONMENTAL CONDITIONS

There are a variety of environmental conditions that affect the safety of a basketball class. These environmental conditions are related to the facility and the equipment used. Being aware of these environmental conditions and eliminating those that have potential to be a safety problem is of extreme importance.

Facility requirements to meet safety standards are listed below.

1. There must be buffer zones between teaching stations and playing areas. Players who are concentrating on the skill or the game will pursue a loose ball into an adjacent court. A buffer zone of at least six feet must separate courts to avoid collisions.

2. Large padded mats should be affixed to the wall behind every baseline of a basketball court. Typically, there are pads behind the baseline of regulation courts, but seldom are there pads behind the makeshift baselines of courts where students play the width of the court. These areas are actually the sidelines of the regulation court and are often ignored. Pads must be placed behind these makeshift baselines as well.

3. Padding on the bottom of rectangular backboards is needed to eliminate an injury when a student with excellent jumping ability jumps and risks hitting part of the body on the bottom of the backboard.

4. Break away rims should be installed and maintained. A break away rim dramatically reduces the potential of a glass backboard shattering. This type of rim also eliminates any jumping up and hanging on a rim.

5. Nets for the basket must be in good repair.

6. Floors must be cleaned on a periodic basis. Both hardwood and synthetic surfaces should be cleaned of dirt on a periodic basis during the day just as the floor is swept at half-time of an interscholastic contest. Also, wet surfaces should be dried immediately with towels.

7. All obstacles and equipment should be placed away from the basketball teaching area. Examples of these obstacles and equipment are:
- basketballs randomly strewn on the floor

- gymnastics apparatus or other physical education equipment located in proximity to the instructional area (even padded and secured apparatus belong in an area away from a basketball instructional area)
- non-class students wandering through the instructional area
- shirts and other clothing tossed on the court in proximity to the instructional area

Equipment requirements associated with the instruction of a safe basketball class include the following.

1. Protection of the students' eyes through the wearing of safety glasses. This is highly recommended to reduce eye injuries that may include detached retinas.

2. Protection of teeth by the use of mouth guards. Again, this is a preventive piece of equipment that is highly recommended to avoid permanent damage to teeth.

3. To avoid scratches that could develop infection, it is advisable that nails be trimmed and that jewelry that might also harm the wearer or participant be removed by the student (e.g., rings, bracelets, etc.).

4. Basketball shoes help to prevent serious ankle and foot injuries. It should be required that a basketball shoe be worn in a basketball class, and a recommendation of appropriate shoes should be made. There are at least 3 quality basketball shoes produced that reduce minor ankle and foot injuries. A good basketball shoe has:
- a high collar on the high top shoe.
- a Y band, which is a leather strap around the ankle that holds the ankle in the shoe
- a heel counter that reinforces the ankle as the ankle rolls in and out.
- a full air mid sole that absorbs shock
- a wide base of the sole that prevents minor ankle sprains.

Students should be informed of the advances in the shoe industry and encouraged to select a shoe that has these features.

CONCLUSION

There are potential hazards in basketball, and with each hazard, there is a preventive safety measure. Proper planning, anticipation of potential safety problems, and capable supervision by the instructor will all contribute to a safe environment for students participating in a basketball class.

REFERENCE

Doane, G. (1983). Basketball. In N.J. Dougherty (Ed.), *Physical Education and Sport for the Secondary School Student* (pp. 63–75). Reston, VA: The American Alliance for Health, Physical Education, Recreation and Dance.

CHAPTER 7

Coed Flag Football

MARYANN DOMITROVITZ
The Pennsylvania State University
State College, PA

The popularity of the game of football is not only reflected by the attendance at high school, college, and professional games, but also by its frequent appearance in the physical education curriculum. Although in physical education classes the game appears in a modified version such as flag football, the skills and strategies inherent in football, exclusive of physical contact, apply equally to flag football.

Prior to participation in this activity, it is imperative that students differentiate between the game as played with protective equipment and that played with flags. Further, since some aspect of the game can appear from the elementary level through the senior high school level, it is critical that the skill level and the physical differences and capabilities of the students are kept in mind when designing the unit and lesson plans. In many situations the activity classes are coeducational, therefore, this must also be a consideration when selecting and programming skills, progressions, drills, lead-up games, and the regulation game.

The attention to appropriate equipment must also be deliberate. The size, weight and composition of the football will vary from the modified equipment appropriate for the elementary level to the regulation football appropriate for the high school student.

Because students may be unaware of or ignore the potential for injury in this activity, it is imperative that a safe learning and playing environment be maintained. Although the correct execution of the activity skills and their application in practice or game play is a priority, enforcement of the rules of the game is of the utmost importance. Inconsistency in officiating and rule interpretation or enforcement, particularly with the non-contact rules, has the potential to contribute to a wide range of injuries. The supervision must be of the highest quality.

The impact that daily use and the weather have on the activity area must also be taken into consideration. An inspection of the playing field to determine its suitability for class must be regularly scheduled. Bare spots, rocks, holes, glass, and obstructions near boundaries are hazards to safe playing conditions and must be removed before approval for use is issued.

Although attention to each of the aforementioned is essential, perhaps the most important ingredient is the selection of a qualified and conscientious physical educator who is knowledgeable and qualified to teach the activity and who will devote the time and effort necessary to provide a safe and enjoyable experience for the students.

CONDUCT OF ACTIVITY

Prior to designing a unit for coed flag football it is essential to identify the skill and ability level of the students for whom the unit is planned. This is a consideration that must be dealt with not only in the preparation of the unit plan, but with each daily lesson as well. One question that must be asked is, "Do these students possess the qualities necessary to allow them to safely and successfully participate in this lesson?"

The following checklist has been compiled to assist in the development of a safe and successful plan.

1. Assess the abilities of the class. Do they possess the skill level to allow them to participate in the day's activity?

2. Assess the physical attributes of the class. Organize the distribution of participants for equitable practice and competition.

3. Develop your unit plan and lesson plans with cognitive, psychomotor, and affective objectives.

4. Develop content appropriate for the age and skill level of the participants.

5. Organize your activity so all directional flow is similar. (Example: all students throwing in the same direction.)

6. Allow adequate distance between drill groups when accuracy and execution may not be consistent. (Example: punting.)

7. Consider the direction of the wind in drills when the ball will be thrown and kicked.

8. Be aware of the location of the sun in drills involving catching and tracking the football.

9. Emphasize the rules interpretation for the day's activity.

10. Demonstrate, describe, and teach the correct skill technique and provide feedback to the students regarding their execution.

11. Remind students of boundaries and limitations of the drill, leadup, or regulation game.

12. Review your expectations for the lesson.

To help you develop and organize your unit or lesson plan, the chart in figure 1 may be of assistance. The three levels can be interpreted as beginning, intermediate, and advanced skill or knowledge.

The use of the chart for each activity class should enable you to evaluate the class and modify your lessons accordingly. Suggested drills and activities for the individual skills may be found in *Physical Education and Sport for the Secondary School Student* (Domitrovitz, 1983).

SUPERVISION

The importance of proper supervision cannot be overly emphasized, particularly with an activity such as coed flag football. To insure the needed supervision for the lesson, it is imperative that the physical educator be well organized and prepared. Following is a checklist that should assist the planning and preparation of the lesson with particular emphasis on supervision.

1. Specify the area where the class should meet.

2. Establish a procedure for dispensing equipment.

3. Organize the warm-ups, drills, lead-ups, etc., so all the activity will be within your field of vision.

4. Establish a pattern of rotation so instruction and specific supervision can

take place without hindering your vision of other activity areas.

5. Determine if the student behavior in the activity is what you had intended and initiate corrective action where appropriate.

6. Observe the officiating and correct any improper interpretation or enforcement of the rules.

7. Specify a procedure for dismissal. Check to see that the area has been vacated by all students.

ENVIRONMENTAL AND SAFETY CONDITIONS

Prior to any activity, it is imperative that a procedure be established for the inspection, maintenance and reporting of hazards. This inspection should occur on a regular basis and any reported hazard must be attended to before granting permission for resumption of the use of the facility or equipment.

The following checklists have been compiled to assist in the inspection of the facility, the equipment, and proper activity attire.

EQUIPMENT CHECKLIST

1. Inspect the condition of the flags and belts and repair when necessary.

2. Inspect the condition of the footballs.

3. Order a variety of sizes and types of footballs to accommodate the various levels of ability.

4. Inspect all markers and determine whether they are safe for the activity.

5. Gather and place unused equipment off the field of play and a safe distance from the activity area.

6. Collect all equipment at the conclusion of the class and store it in a secure space.

FACILITY CHECKLIST

1. Inspect the fields for holes, glass, poles, sprinklers, and obstructions.

2. Inspect the turf for suitability of play.

3. Lay out adjacent fields with enough space between fields to minimize

Class (Grade & Period): _____

Number of Students: Girls:_____   Boys:_____

Overall Ability Level: I _____, II _____, III _____

Skills/Knowledges	Level I	Level II	Level III	Safety	Rules
1. Rules					
2. Body Control					
3. Blocking/Screening					
4. Passing					
5. Receiving					
6. Place Kicking					
7. Punting					
8. Centering					
9. Tagging					
10. Lead-ups					
11. Ball Carrying					
12. Ball Handling					
13. Regulation Game					
14. Team Offense					
15. Team Defense					

Skill Exceptions: (List students of extreme levels of skill)

High   Low

1.   1.

2.   2.

3.   3.

4.   4.

5.   5.

Fig. 1. Class ability levels can be recorded for reference.

the potential for collision between participants on neighboring activity areas.

PARTICIPANT CHECKLIST

1. Check for proper footwear. Do not allow metal cleats.

2. Check for students wearing glasses and provide appropriate glass guards.

3. Stress the rules governing play for the day's activity. Reinforce the non-contact rule.

4. Assign appropriate stretching exercises for the weather conditions and the activity to be presented.

5. Establish a procedure for the reporting and treatment of injuries sustained in the activity.

If the necessary attention is devoted to (a) the conduct of the activity, (b) the supervision, and (c) the environmental and safety conditions, the inclusion of coed flag football in the physical education curriculum should allow for enjoyable participation that is relatively free from injuries and incidents.

REFERENCES

Bayless, M. and Adams, S. H. (1985). A liability checklist. *JOPERD, 2,* 49.

Bucher, C. A. and Koenig, C. R. (1983). *Methods and materials for secondary school physical education* (6th ed.). St. Louis, MO: C. V. Mosby.

Domitrovitz, M. (1983). Coed Flag Football. In N.J. Dougherty (Ed.), *Physical education and sport for the secondary school student* (pp. 115–126). Reston, VA: The American Alliance for Health, Physical Education, Recreation and Dance.

Dougherty, N. J. and Bonanno, D. (1979). *Contemporary approaches to the teaching of physical education.* Minneapolis, MN: Burgess.

Henderson, D. H. (1985). Physical education teachers: How do I sue thee? Oh, let me count the ways! *JOPERD, 2,* 44–48.

Siedentop, D., Mand, C., and Taggart, A. (1986). *Physical education, teaching and curriculum strategies for grades 5–12.* Palo Alto, CA: Mayfield.

Vanderzwaag, H. J. (1984). *Sport management in schools and colleges.* New York: John Wiley and Sons.

CHAPTER 8

Dance

LYNNE FITZGERALD
Morehead State University
Morehead, KY

The variety of programs that fall under the label of "dance" is ever expanding. Most recently, the new dance-fitness form has emerged, permeating our culture and renewing Americas' interest in exercise. Many schools have now added some version of dance-fitness to their already established folk, square, social, modern, jazz, and afro-american dance curricula. With these new programs and renewed interest, physical educators are provided with an excellent opportunity to re-evaluate all of the programs in the dance curriculum.

Some questions need to be addressed in the planning stages of any new dance program. Are the members of the physical education department prepared to design and teach a quality dance-fitness program? Do they understand the concepts and principles of fitness, and the workout framework options? Is anyone certified? Has a safe program, which will promote positive learning opportunities for the students, been constructed? Physical educators today are being held accountable for their teaching, and must be able to demonstrate responsible planning and decision making in the event of an accident or injury. It may seem that dance is not a high risk activity, yet muscles do get strained, ankles get sprained, toes broken, and feet blistered. These kinds of injuries are common to dance, but can be controlled by taking responsibility for the safety aspects of each dance program.

Our task, therefore, is twofold. First, we must increase our awareness of the supervisory concerns of the dance program; and second, we must clarify our obligation to carefully select and construct dance activities to be taught in a safe learning environment. A teacher who addresses each of these concerns by meeting and maintaining the standards set forth in this chapter can significantly reduce the risk of accidents.

SUPERVISION

Dance, like all other forms of physical activity, requires the instructor to take responsibility for both general and specific supervisory concerns. In general, the teacher of dance must be prepared to teach a variety of skills and movement patterns as they relate to the framework of a particular dance form. More specifically, the teacher of dance is responsible for presenting a well planned program in a safe and positive learning environment. Following is a checklist which should be referred to in the planning and evaluation of the supervisory aspects of dance programs.

TEACHER PREPARATION AND ADEQUATE SUPERVISION

A. *Content.* Those aspects of dance one must be aware of, fully understand, and be able to communicate and account for:

1. The movement skills.
2. The movement and rhythmic qualities and characteristics associated with a dance pattern or form.
3. The movement principles that are used to support effective, efficient, and safe learning.
4. Specific techniques or methods that are used to enhance the learning process.
5. The movement, dance, and/or fitness concepts that must be clarified and fulfilled.
6. The specific nature of common dance injuries and the first aid treatment prescribed for these injuries.

B. *Individual readiness.* A teacher must know his or her students:

1. Their physical, mental, and emotional potential and characteristics.
2. The relationship between their abilities, goals, and images of themselves.
3. Any specific medical or learning disabilities or problems which might affect a student's progress.

C. *The environment.* To provide a safe learning context, a teacher must be familiar with:

1. The care and maintenance procedures for a dance facility.

2. The principles of equipment and prop maintenance and use.

GENERAL ORGANIZATION AND ADMINISTRATIVE RESPONSIBILITIES

A. An instructor must be in the dance facility during the entire class. Leaving the dance facility, for any reason, regardless of duration or proximity, would be negligent.

B. An instructor must position him or herself so that the entire class can be within his or her field of vision, even when offering corrections or feedback to a single student or small group.

C. When using audio-visual equipment, the instructor must continue to provide supervision for the class.

D. The instructor must be constantly aware of the individual student's safety as the whole class moves through space, performing imposed movement patterns or solving creative dance problems.

E. The boundaries of a designated safe area of the dance facility must be established.

F. The instructor must be clear about the direction, pattern, starting and ending points of each movement being taught. This helps to organize students effectively and reduce the number of careless collisions, as well as increasing the students' potential to move fully in a safe environment.

G. A clear set of procedures to be followed in the event of an emergency or accident should be established. The instructor must:

1. Communicate these to the students.

2. Run through the procedures with the students so that they understand their responsibility. This is particularly important if the students are very young and/or cannot read.

3. Post a list of the procedures, stated in clear and simple terms.

LESSON PLANS

A. Construct a detailed lesson plan for each class period. Account for content development, organization, and the use of support systems. Eliminate the need to improvise!

B. The lesson plan should clarify specific methods to be used to increase the students' awareness of themselves and their position in space relative to others as they dance.

C. The lesson plan should identify and clarify specific movement risks or environmental hazards, as well as the methods to be used to eliminate these elements.

SELECTION AND CONDUCT OF THE ACTIVITY

Conduct refers to the decisions a teacher makes in regard to the organization and presentation of all aspects of a dance class. Selection refers to the process of determining, for example, which dance forms and what content areas are to be addressed in the framework of each dance form. The scope of decisions made in regard to conduct and selection in dance activities is broad. Two general categories serve as the organizing center for this section: a) general concerns, that is, those principles which should be considered in the selection, planning, or conduct of any dance activity; and b) specific concerns, those factors which should be addressed when teaching a specific dance form. The following guidelines should be followed when planning and presenting a safe and successful dance experience for all students.

GENERAL CONSIDERATIONS

A. *Program selection.*

1. Identify a clear purpose for each dance activity so that each has a clear role in the curriculum.

2. Be sure instructors are qualified to develop and teach each dance activity included in the curriculum.

B. *Planning.* A clear, well organized, and thorough plan will improve one's effectiveness, reduce or eliminate the need to improvise, and if necessary, provide documents for a liability defense.

1. Identify a specific goal or purpose for each class. These should reflect the goals for the dance activity.

2. State objectives which will clarify the specific intentions of the activity.

3. The dance activity content—warmup, cool down, skill development, improvisation, dance making, etc.—should be designed to fulfill the intentions of the objectives.

4. Methodologies should be selected according to the learning process which will promote a positive, informative, and safe learning experience for the students.

5. Specify movement pathways—direction, level, facing, tempo, and any other element which might need to be clarified to assure the safe movement of students through space.

6. Identify options. Students with learning disabilities may need to have a choice in regard to the movement itself, speed of execution, goals, etc. By planning alternatives, the teacher can provide disabled students with movement choices that will allow them to participate fully and safely in dance activities.

7. The level of the teacher's expectation and his or her system of evaluation should account for both the students' growth and the quality of their performance. This will allow students to develop at their own rate and provide them with clear goals, enhancing their level of personal safety and success in dance.

C. *The student*. Identify the level of understanding, ability, and awareness that each student has in the following dance movement categories. This information will help the teacher to provide students with a positive dance experience because they will be prepared to safely explore, learn, and create movement in carefully considered dance frameworks.

1. Motor skill—the level of readiness and ability to perform the basic locomotor, non-locomotor, and movement skills inherent in dance activity.

2. Body awareness—understanding one's ability, limitations, and tendencies as a dancer.

3. Movement principles—understanding and ability to embody the conditions associated with the following will promote the efficient and safe use of the body when dancing: centering, grounding, balance, landing, and alignment.

4. Spatial awareness—an understanding of self as a mover through shared space which has natural or prestated movement boundaries.

5. Comprehension level—understanding the terms, concepts, and characteristic movement frameworks inherent in the dance activity.

D. *Personal safety*. Monitor students' preparation for each class. Students will be ready to dance safely if these policies have been accounted for and followed:

1. Footwear—require appropriate footwear for the dance activity. Account for the conditions in the environment and the special needs of any students when making decisions about footwear.

2. Attire—clothing should be non-restrictive so that the student can breathe and move fully. Layers of clothing should be worn so students can adjust the amount of clothes they are wearing according to the temperature of their bodies. Over heating or being cold can create personal health and safety problems when dancing.

3. Jewelry—sharp, dangling, or protruding objects should be removed because these are potentially harmful to the dancer.

4. Gum and candy should not be allowed.

5. Long hair should be tied back.

6. Glasses should be secured to

the student's head so they don't fall off when bending or turning.

DANCE FORM SPECIFIC CONSIDERATIONS

A. *Dance-Fitness Activities.*

1. Pre-screen students to determine their level of fitness.

2. Each student should be informed about his or her fitness level and be supported in the clarification of appropriate personal dance fitness goals.

3. Plan for a warmup, workout, and cool down segment for each class period.

4. Clarify personal options as these pertain to the intensity, frequency, duration, and movements selected for the dance aspects of each class. Informed students can monitor their own safety when the choices are clear.

5. Continually scan the students as they move and make personal corrections when a student is moving in a way that is not structurally sound.

B. *Folk, square, and social forms.*

1. Warm students up.

2. Introduce new dance skills prior to the teaching of a dance. Students will feel more able to perform a dance when they are familiar with all the movement elements of that dance.

3. Orient students to the movement patterns inherent in a specific dance. This will reduce the level of confusion and therefore the number of collisions.

4. Each student should know his or her role and the related movement responsibilities (e.g., lead couple).

5. When using a musical recording, identify starting cues and introduce listening techniques so students can effectively execute the dance in relation to the music.

6. Provide students with a cue which can be used to stop a partner, square, line, or circle when confusion occurs. This will reduce

the number of accidents that result from moving when disoriented or confused.

C. *Art forms: ballet, modern dance, jazz, afro-american dance.*

1. Orient students for the day's dance activity by presenting them with a warmup which will prepare them to succeed physically, emotionally, and mentally.

2. Be sure the technical aspects of the movement and dance skills are demonstrated and performed correctly.

3. The development of each class should be progressively sound.

4. When teaching a complex or long dance sequence or pattern, ask students to "mark" through the sequence first so they have an understanding of all its parts prior to performing it in its entirety.

5. Identify any typical problem areas in a sequence or in a student's performance so they can monitor themselves as they move, enhancing their potential to dance fully and safely.

6. Be prepared to modify a task for any or all students who have difficulty understanding or doing a dance task so all have an opportunity to participate and succeed at their own level.

7. Clarify any specific movement qualities or characteristics the students are expected to fulfill through their dance.

ENVIRONMENT

There are two general areas of responsibility which must be fulfilled when providing students with a safe and positive dance learning environment. First, the facility in which the dance classes are conducted must be well maintained. Second, the equipment, for example, audio-visual or any props being used, must be mechanically sound and safe. The following guidelines are provided to help the teacher plan for an maintain a safe environment for a dance program.

FACILITY

A. *The condition of the floor.*
   1. Is it clean? This is especially important when students dance in bare feet.
   2. The floor must be free from splinters, cracks, chips, or holes. If any of these conditions exist, the specific area(s) should be marked off. If the general condition of the floor is bad, dance shoes should be worn at all times and dance activities should be modified appropriately.
   3. The floor surface should be resilient, and have some "give." If the floor is hard (wood or tile over cement), the amount of jumping, hopping, running, and leaping that the students are asked to perform should be reduced or eliminated. This will reduce the potential for such problems as shin splints and the leg, foot, and ankle injuries which result from stress induced by dancing on a hard floor surface.
   4. Check the floor for sticky or slippery conditions. The instructor should test the floor with each kind of acceptable dance footwear. Extremely slippery or sticky floors are dangerous and may interfere with performance success. Account for these conditions when planning by either adjusting performance speed or the movement elements of a dance pattern.
B. *Other considerations.*
   1. Whenever possible, move all unnecessary equipment off the dance floor or out of the area. If this is not possible, move the equipment to one side of the facility, pad and/or mark off the area. Make sure that students recognize the boundaries of the safe dancing area.
   2. Note extremes in temperature. When a facility is extremely hot or cold, modifications of the warm-up, cool down, and intensity or duration of the activity may be warranted.

EQUIPMENT

A. *Audio-visual aids* are often used in conjunction with dance programs. The instructor must take responsibility for the following:
   1. The record player, tape deck, and video equipment should be in good working order.
   2. The plugs for the equipment and the outlets in the facility should be electrically sound and in good working order.
   3. The instructor must be trained to operate the equipment safely and effectively.
   4. Operation of the audio-visual equipment is the sole responsibility of the instructor, unless a student has been specifically trained for this duty.
   5. Be prepared with an alternative lesson plan. Mechanical problems are unpredictable.
   6. Class time should not be spent in honing an instructor's equipment skills or making repairs. Proper supervision of students cannot be given if all the teacher's attention is on the equipment.
B. *Props and performance items.*
   1. When using props, be sure that all students are clear about how and when they are to be used.
   2. Make sure that students understand the proper ways to handle and move props. Accidents and injuries can occur when props are misused.
   3. Inspect all props (e.g. tinikling or bamboo poles) prior to use. Any damaged equipment should be eliminated or repaired before students are allowed to handle it.

CONCLUSION

The suggestions made in this chapter have been presented as guidelines to support the teacher's efforts to provide a safe learning experience and environment for the dance program. Meeting and maintaining these standards will help to reduce the risks associated with dance. Students who feel safe will feel more comfortable, and therefore will be more likely to move and express themselves fully while dancing. A safe dance experience will bring joy and satisfaction to the student.

REFERENCE

Fallon, D. (1983). Dance in education. In N. J. Dougherty (Ed.), *Physical education and sport for the secondary school student* (pp. 93–101). Reston, VA: The American Alliance for Health, Physical Education, Recreation, and Dance.

CHAPTER 9

Field Hockey

BARBARA J. BELT
John F. Kennedy High School
Silver Spring, MD

Field hockey is a sport for boys and girls, men and women of all ages. There are organized opportunities to play in elementary and secondary physical education programs, interscholastic and intercollegiate programs, recreation and club programs, and competitive regional, national, and international programs. As a physical education activity, field hockey can be a positive coeducational experience in which students develop coordination, speed, stamina, and teamwork skills.

As in any physical activity involving an implement, a propelled object, and a confined area of play, there is a need for careful consideration of safety. Field hockey can be a safe, fun-filled experience if common and specific problem areas are considered before introducing the activity to students. Areas of concern include proper supervision, the selection and conduct of the activity, and the care and maintenance of facilities and equipment. Thorough planning and preparation are the keys to providing a positive learning experience for all participants.

Competent supervision is a very important element in any teaching unit. The more qualified the staff member, the more effective the supervision. A teacher with experience as a player, coach, or umpire in field hockey is more likely to have a complete knowledge of the sport and to be aware of potential dangers. If an inexperienced staff member is assigned to teach this activity, ample time should be given to become familiar with the sport. The quantity and quality of supervision improves as a teacher becomes more familiar with the activity.

Proper conduct of a field hockey unit includes the appropriate selection of specific activities for the age and ability levels of the students. The scoop and the flick are difficult skills to control during game play and they can be omitted from an instructional unit for safety purposes, thus placing the focus on keeping the ball on the ground during skill instruction and game play. Providing correct instruction in various skills,

enforcing guidelines for safe game play, and providing the necessary safety equipment are part of the proper conduct of a field hockey unit. Written lesson plans are essential.

Maintaining safe playing areas and equipment is another concern when teaching field hockey. Playing areas must be free of obstructions or loose impediments and the grass must be kept short to allow for better stickwork. If adjacent fields are used, space should be left between them to avoid an overlap of activity from field to field. Protective equipment such as shin guards should be provided and used by every student. Goalie leg pads and kickers should be used for protection if the goalie is a designated position during class play.

Risk management comes through an awareness of the potential problems or hazards associated with a specific activity. A teacher who is aware of such problems can plan activities that minimize the risks to the participants. Sound planning and good judgment are important background elements in a positive learning experience.

The following checklists have been developed to provide a quick reference for teachers as they plan an instructional unit in field hockey. They cover the areas of supervision, selection of content and conduct of activity, and the care and maintenance of facilities and equipment.

SUPERVISION

1. Only qualified instructors should teach field hockey. Qualifications include:
   a. thorough knowledge of the sport
   b. up-to-date techniques and teaching methods
   c. first aid and emergency training
2. Maintain visual contact with all groups in the class during the entire class period. Do not leave the activity area.

3. Maintain awareness of total class activities while giving instruction or assistance to individual students.

4. Students should not have direct access to the equipment. Equipment left out is an invitation to participate in unsupervised activities.

5. Establish policies and procedures for safety during the class.

6. Students should have access to the instructor at all times.

7. Lesson plans should be detailed to show supervisory efforts used to maintain a safe learning environment (see next section).

8. Be prepared to provide both general and specific supervision during the course of each class.

SELECTION AND CONTENT OF ACTIVITY

1. Use an established curriculum guide as a comprehensive reference for course content. An excellent resource is chapter 8, by Belt and Reimann, of *Physical Education and Sport for the Secondary School Student* (Dougherty, 1983).

2. Select tasks that are appropriate for both the ages and ability levels of students.

3. Prepare and maintain written unit and lesson plans for all activities. Specific plans include objectives, learning experiences, teaching methods, and assessment measures.

4. Individual lesson plans should indicate a progression of appropriate skills and learning experiences. Sample drills and suggestions for self-evaluation may be found in *Physical Education and Sport for the Secondary School Student* (Dougherty, 1983).

5. Provide warm-up sequences that include fitness activities such as jogging and flexibility exercises.

6. Keep accurate records of all class activities.

7. Prepare procedures for dealing with accidents and/or other emergency situations.

8. Prepare lesson plans for indoor activities that provide the opportunity to continue working on field hockey skills or game tactics if space is available.

9. Stress the non-contact aspects of the game.

10. Include student officiating as a skill activity that facilitates game play during class.

11. Warn students of the risk of injury if the hockey stick is used for purposes other than those intended or if the stick is raised too high during skill-work and game play.

12. Develop a personal safety checklist for students that includes removing all jewelry, eliminating gum chewing, and securing eyeglasses in some way.

13. Group students according to size, strength, and skill.

14. Following are suggested modifications to skillwork and game play in physical education classes.

a. Do not teach the flick or the scoop. These are aerial strokes that increase the potential for dangerous play.

b. Limit the backswing and follow-through to waist height.

c. Limit the game play to 5 v 5, 6 v 6, or 7 v 7. Small games develop the larger game concepts and allow students more opportunities to be involved in the activity.

d. Eliminate the goalie position unless proper protective equipment can be provided. If using a player to cover that position without protective equipment, limit shots on goal from outside a certain distance in front of the goal. This will avoid chaotic play in front of the goal.

e. Use playing areas as small as 30 × 50 yards depending on the size of the teams.

f. Discourage the use of reverse sticks when playing because it leads to over-reaching and committing such fouls as obstruction and stick interference. Students should be taught to move into proper position to avoid the reverse play.

g. Substitute cones or other field markers for regulation goals when using smaller fields (or if goals are not available).

CARE AND MAINTENANCE OF FACILITIES AND EQUIPMENT

FACILITIES

1. Playing areas must be kept free of obstructions (examples: football and soccer goalposts, bleachers, drainage grates).

2. Remove loose impediments (rocks, sticks, broken glass).

3. Goal cages (if used) must be assembled properly and anchored to the ground.

4. Adjacent fields must be separated by open space to avoid an overlap of activity from field to field.

5. Sidelines and goal lines must be marked with field white and/or cones.

6. Scoring circle must be marked in front of each goal or activity modified to omit these areas.

7. Provide space for non-participants that prevents interference with class activities.

8. Provide easy access for emergency first aid personnel.

EQUIPMENT

1. Apply linseed oil to cleaned and sanded sticks to prevent drying and cracking during storage.

2. Discard sticks that are splintered and cracked.

3. Replace torn or frayed grips on sticks.

4. Provide plastic (inside-the-sock) or canvas and cane shin guards for every student. Buckles of cane shin guards must be worn on the outside of the leg to prevent chafing.

5. Provide protective equipment for goalie if that position is designated during class play: helmet, leg guards, kickers, chest protector.

6. Discard cracked hockey balls.

7. Clean or paint hockey balls (white) periodically for better visibility.

8. Provide cones or corner markers for designated playing areas. Boundaries for available playing space must be marked and visible to all participants.

9. Select sticks of a proper length for each individual student (26″–38″).

REFERENCE

Belt, B. and Reimann, B. J. (1983). Field Hockey. In N. J. Dougherty (Ed.), *Physical education and sport for the secondary school student* (pp. 103–113). Reston, VA: The American Alliance for Health, Physical Education, Recreation and Dance.

CHAPTER 10

Fitness/Weight Training

CLAIR JENNETT
San Jose State University
San Jose, CA

Exercise programs have been in existence for centuries. There remains, however, a great need to reach more people of more age groups with these programs. One question frequently asked by those contemplating the development of an exercise program is, "How shall I begin?" The safety ramifications of this question *must* be considered when answering. Too frequently, mistakes have been made in answering the question by lay persons, health spa employees, gymnasium directors, teachers, physicians, and others. These persons, lacking an understanding of the specific safety hazards which exist in the conduct of programs of exercise and fitness, may unwittingly be putting the participant at risk.

The purpose of this chapter is to present the risks involved in exercise programs, and to suggest procedures for conducting safe programs of exercise for all. When the elements of risk have been considered during program planning, exercise programs can provide a valuable addition to one's recreational and professional life. The following material is, therefore, presented as a guide for safety in exercise programs. Supervisory concerns, conduct of the activity, and environmental conditions are presented with a focus on the prevention of injury. Safety procedures for exercise programs which include cardiorespiratory endurance activities, flexibility activities, and strength activities (e.g. weight training) are presented within each of the three areas.

SUPERVISORY CONCERNS

A. Knowledge of the subject matter dealing with exercise is essential. Certification programs are available which include both study and supervised internships for exercise specialists, strength training specialists, and aerobic specialists. Completion of an approved course of study in exercise physiology is highly recommended.

B. The ability to assess the fitness level of each student and prescribe appropriate exercises based upon the assessment is essential.

C. Instructors must possess a knowledge of progressions in exercise prescription in terms of frequency (how often), intensity (how stressful), duration (how long), and mode (type of exercise).

D. A thorough knowledge of first aid procedures including cardiopulmonary resuscitation (CPR) is required.

E. Instructors must be familiar with the proper use of the equipment common to exercise programs.

F. A knowledge of the current and past research concerning exercise programs is necessary.

G. Safety procedures for the conduct of exercise programs must be established and implemented by the instructor.

FACILITIES MANAGEMENT

A. Exercise rooms or gymnasiums must be supervised by qualified instructors.

B. The instructor must be aware of the space demands of each exercising person as well as the space demands for each piece of exercise equipment.

C. The instructor must be aware of the movement patterns of each exercise activity in order to allocate adequate space.

D. Rules of conduct and safety should be developed by staff and students, including:

1. When the area is to be used (hours and days).
2. Who may use the area.
3. Who is in charge of the area.
4. How each piece of equipment is to be used.
5. Where exercises occur in the area.
6. Where equipment is placed and stored.
7. What equipment can be used in the area.
8. What patterns of movement can be used in the area.

E. Each exercise area should have rules of conduct and safety posted.

F. In addition to the proper posting

of rules, students should be informed verbally of the rules of conduct and safety.

PLANNING FOR INSTRUCTION

A. Teaching plans should include:
1. Consideration for safety matters.
2. Placement of equipment.
3. Placement of students for exercise activities.
4. Placement of the instructor for teaching and supervision.
5. Assessment of students' physical status and plans for mode, frequency, intensity and duration of the activities.
B. The teaching plan should be prepared after consideration of the risks involved in the activity and procedures by which the risks can be reduced and avoided.

CONDUCT OF THE ACTIVITY

Everyone can improve their cardiorespiratory endurance, flexibility, and strength. When a person begins an exercise program, the body adapts. The adaptive responses are the "training effects" of the program. Everyone, therefore, is physically ready for exercise, but everyone is ready at a different level. Assessing that level is essential to proper exercise prescription. An increased potential for injury exists whenever an improper assessment is made. While underassessing participant capabilities may not present an immediate physical hazard, the resultant loss of motivation can easily lead to a multitude of other problems. The dangers of overassessing a participant's capabilities are obvious. The instructor must, therefore, refer to accurate assessment measures when assigning the frequency, intensity, duration, and modes of exercise. Following is a guide for assuring safe conduct for exercise programs.

PARTICIPANT READINESS

A variety of exercise programs are used to improve fitness. Continuous activities such as walking, swimming, bicycling, rowing, dancing, jogging, rope jumping, bouncing, and large muscle exercises with the whole body moving are activities commonly used for the improvement of cardiorespiratory endurance. Calisthenics exer-cises are used for strength, flexibility, balance, and agility improvement. In addition, a large number of weight training devices have been developed to improve strength and flexibility. Assessing the readiness of an individual for each exercise is a difficult task. Assessing the readiness of a class of students presents an even greater challenge. Some general rules of readiness are suggested in the following four areas of concern.

A. *Physical readiness.*
1. Review medical records for all students before activity. Exercise limitations may be necessary in the presence of some medical conditions. Medical records should provide historical data as well as the results of recent examinations.
2. Determine the level of endurance, strength and/or flexibility slowly, allowing ample time for assessment and recording the level for each activity. Begin the exercise program at a relatively low level which offers the safety of readiness and the motivation of achievement.
3. Allow parent participation in the assessment by discussing results of any medical examinations or early assessments which indicate a deviation from standard expectations.
4. Keep records of initial and subsequent assessments and use them for individual advising and guidance.
5. Use a continuous activity as a warmup to the exercise program each day. Vary the warmup to maintain motivation. Include strength and flexibility activities as well as cardiorespiratory activities. Students should begin to experience sweating before difficult strength, flexibility, balance, or

agility activities are added to the routine.

6. Require written permission from a physician to begin activity after an injury or serious illness. Special activities for the injured and low-fitness students are important. It is essential, however, that the aid of a physician be enlisted in the development of such programs.

7. Provide individual programs for all students who have special needs. All students can benefit from some type of exercise. Modifications of intensity, duration, frequency, or mode facilitate the adaptation of exercises for individual needs.

B. *Skill readiness.*

1. Review the skill level of all activities to ensure a sequencing from easy to difficult.

2. Be sure that thorough instruction and feedback are provided with regard to all skills and techniques.

3. Start the class at an appropriate level of skill to ensure safety and motivation.

C. *Emotional readiness*

1. Provide sufficient activity levels to ensure success.

2. Keep interest high by providing variety in frequency, duration, intensity, and mode.

3. Pressure to increase the frequency, duration, and intensity should come from the student rather than from the instructor.

4. Self-regulation of frequency, duration, and intensity should be instilled in each student. Recognition of preliminary signs of overstress or injury should be taught. Students should learn to understand their bodies and how to recognize when more or less intensity, frequency, or duration is needed.

5. A statement of the risks involved in exercise programs and techniques for avoiding injury should be presented to each student. This should be a written statement in language that all students can understand. After the students read the statement, discussion and an opportunity for questions should follow. These documents, called informed consent forms, should be used to inform the parents as well as the student. While they do not relieve any party of responsibility, students, parents, and school personnel will have a better understanding of the program and their responsibilities and will feel free to consult with the program director when given the opportunity to read and sign consent forms. Figure 1 provides an example of an appropriate informed consent document.

D. *Social readiness.*

1. Group activities are usually more motivating than working alone. Students should be taught to support each other in their exercise activities. This support should not be pressure; it should be encouragement and acceptance.

2. Students should have fun while working hard. Group support enhances the enjoyment.

CURRICULAR CONCERNS

A. The aim of the fitness/weight training unit should be to meet the needs of the students enrolled.

B. Objectives should be established which lead to fulfillment of the aim.

C. The exercise activities should relate to the objectives.

D. The following general guidelines for the fitness/weight training unit may also be used to further assess the individual exercise activities. The activities should:

1. Increase tone, stability and control of the body.

2. Prepare the student for more strenuous exercise activities.

3. Meet student needs.

4. Be good for overall fitness.

5. Be progressively sequenced from easy to difficult.

In the prevention of injury in exercise programs, it is important to understand the causes of injury presented below. Injury prevention procedures are listed after each causal factor. Be aware of risks and conduct your personal program in a safe manner.

Causes of Injury	Preventive Techniques
Lack of adequate warmup	• Use related rather than unrelated warmup activities • Use active rather than passive warmup activities • Bring the body to sweating temperature gradually during warmup activities
Lack of adequate cool down period	• Keep moving at a gradually slower pace after exercise • Avoid hot showers, hot tubs, and saunas after exercise
Lack of adequate rest (overexertion)	• Use a frequency of 3–4 days per week for beginning exercise programs • Use low intensity for beginning exercise programs • Use short duration for beginning exercise programs • Avoid competition for beginning exercise programs
Overextending range of joints	• Use short range of movement for beginning exercise programs • Avoid painful stretching for beginning exercise programs
Excessive heat, humidity, pollution, or altitude	• Decrease intensity and duration in these conditions • Drink water freely during exercise
Using sudden stops or starts or exercising on hard surfaces	• Use smooth movements • Avoid hard surfaces and sudden stops
Failing to use progression or increasing intensity and duration too early	• Slow progression avoids injury • Increase intensity and duration when it feels good to the body • Reduce intensity and duration when soreness or pain are felt
Failing to listen to the body	• Avoid overexertion when sick, fatigued, or injured • Avoid being compelled into activity because of habit, friends, or competitive reasons • Avoid continuing exercise or completing an activity when the body says stop
Failure to dress for the activity	• Dress for warmth and for cooling as dictated by temperature • Avoid restrictive clothing • Use shoes that fit the activity and protect the foot and leg joints
Failing to check equipment before use	• Check all equipment before exercising • Use all equipment as specified • Clear area for equipment use

Figure 1. Statement of informed consent.

Continued

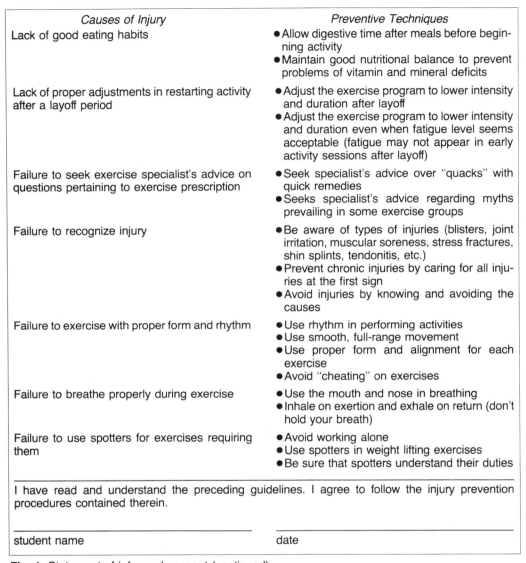

Causes of Injury	Preventive Techniques
Lack of good eating habits	• Allow digestive time after meals before beginning activity • Maintain good nutritional balance to prevent problems of vitamin and mineral deficits
Lack of proper adjustments in restarting activity after a layoff period	• Adjust the exercise program to lower intensity and duration after layoff • Adjust the exercise program to lower intensity and duration even when fatigue level seems acceptable (fatigue may not appear in early activity sessions after layoff)
Failure to seek exercise specialist's advice on questions pertaining to exercise prescription	• Seek specialist's advice over "quacks" with quick remedies • Seeks specialist's advice regarding myths prevailing in some exercise groups
Failure to recognize injury	• Be aware of types of injuries (blisters, joint irritation, muscular soreness, stress fractures, shin splints, tendonitis, etc.) • Prevent chronic injuries by caring for all injuries at the first sign • Avoid injuries by knowing and avoiding the causes
Failure to exercise with proper form and rhythm	• Use rhythm in performing activities • Use smooth, full-range movement • Use proper form and alignment for each exercise • Avoid "cheating" on exercises
Failure to breathe properly during exercise	• Use the mouth and nose in breathing • Inhale on exertion and exhale on return (don't hold your breath)
Failure to use spotters for exercises requiring them	• Avoid working alone • Use spotters in weight lifting exercises • Be sure that spotters understand their duties

I have read and understand the preceding guidelines. I agree to follow the injury prevention procedures contained therein.

_____   _____
student name   date

Fig. 1. Statement of informed consent (continued).

6. Be fun and suited to the age and ability of students.

7. Be safe—conducted without injury to students.

E. The lesson plans should be developed from the unit plan and the lesson objectives should grow out of the unit plan objectives. The following should be considered in the development of individual lessons.

1. Progressively more difficult exercise activities should be planned for each lesson.

2. Safety consideration should be part of each lesson plan.

3. Plans and procedures for safe use of the equipment should be part of each lesson plan.

4. Questionable movement patterns (deep knee bends, straight-knee leg lifts, straight-knee sit ups, bouncing toe touch, etc.) should not be included in the exercise program.

ENVIRONMENTAL CONDITIONS

GENERAL CONSIDERATIONS

A. Exercise areas must be supervised by qualified persons when in use.

B. All equipment should be returned to the proper storage area after use.

C. Safety rules for each exercise area should be posted in highly visible locations.

D. Only proper use of the facilities and equipment is allowed.

E. Safety inspections of facilities and equipment should be planned on a regular time schedule and records of the inspection should be kept on file.

F. Regular cleaning of the equipment and facilities is an important safety measure.

EXERCISE AREAS

A. *Weight training room.*

1. Placement space for all equipment should be clearly marked.

2. Space allocations for all equipment should meet the manufacturer's specifications.

3. The maximum number of participants that can safely use the space should be posted in highly visible locations.

4. Emergency procedures in case of injury should be posted in highly visible areas.

5. Ventilation and lighting must be adequate for the exercise activities.

6. Traffic patterns should be clearly designated.

7. Equipment should be used for specified exercises only.

8. Equipment and facilities should be inspected daily. Careful inspection records must be maintained indicating:

- Security of all floor and wall anchor points.

- Safety stop pins present on exercise machines and weight racks.

- Floor surface free of dust, debris and moisture.

- Bars, plates and machinery are free of rust.

- All free weight bars have proper fastening hardware.

- Security of all joints and fastenings.

- Stability of all benches and platforms.

- Security of all chains, cables, pulleys, and other moving parts.

- Cleanliness of mats, benches, seats, etc.

9. Noted deficiencies should be immediately corrected or the faulty equipment taken out of service.

B. *Exercise rooms or gyms.*

1. Ventilation and lighting must be adequate for the exercise program.

2. Storage space for all equipment should be clearly marked and the storage space should be secure if the room is used for other activities.

3. Space limitations and number of participants should be posted in highly visible areas.

4. Traffic patterns for some exercise activities should be established before students begin the activity.

CONCLUSION

There are a great many ways for people to become physically fit. In conjunction with the attainment of fitness goals, however, safety considerations must be a planning priority. The guidelines presented in this chapter should help attain both fitness and safety goals so that everyone can enjoy a safe, healthy and worthwhile experience.

REFERENCE

Ward, Bob. (1983). Weight training. In N.J. Dougherty (Ed.), *Physical education and sport for the secondary school student* (pp. 365–380). Reston, VA: The American Alliance for Health, Physical Education, Recreation, and Dance.

CHAPTER 11

Golf

DEDE OWENS

University of Virginia
Charlottesville, VA

The nature of the game of golf invites potential safety hazards. Swinging an implement in excess of 90 mph in an attempt to propel a solid sphere 1.68 inches in diameter and weighing 1.62 ounces can be both exhilarating and dangerous. The manner in which the game is introduced and organized for instruction and practice can greatly reduce the danger and enhance the exhilaration. The key to safety in golf is *awareness*. Awareness must be developed through three levels: the administration, the golf instructor, and the student. Each has a major responsibility in regard to safety considerations.

Administration. Golf is becoming more popular in physical education curricula and in recreational programs. However, the question of whether *qualified* personnel are on staff to supervise and/or instruct golf is rarely addressed by administrators. Often, an individual who plays golf is assigned to the activity with the assumption of instructional ability. This may be a faulty assumption and could lead to safety hazards.

The administration must determine if an individual is qualified to teach golf. If not, adequate time must be provided for training to insure that technical, organizational, and safety skills are acquired.

If a person accepts the responsibility for teaching golf, he or she is acknowledging the preparation to do so. If the teacher does not feel prepared, additional training should be secured before assuming those responsibilities.

Golf Instructor. The greatest responsibility for safety awareness resides with the instructor. Readiness to instruct requires the technical knowledge to insure the understanding and development of efficient and effective swing mechanics; organizational knowledge for safe student practice and movement in the instructional and practice area; an understanding of individual needs and contraindications for golf drills and techniques; knowledge of the selection and care of equipment; and knowledge of appropriate procedures for the care and maintenance of facilities. Constant awareness of the safety issues in each of these areas is needed, regardless of how much or how little experience an individual has had in golf instruction.

Students. Students are the third link in safety. They should be made aware of safety concerns and required to assume a major role for their personal safety and the safety of others while in a golf class. This is critical if safety is to be practiced when students are on their own during actual course play.

COMMON INJURIES IN GOLF

The potential for injuries during golf instruction is far greater than the actual severity of most injuries which occur. The most common minor injury in golf classes is blisters. These are caused by excessive movement of the club in the hands. A faulty grip or improper grip size is usually the problem (see figure 1). Both can be remedied by awareness of individual hand size and grip technique relative to the size and condition of the club grip.

The less frequent and more serious injuries occur when individuals are hit by a club or golf ball. Being hit by a club usually occurs when an individual walks into the path of a swinging club. Such injuries can be avoided by establishing and enforcing rules which govern *where* and *when* a club may be swung. Each instructional area should have designated areas for student movement in the instructional/practice environment and hitting field (see figure 2).

Injuries due to golf balls occur more frequently on golf courses with parallel fairways than in physical education or recreational golf classes. In fact, they should never occur during instruction if appropriate safety rules are followed. This is especially true if individuals are properly instructed never to retrieve balls prior to a designated signal by the instructor. Walking in front of the designated area or into the hitting field should never be allowed while anyone else is swinging a club.

Fig. 1(a). Proper grip size.

Fig. 1(b). Grip size too small—unsafe.

Fig. 2. Safe practice environment.

Fig. 3(a). Proper position for one-legged drill.

Fig. 3(b). Potentially unsafe modification of one-legged drill.

CONDUCT OF THE ACTIVITY

Student information sheets. Student information is important for establishing a safe and effective environment. The following type of information is particularly beneficial in golf:

1. Experiences in golf.
   - grouping by ability
   - selection of peer teachers/aides
   - determination of starting level
2. Disabling conditions.
   - potential equipment and technique modifications
   - contraindications of specific drills
3. Allergies.
   - awareness to potential allergic reactions
   - medication side effects

Progressions. Skill progressions in golf are not always based on safety considerations as in gymnastics or swimming. The progression selected is determined by instructor preference with regard to beginning with the long game and progressing to the short game, or the reverse. No specific progression has been supported by research as being more effective in skill development. Safety, however, must be instilled in the organizational structure and instruction regardless of the selected progression.

Drills. Golf drills greatly enhance the learning process and are beneficial for group instruction. There are, however, drills which are contraindicated for particular individuals due to pre-existing conditions such as back problems, shoulder or knee dislocations, and arthritis.

As an instructor, it is important to be aware of the potential good or harm specific drills may cause. Drills should be explained clearly, demonstrated correctly, and used appropriately. Figure 3 (a) is an example of the "one-legged" drill which has become popular for helping students develop an arm swing. Note the position of the rear foot placed up on the toe. This allows the lower back to be free of tension. Figure 3 (b) is a dangerous position. It shows a modification of the basic drill which has caused back problems to occur in people with no previous history of back trouble. These positions may also exacerbate or irritate already existing problems, or back weaknesses.

TABLE 1
Examples of Safety Rules in Golf

Where	Clubs may be swung and balls hit only in the designated area.
	Note: Designated areas should be clearly delineated with *visual markers*, and *verbally* described to students.
When	Clubs may be swung and balls hit only when indicated by the instructor.
	Balls are to be retrieved only when indicated.
	Note: The "when Indicated" should be an established signal such as a whistle or verbal command.
Direction	Clubs are to be swung and balls hit toward the designated target(s) only.
	Note: Targets should be set toward which balls must be hit.
	They should be placed toward the center of the hitting area and at a variety of distances to accommodate for swing lengths.

The use of the student information sheets is a valuable tool in the selection and omission of drills when problems are noted. Know your students and the drills you select.

Safety awareness should begin as the activity is introduced. Similarities and differences relative to safety and equipment in other activities need to be stressed. The length of the club, subsequent differences in the space required to swing, and the potential speed of the swing should be noted and compared visually and verbally by demonstration with bats, tennis rackets, and/or other implements familiar to the students.

Rules should be established to help the students become familiar with their responsibility in promoting the safety of the game for themselves and others. It is important to relate the rules for your class activity to specific implications at a driving range, golf course, or practice in the park or backyard. The safety rules should specify *where, when* and the *direction* in which clubs can be swung and balls hit. Once set, the rules should be strictly followed.

Table 1 is an example of a rules format that may be used in your classes. The *note* insertions are clarifications provided for instructors, and not for inclusion in the handouts.

Copies of the rules should be dated and distributed to each student as well as posted in areas which are clearly visible to the students. Computer graphics and attractive posters can enhance the visibility of the rules and provide subliminal reinforcement. Examples of such signs are provided in figures 4 and 5. When laminated, the signs can be used for both inside and outside activity areas.

ENVIRONMENTAL CONDITIONS

Golf can be taught effectively in a gym or on a playing field. Larger areas are more conducive to safety because students can be provided more space in established hitting areas and stations. Anytime space becomes restrictive or less than three yards of space is allowed for a swing station, safety becomes a problem.

INDOOR PLAYING AREAS

The designated swing stations should be marked and safety rules clearly posted. The swing stations should be free of extra clubs, bags or ball baskets.

Mats. Brush mats with rubber mat supports should be used when possible for safety. The brush mat provides a thick protective hitting surface (particularly for beginners) while the rubber mat creates a non-slippery surface for stance and brush support.

Full swing stations in which plastic balls are hit against walls should be placed away from doorways and a minimum of 7 to 8 yards from the wall. There should be a minimum of 3 yards between stations (see figure 6). This

Fig. 4. Sample safety awareness poster.

allows ample room for the plastic ball to bounce off the wall and roll safely back toward the mats. If the mats are placed too close to the wall, students may become swing-shy, feeling too cramped.

The physical arrangement of the stations should be checked frequently dur-ing class, and between classes. It is particularly important to check the dis-tance between stations, and be sure to maintain the 3 yard minimum.

Traffic flow. Traffic flow needs to be considered in the gym, particularly when various stations are implemented. Designated pathways can be marked

Golf Safety Rules

WHERE?

Swing & Hit only in
Designated Areas.

WHEN?

Swing & Hit only on
Signal.

DIRECTION?

Swing & Hit only to
Targets.

Retrieve only on
Signal.

Fig. 5. Sample safety rules poster.

using cones, jump ropes, chairs, brooms, etc.

Changing stations should be done on a signal and in a single direction. This systematic procedure, under the control of the instructor, helps to assure safety of movement. Once the change is complete, activity should be allowed only on a signal from the instructor.

Stations. The swing stations should be marked clearly as putting, chipping, and full swing. This will help the stu-

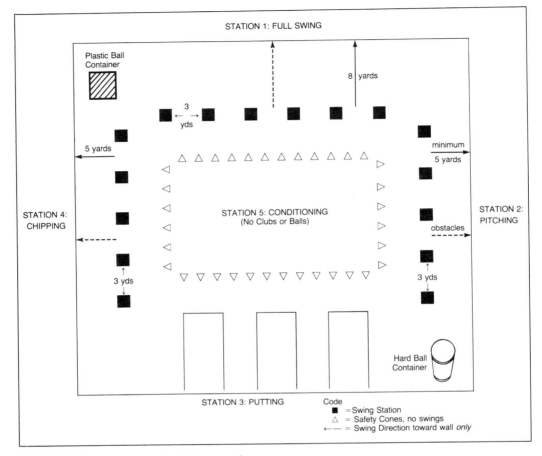

Figure 6. Illustration of a safe indoor practice area.

dent understand the proper swing length in the given area. For example, a full swing should not be made in the putting or chipping areas. It should be indicated that this is also true when practicing at a golf course.

Balls. When using plastic balls for swing practice and hard balls for putting, the ball containers need to be clearly marked. It would also be helpful to have different colored balls (e.g. blue stripe on hard balls). The plastic ball container should be carefully checked before each class to assure that hard balls have not been mixed in. Students should be made aware of the differences and instructed to check each ball for type prior to hitting. It is easy for a beginner to become engrossed and not

be aware of the ball he or she is about to hit.

Dress. Loose fitting clothing and tennis shoes should be required. Tight clothing can be uncomfortable as well as restrictive in the swing. Street shoes are unsafe in that they lack support and are sometimes slick on the floor.

Cleaning up. The area in which you are practicing should be clean and neat. It should be dust mopped each day, and preferably between each class. Brush mats and rubber mats create a dust film on the floor which can be hazardous to others using the gym.

Equipment. The clubs and balls should be collected at the end of each class and secured if the gym is left open or without supervision. Each area should be checked frequently to assure that the stations are the proper distance apart.

OUTDOOR PLAYING AREAS

Hitting Surface. Mats may or may not be used in outside hitting areas. A grass area is preferable to mats if at all possible. Grass provides the best learning environment and will assist in the direct transfer of the skills to the actual golf course. Whether mats or grass are used, the hitting surface should be free of rocks or any obstacles which could be hit accidentally.

Swing stations. Swing stations and the safety considerations discussed earlier are equally important outside. The open space may tend to give students a false sense of security. When students are not swinging or awaiting their turn, there should be an area designated in which they should stand or sit. This area should be away from the swing stations.

Balls used outside. As with indoor practice, plastic balls and hard balls should be separated and *not used simultaneously* at any one station. A hard ball hit accidentally in a confined area could be dangerous.

Hard balls are fun to hit, however, they need to be used with discretion when instructing the full swing. Adequate space, both length and width, is needed to accommodate the novice who lacks control of distance and direction.

The grass space should be clear and cut close to the ground. This will help in finding golf balls. Balls which are not found can be hazardous to others using the field for activity classes and after school sports. The same is true when practicing in parks or other fields.

The total number of golf balls should be counted at the beginning and end of each class. Students should be instructed to count the number of balls they have before hitting and pick up as many balls as they hit. Students should pay particular attention to any misdirected shots (i.e. balls that go an unusual distance or direction) and be instructed to pick them up when it is time for all balls

to be retrieved. This takes time, but is critical to the safety of others.

Most secondary education facilities do not have appropriate outdoor space for safe use of hard balls. Plastic balls can be stuffed with cloth to produce a firmer feel and flight similar to the hard ball. An advantage of the plastic or stuffed ball is that they require less time to retrieve since they can not be hit as far. They are also much safer—just be careful not to use tightly stuffed balls inside the gym if space is restricted.

RESTRICT THE AREA

When golf classes are in session, signs should be posted around the area. This is needed particularly in areas where the fields are used by community joggers or others as a thoroughfare.

EQUIPMENT

Appropriate equipment. Golf clubs should be purchased which vary in length, weight, and grip size. If the club is not appropriate for the learner, it can have a negative effect on the rate and progress of learning, as well as compromise safety. If you are not sure how to "size" clubs for a class, be sure to check with a local professional, or ask the golf club manufacturer for advice when ordering equipment.

The students in figure 7 could be in a golf class in the 10th grade. The golf club held by each is the same club, a standard men's 7-iron which is generally longer and heavier than a woman's club. The same students in figure 8 are holding a woman's standard 7-iron. Will they benefit in a golf class using the clubs they are holding?

Clubs which are at the extremes in weight or length for individuals affect their ability to swing the club effectively and efficiently. These extremes decrease the potential for success.

Grip sizes in the extremes can cause blisters. Sore hands from trying to maintain club control, and "flying clubs" can both be the result of a grip which is too large or too small for the hand size. These are safety hazards

Fig. 7. Men's 7-iron.

Fig. 8. Women's 7-iron.

which can easily be prevented, but not without awareness.

Maintenance of clubs. Three areas of a club should be checked for wear and damage: the grip, shaft, and hosel.

Grips which get worn or frayed can cause blisters and slippage in the hands. These should be checked and cleaned frequently. Composition grips are recommended for use in most classes because they are safer on the hands and easy to clean and replace (inexpensive). Grips should be cleaned with soap and water on a frequent schedule since they become slippery when dirty.

Clubs receive unavoidable wear and tear through extensive use. Shafts can bend as a result of hitting the ground repeatedly during swings, getting stepped on, or improper storage. They should be checked daily. If a shaft is bent it should be broken completely. A bent shaft is much weaker and if used, could snap in two. This is quite dangerous. Depending on the condition of the head, including the hosel, it can be used again by having it re-shafted. Otherwise, if it is too worn, it should be thrown out. If a shaft is only slightly bent, it can be straightened—just be sure to check it frequently.

The head of the club, where the shaft enters the hosel, receives tremendous abuse and may weaken over time. The club heads can snap without warning. Frequent checks are needed and often weaknesses can be detected by holding the head of the club and trying to turn the shaft. A squeaking sound indicates a potential weakness and it should be repaired (by a club repair expert) or destroyed.

Inspection. An equipment record should be kept. As golf equipment is received it should be numbered and the date noted. A written record should be established for a periodic inspection of all equipment. This is in addition to the daily inspection which should be noted in lesson plans or logs of activity sessions.

An ongoing record of equipment may provide information relative to the longevity of equipment purchased from various companies. Clubs which are inexpensive and therefore often attractive for purchase may not be as durable, or safe, when they receive excessive use. Such records may later be used to justify budgets when ordering a different quality club.

Students should be encouraged to help in checking and inspecting their golf clubs. Before hitting balls, all students should check their clubs. This aids in raising their awareness to the care and maintenance of clubs, and the importance of safety.

SUMMARY

Safety issues in golf instruction are keyed on developing *awareness* through classroom organization and instructional procedures. Awareness to safety in and beyond the school program is critical to the students themselves and others. As a teacher, your task is to set the environment for learning and continued involvement beyond the school setting.

The following checklist is provided as a tool for developing a safe golf program.

GOLF SAFETY REVIEW CHECKLIST

Instructor

_____ previous instruction/training
Knowledge of:
_____ group techniques
_____ drills
_____ selection/care of equipment
_____ adaptation of facilities

Environmental Conditions

Rules
_____ rules handouts
    (e.g. discuss/date)
_____ rules poster
Facility (indoor–outdoor)
_____ hitting surface cushioned/ secured
_____ area free of obstacles
_____ traffic flow established/discussed
_____ stations minimum of 3 yards apart (check during activity)
_____ stations indoors minimum of 7 yards from wall and away from doors and hallways (check periodically during activity)
_____ warning signs posted around outside area if thoroughfare
_____ signal established for beginning and end of hitting

Equipment

_____ file established for periodic checks
_____ daily check for condition and repair of clubs
_____ storeroom and gym secured or locked between classes

Balls

_____ containers marked and separated for hard versus plastic balls
_____ check plastic ball container before each class
_____ instructor directs students to check balls before hitting
_____ count hard balls prior to hitting and after each class

REFERENCES

Owens, D. (1983). Golf. In N.J. Dougherty (Ed.), *Physical education and sport for the secondary school student* (pp. 129–148). Reston, VA: The American Alliance for Health, Physical Education, Recreation and Dance.

CHAPTER 12

Orienteering

ARTHUR HUGGLESTONE
Smith Environmental Education Center
Rockville, MD

There comes a point in most orienteering programs when the students are out on the course and you find yourself alone with the feeling that the program you planned is now well underway. It doesn't take long, however, to begin wondering what is really happening out there on the course. Is everything all right? Will each of the students make the correct decisions? Why hasn't anyone finished the course yet? If only you could see them. At this point, you have three alternative courses of action: (a) sit and worry; (b) run out and spot check the course which will, at least, keep you busy; (c) plan for the next "bring 'em back alive" orienteering class which will stress safety and "lost-proofing" the students. How much better it would have been to have included safety planning and instruction in the program from the outset.

EQUIPMENT

Begin the safety planning process by checking your equipment. Any compass can be used for orienteering, and regardless of the type that is used, you must first verify that each is in working order. The easiest way to check a compass is to ask the students to point in the direction that the north seeking arrow is pointing, then turn 180° and do the same thing again. The most common problem with a new compass is reversed polarity, that is, the north arrow points south. When this is found to be the case, either return the compass to the vendor or dispose of it. You may wish to keep one compass with reversed polarity for use when demonstrating compass handling. A reversed polarity compass can be used while facing the students, thus allowing you to easily maintain visual contact with them. Keep a special lanyard on this compass for easy identification and to prevent confusion with the properly oriented compasses.

With older compasses, there is often a loss of dampening fluid. If it is a relatively small loss, the compass will probably still be usable. Too large a bubble can, however, obstruct the free movement of the needle. If this is the case, the compass should not be used.

Our school system lost a lot of compasses until orienteering maps were glued on boards, varnished, and then had a compass tied to one end and a whistle tied to the other. Even if everything is not tied to a board, the compass and the whistle can be tied to a cord and worn around the neck or wrist. Students should be instructed that the whistle is to be used only in an emergency. Three repeated short blasts are a summons for help, while a single short blast identifies the searcher who has heard the three short blasts and wants them repeated.

A small brightly colored daypack or fanny pack equipped with some emergency supplies should be carried at all times except in competition. There are good first aid kits on the market. One of these should be chosen and supplemented from the following list, depending on the area and time of year.

- bandaids
- butterfly closers for large cuts (practice using)
- sanitary napkin for large wound dressing
- plastic adhesive, wide roll
- safety pins
- medicated soap, small bar
- matches, waterproof in waterproof container or magnesium fire starter
- tinder in ziplock bag (practice being able to build fires under any circumstances)
- water in canteen and/or clear, plastic detergent bottle with push-pull cap
- insect repellent
- sting swab
- sunscreen #15
- magnifying glass
- woolen sweater or down vest
- garbage bags—use as rain gear, sleeping bag, or even litter bag
- signal mirrors—available from marine and surplus stores (practice using)
- freeze dried food
- candle

- whistle that is loud but does not require much wind
- small flashlight with alkaline batteries
- knife
- heavy fishing line
- extra socks and bread wrappers or plastic bags (put on dry socks and plastic bread wrappers and you will not know shoes are wet)
- extra compass, map, paper, pencil (glasses if needed)

The list could go on depending on how much you are willing to carry.

Although it is possible to purchase maps with declination lines already in place, it will often be necessary to draw them yourself. When drawing magnetic north/south lines on a map, use a protractor or Silva type compass to lay out the number of degrees of declination. The U.S. Geological Survey warns that the diagram pictured on the lower left margin of their maps is only an approximation of the actual number which is printed next to the magnetic north arrow. This number is accurate for the year printed just below the diagram. Deviation may change very little or as much as one degree in five years. You can get the current deviation for your area by calling the National Cartographic Information Center, Reston, Virginia. The toll free number is 1-800-USA-MAPS.

If you place the magnetic north/south lines at a convenient and uniform distance apart (500 feet, or 1,000 feet, or ½ mile), they can aid the orienteer in judging distance. Any time when drawing lines or making marks on a map, be careful not to cover or obscure any important symbols. A piece of clear plastic can be used as a straight edge which makes it possible to see whatever symbols are along the line. Leave a break in the line where symbols occur. If a 6mm hole is drilled in the plastic straight edge, it can be used to make the circles that mark the control points on the map. When making circles, skip a space if any symbols would be obscured. Do not put a dot in the center of the circle.

It is important to draw parallel magnetic north lines (arrows) on the map

you reproduce because if you do not, it is likely that students will draw magnetic north/south lines using the diagram or, worse yet, confuse magnetic north and true north.

SUPERVISION

Because of the nature of orienteering, it is impossible to maintain visual contact with all students at all times. After the initial learning experiences, during which the students can and should be grouped in an open area and constantly observed, the students will, of necessity, be released onto orienteering courses of gradually increasing size and difficulty. Once this phase of the activity has begun, it is no longer possible to maintain visual contact with the entire class. It is important, under these circumstances, that an area be set aside where the students can always find help if it is needed or desired. The base area should be relatively central in location and easily found. Placement near some prominent and recognizable feature such as power lines, or atop an easily distinguished hill would assist the students in quickly locating assistance if needed.

CONDUCT OF THE ACTIVITY

Since the students will be on their own for a significant portion of the orienteering unit, proper preliminary instruction and safety training is essential. Orienteering skills should be learned and practiced under supervision to guarantee full knowledge of and compliance with safe practices and procedures. Course and safety rules should be understood and followed by all and should be printed either on the back of each map board or on a separate sheet included with it. In addition to orienteering skills students should be provided with an understanding of basic survival techniques. This will increase their confidence in the field and provide an added margin of safety in the unlikely event that someone is lost for more than a matter of minutes or hours. An introductory survival course should include:

- how to use the equipment and supplies in your emergency kit
- how to help searchers find you
- how to treat an injury or sudden illness
- how to build a shelter
- how to conserve energy and temperature
- how to signal for help
- how to forage for food
- how to be safe in a storm
- how to remain calm and wait for help (this will be the adventure that you talk about later)

It is generally best to send students onto the orienteering course in groups of three. If teams of three are used and one person is injured, another can stay with him/her, while a third goes for help. While larger groups provide the same advantage, they tend to become unwieldy and result in lowered involvement for individual students.

If you don't know the students and would like to send them out in teams of two or three with at least one capable student in each team, use the Beginner Compass Game available from Orienteering Services, USA, P.O. Box 1604, Binghamton, New York 13902. This game may be played in any open area approximately 100 × 100 feet. To play, the participant must be able to find directions with a compass. No pacing of distances is necessary. There are 90 courses, using eight labeled markers placed at exact spots in a large circle. While playing the game, all players are contained in the circle. You can easily identify the students with the most and least aptitude. As the students complete the game they will come to you to find out if the courses they've charted are correct. If they are, put their names at the top of a roster and ask them to help students who do not have everything right. The list formed this way will rank the students from most proficient to least. When it is time to make up the teams, they can be made up of one person from the top, middle, and bottom of the list. Another option is to send the first time orienteers on an open

mini-course that will take only a few minutes and allow them to demonstrate their ability to manipulate a map and compass.

In deciding how difficult or easy to make the orienteering course, you must take into consideration the age, experience, and skill of the participants as well as weather conditions and the time of the day and year. If you run a course in the morning and the afternoon, it would be much better for the more experienced group to run a more challenging course in the morning and the less experienced group to tackle an easier course in the afternoon, especially in the winter when the days are shorter. Courses laid out for beginning orienteers should have all stations accessible from trails.

Even if you have an alarm that can be sounded in the event of a problem, everyone won't hear it. It is important that you establish an understanding ahead of time concerning cancellation of the event due to storms, falling trees, or other emergency. Trees may fall at any time. When the ground is soft after a soaking rain, trees may fall even without wind. Anyone who sees or hears two or more trees fall of natural causes in a short period of time should take a direct route to the nearest road or clear area and report this information to the person in charge.

Even if students understand all the fundamentals of orienteering, they should be "lost proofed," or taught to orient themselves to the larger geographic area before they go out. This can be accomplished by using a large wall map that covers a greater area than the orienteering map. Prominent mountains with specific shapes can serve as gross reference points. Indentify any off limits or dangerous areas and the farthest limits they should go. There might be a long straight road on one side, a river on another, and a power line on the third. Anyone who goes far enough in a straight line will end up at one of these features which serves as a perimeter and as a reference point for those who get that far. If operating in an area

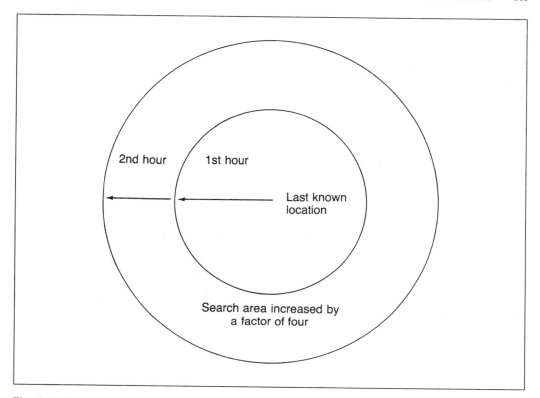

Fig. 1. An hour's delay means that the search area will be four times larger.

where most of the above features are not to be found, advise students to trust their compass. It will get them very close to where they want to be or back to where they started.

In the event that participants lose their compass or feel hopelessly lost, they should be instructed to hike down hill until they find a trail or stream. Water will eventually lead to some sign of civilization. Instruct them on how to ask for help and point out that the phone number where the instructor can be reached is on the map. (Be sure always to include a phone number on the map.)

If students are only going to be out for a short time, they should take a bearing on the sun and notice the direction their shadows cast. It is a good idea to point out the approximate direction the sun will be in two hours from now and its course across the sky. Even after sunset

the western part of the sky will be brighter for hours unless there is a bright moon or the reflected lights of a city.

If some students do not return at the expected time, they may be lost, in need of emergency care, or if they are unreliable, may have abandoned the course and wandered off to their own interests. Schools often run one orienteering course in the morning and another in the afternoon. If someone is late returning in the morning, you may have the leisure to wait a while. If someone is later in returning in the afternoon, especially in the winter when it gets dark earlier, time is more critical. An unaccounted for person can create an urgent situation that requires response in the form of search procedures. A delay of two hours instead of one means that the search area will, of necessity, be four times larger. Figure 1 illustrates the effect of time on a search area.

In a search situation, do not delay. Decide who is going to be in charge (stays in central area and maintains communications), then fill out a missing person questionnaire (see sample, figure 2).

Send out a few people who can patrol the perimeter of the search area. These searchers should travel in the fastest way possible, car, boat, all terrain bicycle, or on foot.

Try to attract the lost person by ringing bells, blowing vehicle or air horns, or using whistles. This "attention getting" should be done from an open area so that sound will travel better. Searchers should be careful not to make any sounds that could be mistaken for a series of three that would be the call for help from the lost orienteer. It is important to frequently pause to listen for a call from the lost orienteer.

If there is a narrow off-road area through which a disoriented person might wander, and thus enlarge the search area, this area should be heavily patrolled. It is important to confine the search area to as small a plot as possible. In off-road areas it is more important to look for signs or clues of the missing person. If you are looking only for the person, you could very easily miss the traces or other evidence that could concentrate the area of search and insure a quicker discovery.

If there is a high point from which much of the search area can be surveyed, assign at least two people to this point so that they can take turns scanning the area. Binoculars should only be used to identify something already spotted.

In the rare case where someone is not found after a reasonable time, check his or her home, friends' houses, hospitals, and favorite hangout. As a last resort, the sheriff or police should be called. Once this decision has been made, resist the temptation to go into the general area where the lost person is suspected of being. Since tracking dogs may be used, do not allow anyone to touch any articles of found clothing. Pick up articles with a stick and put in a clean plastic bag and store in a cool place. If more than one person is lost, store items in separate bags and label them.

The police or sheriff will interview you, scan the area, and call a rescue team. They will probably have tracking dogs that will search for a particular scent left on the ground by the lost individual. They may have air scent dogs that can quickly smell the air for any human scent, not just the lost persons. A trained handler and his dog can be as effective as 20 or 30 human searchers. If you can keep well meaning but inexperienced individuals out of the area, trained search and rescue personnel and their dogs will have a much better chance of finding the missing person.

Initially, all rescue actions are limited to perimeter patrols, attraction, and survey search. The effort is to confine the search area by patrolling natural perimeters or areas that would be outside the distance the victim could have traveled since last seen. An exception to going inside this area could occur if a person were lost overnight and you could define a central area in which a group could camp. These people would have to confine themselves to a specific area for a specific time and enter and leave by the same route. Singing and a campfire might help attract the victim to the group.

You and the orienteers constitute the largest group with the most immediate knowledge of the area. Should you use this group to try to find the subject or use them to confine the search area? This will always be the dilemma faced by the person in charge. The National Association for Search and Rescue offers training, data collection, educational programs, and conferences that could give you the skills necessary to manage a complete search and rescue operation. If you are conducting orienteering meets in areas where participants could be lost for long periods of time, you should avail yourself of their services.

Name _____ Age _____ Sex _____ Race _____ Ht. _____ Wt. _____

Build _____ Hair _____ Length _____ Other _____

Shirt _____ Sweater/Jacket _____

Pants _____ Shoes _____

Hat _____ Gloves _____ Glasses _____

Raingear _____ Other _____

General Condition _____

Medical Problems _____

Psychological Problems _____

Handicaps _____ Medication _____

Smoke/Drink _____ Drugs _____

Outdoors Interest _____

Outgoing/Quiet _____ Hitchhike? _____ Ever Run Away? _____

Depression? _____ Give Up/Keep Going _____

Stop/Keep Moving _____ Other _____

Last seen: Time _____ Place _____

By Whom _____ Direction _____

Reason for Leaving _____

Destination _____ Pickup? _____

Unusual Behavior _____

Pack _____ Tent _____ Sleeping Bag _____

Food _____ Drink _____ Map/Compass _____

Matches _____ Flashlight _____ Firearm _____ Camera _____

Other _____

Outdoor Skills _____

Familiar with area? _____

Ever out overnight? _____ Ever Lost Before? _____

Trails/Crosscountry _____

Talk to Strangers? _____ Accept Rides? _____ If Lost _____

Specific Fears/Interests _____

Other _____

Tendency to Hide? _____

Old Haunts, Special Places _____

Other _____

Anything Else?

Fig. 2. Missing person questionnaire.

They can be contacted by writing to NASAR, P.O. Box 50178, Washington, DC, 20004.

The United States Orienteering Federation (P.O. Box 1444, Forest Park, Georgia 30051) was established in 1971 to promote orienteering in the United States. It can put you in touch with a club in your area or help you start one if none is close by. Their magazine, *Orienteering U.S.A.*, is published nine times a year and contains information on improving orienteering skills, map making, rules for competition, safety, and orienteering for different ages and skills. Belonging to USOF includes automatic membership in the International Orienteering Federation. At a recent convention workshop, the USOF produced the following document.

SEARCH AND RESCUE

To avoid unnecessary searches the organizing personnel should:

1. Make sure the meet area has clear boundaries such as roads or rivers.
2. Make certain that a person not only has registered but has started the course.
3. Know how many participants there are and have a brief individual description, i.e., age, sex.
4. Make certain to impress upon all meet participants the necessity to check in even if the course is not finished.

Recommendations for preliminary meet preparations to insure a successful search and rescue:

1. Know your victim! A novice orienteer is likely lost and may have wandered far from the chosen course. An experienced orienteer is likely injured and near the route.
2. Require all orienteers to carry a whistle. A different code for victim and searchers must be decided on beforehand.
3. Have some emergency instructions for the orienteer incorporating common wisdom of steps to take when lost.

4. Have a club first aid kit with a list of emergency numbers for the nearest professional medical assistance, ambulance, sheriff's department, club members with CPR and first-aid training, etc.
5. Have a prepared list of personnel able and willing to be part of an emergency team.
6. Organize a group CPR and first-aid course for club members.
7. Carry equipment helpful in a search in your car's glove compartment. Items to include would be a whistle and a Night-O headlamp.
8. Have meet director know location of nearest telephone.
9. Decide on the particular type of communication control equipment to be used in the meet area. (United States Orienteering Federation Workshop, 1986. Reprinted with permission.)

In the event of an actual search it is absolutely essential that a search coordinator and a control center be set up. The duties of coordinator include coordination of efforts with other groups (e.g., forest rangers), exact knowledge of the search parties' locations, and recall of the searchers. Knowledge of terrain will modify conditions and alter plans.

As knowledge accumulates in search techniques it should be shared with other clubs and USOF. Orienteers at all levels feel more secure knowing that their club can demonstrate expertise in searching (USOF, 1986).

Most outdoor emergencies can be dealt with satisfactorily given the proper training. The fact that students are in the field navigating with map and compass means that they have a valuable survival skill. They are also more likely to go out on their own and venture further afield. The teacher who has given students the confidence to navigate through the wilderness should also be sure that they know the importance of informing someone of their whereabouts and carrying certain emergency supplies. Whether someone goes out alone or with a partner, a responsible person should always be informed of where they are going, what they are doing, and when they expect to be back.

Because the emphasis has been on safety throughout this chapter, one might get the impression that orienteering is dangerous or risky, but this need not be the case. In over 15 years of conducting orienteering activities involving thousands of students, the author has had no one seriously injured or even lost for a long period of time. However, knowing what to do should such emergencies arise can give the teacher confidence to offer activities such as orienteering that otherwise might be avoided. From an instructional point of view, orienteering is an ideal

activity because it is enjoyable as well as educational, and students find it both challenging and satisfying.

REFERENCES

Hugglestone, A. and Howard, J. (1983). Orienteering. In N.J. Dougherty (Ed.), *Physical education and sport for the secondary school student* (pp. 191–198). Reston, VA: The American Alliance for Health, Physical Education, Recreation and Dance.

United States Orienteering Federation (1986). *Search and rescue.* Workshop presented at the USOF convention, Plymouth, NH.

CHAPTER 13

Racquet Sports

JOHN SMYTH
The Citadel
Charleston, SC

Racquet sport participation is growing at a rapid rate. The injuries associated with racquet sports, naturally, are showing increases proportional to the growing participation. The most common injuries in racquet sports have been to the eye, elbow and shoulder, and the strains and sprains related to poor conditioning and/or failure to warm up properly. Direct eye damage from the ball, eye and facial damage from the racquet, tennis elbow, rotator cuff tears, and swing-related bursitis and arthritis collectively form the primary concerns for the racquet sport player.

SUPERVISION

Proper supervision in racquet sports requires adequate planning, risk management strategies, prudent judgment, and elimination of site/equipment hazards. The participant should be warned of the inherent dangers of the activity and any specific hazards. Pre-activity warning should be followed by regular oral reminders and posted visual aids listing safety measures in a manner appropriate to participants.

SELECTION AND CONDUCT OF THE ACTIVITY

The instructional curriculum should be educationally sound. One characteristic of good teaching is the identification of and provision for a learning progression. Racquet sports require proper throwing mechanics which can transfer to hitting mechanics. The participant should demonstrate physical and psychological readiness in all areas. Physical readiness should include proper warm-up, satisfactory health, demonstrated fitness levels, demonstrated performance in prerequisite neuromuscular skills, and proper post-activity cool down routines. Psychological readiness includes the player's ability to act responsibly in competitive situations, to enjoy the participation, and to grow from positive interactions with partners, opponents, and mentors.

Rules should be established, communicated, frequently repeated, and prominently posted. The reading level of the students or players should be established and the rules targeted at that level. The rules must be modeled by the instructor and enforced unilaterally. Where special populations or conditions exist, rules must be modified to match the activity to the participant. Printed handouts should be prepared and distributed to each student.

Common sense rules in regard to replacing fluids, pacing oneself, attending to one's body in instances of pain and fatigue, and wearing proper clothing and safety equipment are no less important in racquet sports than in any other activity. Proper conditioning for the specific sport is a prerequisite. Other more subtle areas of safety include knowing the competitive habits of your opponent and resisting the overly aggressive "big play." Another safety measure might be limiting matches to as few players as possible, since cutthroat and doubles generally produce more injuries than singles.

Organizational control should be demonstrated by professionally trained personnel who can observe the playing area to determine that conduct and safety rules are followed. Through planning, the instructor should provide for reasonable participant/space ratios and practice formations which include adequate space for swing planes and ball flight. Racquetball and squash courts are logically supervised from an elevated vantage point to provide an overall view, but the instruction generally must be conducted on a court-by-court basis. This can create supervision concerns in the remainder of the courts. It is critical, therefore, that students be taught to accept responsibility for their own welfare, as well as relying on the guidance of the teacher.

THE PLAYING ENVIRONMENT

The playing environment is a primary concern for the racquet sport instructor. The playing courts need to be free of all extraneous equipment, including maintenance and sports items. The playing surface should be flat, well-groomed, and its composition such that safe footing is provided. There should be no protrusions from side walls or fences, especially at player or racquet level. The court layout should provide for a safe playing area, adequate intercourt space, and ample baseline area off court. There should be a plan for players and observers to move to and from the playing courts. Facility guides give official court dimensions and give suggestions for the design of active court areas and the necessary inter- and off-court space.

Written policies and procedures should include the court maintenance procedures, safety inspection procedures, use policies, equipment maintenance procedures, and participation agreement forms. Court maintenance documents should reveal the surface treatment schedule, cleaning or clearing schedule, and the itemized maintenance checklist. The safety inspection procedures should include a time table, key element precautions, and some indication of the personnel responsible for safety in the area. Use policies should indicate eligible users, conditions, risks, hours of use, and user responsibility. The equipment should be checked regularly for deterioration, damage, and compliance with manufacturer maintenance suggestions. The participant agreement should include the primary risks, inherent safety concerns, and a place for the player or responsible adult to indicate an awareness of the stated concerns and give consent to play with that understanding.

AVOIDING COMMON INJURIES

EYE INJURIES

The aspect of ocular injury is the greatest hazard in racquet sports. The National Society to Prevent Blindness reports that 10% of all sports related eye injuries are incurred in racquet sports. In Malaysia, where badminton is a popular sport, two-thirds of all injuries are

to the eyes. Tennis balls measure from 6.25 to 6.57 centimeters in diameter and reach speeds of 50 to 85 miles per hour as they cross the net. The size of the tennis ball makes it less likely to enter the eye socket, but the ball's texture and the dirt it collects make corneal abrasion more likely than with a racquet ball.

Racquet related injuries in tennis and badminton are not as prevalent as in squash and racquetball. This may be due to the more confined area and multi-directional swing planes created by the four wall court games. Ball speeds in racquetball can reach 125 miles per hour. The smaller ball in squash (1.56–1.75 centimeters) and the more pliable racquetball fit into the orbit of the eye and create an increased probability of ocular injury. There are more injuries from the racquet in squash than in racquetball because of the greater racquet length and the somewhat shorter court.

As a result of these dangers, eyeguard lenses and frames have been the subject of considerable investigation. Although development in the protective devices has been an ongoing process, there is still room for improvement in design and materials. The weakness of the open eyeguards is that they do not prevent the penetration of a compressed ball between the rims into the orbit of the eye. Hardened glass, while more protective than regular glass, is still subject to shattering when the lens has been scratched. Plastic streetwear glasses are not generally break resistant in spite of the widespread perception to the contrary. The wrap-around eyeguards with lateral coverage and protective frame for the nose appear to provide safer protection than the open model. Models utilizing a polycarbonate lens have been demonstrated to resist ball contacts up to 100 miles per hour. The CR-39 prescription lens should be of industrial thickness (3 mm) at the center, or a polycarbonate lens should be used. The primary weakness of the bubble and wrap-around guards appears to be one of ventilation.

Eyeguards suffer from people's perception of problems with restricting peripheral vision, being unattractive, and/or being uncomfortable. It is because of these perceptions that players often will not voluntarily wear the guards, with the exception of those who have previously suffered injuries. Predictably, it is the unprotected player who is injured most often. The teacher, therefore, must take the lead in guaranteeing player safety by requiring the use of proper eye protection.

The degree of experience in racquetball play does not seem to affect the probability of eye injury. One reason for this may be that novice players, while less controlled in their movement, tend to watch the front wall; more skilled players, while exposed to higher ball speeds, seldom take their eyes away from the ball. A very common safety problem in racquetball and squash occurs when the front court player faces the back wall as his opponent returns a shot. Another potential eye injury is a richochet from a racquet or off a back or side wall.

Players should concentrate on court awareness: their position in relation to the walls, their racquet, their opponent, and his or her racquet. When there is any danger of striking an opponent, a "hinder" should be called and the point replayed. Court awareness is particularly important in avoiding the hinder and the danger inherent in that situation.

Although eye injuries in tennis are somewhat less frequent than in the closed court racquet sports, awareness of potential eye hazards is important. The probability of eye injury in tennis increases as the player approaches the net. The speed of the ball and the reduced reaction time are contributing factors in this situation.

ELBOW AND SHOULDER INJURIES

Recurrent microstress of the elbow is known more commonly as "tennis elbow." This name is used even though probably less than five percent of those who suffer from the condition are actually tennis players. Tennis elbow is not a new problem; in fact, it was first described in medical journals in 1863. Even now it is thought that approximately ⅓ of all tennis players experience this condition at some point in their playing careers. Proper swing mechanics is good preventive medicine for tennis elbow. The proper swing mechanics should include a backswing involving the rotation of the trunk, with the upper arm close to the body and the forearm in the pronated position. Upon impact and during the follow-through, the player should generate external rotation with shoulder abduction. As the trunk unwinds, the elbow is extended while the racquet is held with a fixed wrist from a pronated forearm. This pronated position is thought to be the most stable for the forearm. The forward transfer of weight occurs with the forward momentum of the racquet head. The two-handed backhand may also reduce the incidence of tennis elbow by forcing the proper shoulder turn and spreading the shock of contact through both arms, thereby decreasing the force on either arm. Off center hits, frequency of play, grip strength, string tension, grip size, racquet head size, court surface, shock from returning powerful strokes, and ball weight have all been related to the incidence of tennis elbow.

The occurrence of shoulder injury in racquet sports is most common in the overhead strokes, primarily the serve. In tennis, rotator cuff tears and subacromial impingement are two of the most common injuries associated with this tendonitis-related problem. The throwing action and the trauma of continued contact can aggravate this condition.

CHECKLIST FOR SAFETY

Tables 1–4 should help in developing and implementing a safe and effective instructional program in the racquet sports.

TABLE 1
Tennis Elbow Checklist

STROKE MECHANICS

DO
   Use a two-hand backhand
   Use a shoulder turn
   Use a pronated forearm position

DON'T
   Lead with elbow on backhand
   Swing with arm only
   Use a supinated forearm stroke

EQUIPMENT TIPS

DO

   Use an oversized racquet (larger sweet spot)
   Reduce string tension
   Use the proper grip size (larger grip size reduces wrist play)
   Use a lightweight ball for practice
   Play on softest surfaces possible

PLAYING TIPS

DO

   Play less frequently if tennis elbow symptoms appear
   Play with an opponent who doesn't continually use "power" strokes
   Work to increase grip strength and flexibility
   Use a counterforce brace
   Practice proper stroke mechanics
   Develop and maintain proper conditioning

TREATMENT NOTES

DO

   Use anti-inflammatory medication as prescribed
   Heat elbow prior to playing
   Ice elbow with massage after playing
   Wait—surgery is generally not advocated until after a 6 to 9 month rest period followed by a rehabilitative exercise program and possibly prescribed injections. Surgery is not a first step.

TABLE 2
Badminton Safety Rules

EQUIPMENT

Check Racquets
  proper string tension
  safe grip
    tightly wound
    tacky/not slippery
  no loose, broken, or missing parts
    cracks in head
    cracks in shaft
Check Shuttlecocks (Birds)
  no sharp feather quills or sharp protruding plastic
  balanced shape (proper flight symmetry)
  proper weight for environment (indoor/outdoor)
Check Net and Standards
  net secured properly
  standards adequately weighted or anchored
Check Court
  floor clean and dry (adequate traction)
  lines clearly marked
  playing area free of extraneous equipment

PRACTICE

Allow adequate space between players for swing formations
Allow for safe distance in stroke practice
Use fleece balls when appropriate
Stretch the major muscle groups generally and the upper arm and shoulder specifically

GAME SITUATION

Match the players by ability
Provide recommended space around the court
Make eyeguards available and encourage their use
Assist the players in gaining and maintaining proper level of conditioning for competition

TABLE 3
Racquetball and Squash Safety Rules

EQUIPMENT

Check Racquet
    proper string tension
    safe grip—tightly wound, tacky/not slippery
    no loose, broken, or missing parts
        cracks in head
        cracks in shaft
    check wrist thong (racquetball only)
        test the tensile strength of the thong
        test the knot/connection of the thong
    provide and require eyeguards
        lens material—polycarbonate recommended; if CR-39 is used, require 3mm thickness at
          center
        do not allow street eyewear for protection
        do not use eyeguards without lenses
        type
          use lens model
          use wrap-a-round model
          protect eyes and nose
          avoid temporal hinges
    ball—check for proper pressure, keep ball clean and dry
    court
        check door for fit and security
        leave all non-essential equipment outside of the court
        be sure the floor is clean and dry

PRACTICE

Establish safe drills
    check swing space for all drills
    check ball path for all drills
    establish ball retrieval strategy
    establish court communication responsibilities
Require eyeguards
Require thong (racquetball only)

PLAY

Require eyeguards
Stretch major muscle groups and specific swinging muscles
Avoid hinders; Call hinders, if unavoidable
Play under control, don't be aggressive beyond skill level
Face the front wall
Swing under control
Use the wrist thong (racquetball only)
Use proper swing mechanics
Play the ball from low position to low target
Play singles rather than cutthroat (3 players) or doubles (4 players) and cutthroat rather than
    doubles to reduce risk from other players
Wear the proper shoes (thick soles)
Call warning "coming around" (back corner shot in squash only)
Use a short follow through toward the front wall
Avoid contact with the walls
Communicate with partner and opponents
Don't misuse the rule loophole of playing the ball off an opponent
Gain and maintain the proper level of conditioning for competition

TABLE 4
Tennis Safety Rules

EQUIPMENT

Racquet
  check string tension (reduce to ease or help prevent tennis elbow)
  grip characteristics
    tightly wound
    tacky/not slippery
    proper size (increase to ease or help prevent tennis elbow)
  head size (increase to ease or help prevent tennis elbow)
  no loose, broken, or missing parts
    cracked head
    cracked throat
    worn or broken strings
Balls
  proper pressure
  proper nap
  proper weight (reduce to ease or help prevent tennis elbow)
  keep clean and dry
Net and Standards
  net secured properly
  standards adequately weighted or anchored
Court
  surface clean, responsive, and level (slower to ease or help prevent tennis elbow)
  lines clearly marked
  sufficient border space around/between courts
Shoes
  suitable tread
  thick soles

PRACTICE

Use proper stroke mechanics
Use safe formations
  adequate swing room in drill formations
  safe distance from ball in stroke formations
Stretch the major muscle groups generally and the upper arms and shoulders specifically

PLAY

Match the skill levels of the players
Approach the net only when under control
Use proper swing mechanics
Replace fluids lost during play
Stretch the major muscle groups generally and the upper arms and shoulders specifically
Play within skill and conditioning limits
Develop and maintain proper level of conditioning for competition

REFERENCES

Bernhang, A. (1979). The many causes of tennis elbow. *New York Journal of Medicine*, 79(9), 1363–6.

Cofield, R. H. and Simonet, W. T. (1984). The shoulder in sports. *Mayo Clinic Proceedings*, 59(3), 157–63.

Cooney, W. P., III (1984). Sports injuries to the upper extremity: How to recognize and deal with some common problems. *Postgraduate Medicine*, 76(4), 45–50.

Doxanas, M. T. and Soderstrom, C. (1980). Racquetball as an ocular hazard. *Archives Ophthalmology*, 98(11), 195–6.

Easterbrook, M. (1981). Eye injuries in racket sports. *International Ophthalmology Clinic*, 21(4), 87–119.

Feiglman, M. J., Sugar, J., Jednock, N., Read, J. S., and Johnson, P. L. (1983). Assessment of ocular protection for racquetball. *Journal of the American Medical Association*, 250(24), 3305–9.

Kohn, H. S. (1984). Current status and treatment of tennis elbow. *Wisconsin Medical Journal*, 83(3), 18–19.

Sports related eye injuries for selected sports. (1980). National Society for the Prevention of Blindness. 1.

Priest, J. D. (1982). Elbow injuries in sports. *Minnesota Medicine*, 65(9), 543–545.

Smyth, J. P. (1983). Racquetball/Handball. In N.J. Dougherty (Ed.), *Physical education and sport for the secondary school student* (pp. 223–233). Reston, VA: The American Alliance for Health, Physical Education, Recreation and Dance.

Soderstrom, C. A. and Doxanas, M. T. (1982). Racquetball: A game with preventable injuries. *The American Journal of Sports Medicine*, 10(3), 180–183.

Stamford, B. (1986). Can you get fit playing racket sports? *The Physician and Sportsmedicine*, 14(1), 208.

Stotlar, D. and Lasley, D. (1985). Racquetball eye injuries: An analysis of student attitudes and behaviors. *National Intramural-Recreational Sports Association Journal*, 10(1), 16–18.

Vinger, P. F. (1986). How I manage corneal abrasions and lacerations. *The Physician and Sportsmedicine*, 14(5), 179.

CHAPTER 14

Self-defense

KENNETH TILLMAN

Trenton State College
Trenton, NJ

The key to safety in a self-defense class is to instill, in each student, the proper attitude toward the activity. Students must have a different view of self-defense than they have of other activities that are included in a physical education program. Basketball, tumbling, wrestling, dance, and other sport skills are learned to provide enjoyment and develop competency in performing an activity for recreational and/or competitive purposes. The goal is to *use* the skills that are learned. In self-defense it is hoped that many of the techniques will never be used. The skills are not learned for use in a competitive situation with friends or in an interscholastic athletic setting. The dangerous nature of attacking and retaliatory self-defense skills mandates that students know that these skills are to be used *only* when someone's safety is threatened and they must not be used with full force in the practice situation.

Students must have ingrained in them an understanding of the serious consequences that can result if they approach the learning of self-defense skills in a flippant manner. They must accept the fact that the skills they are learning can cause serious injury and even death. They must follow all safety precautions established in the class.

As part of the instructional approach, the teacher must emphasize that self-defense skills should be used only as a last resort technique. Avoidance of dangerous situations, fleeing when threatened, and discouraging an assailant must precede the use of physical force. This concept is important for students to accept if they are to participate safely. A macho attitude has no place in a self-defense class.

The tenor of the class should be that of helping each other develop skills, not competing against another person. The skills are being developed, not for sport, but for protection. Practice must be safe, even though the techniques will be damaging to an assailant if they are used in a life threatening situation.

Classes are structured to maximize safeguards against injury. Falling, strik-ing, and throwing are skills that are used in self-defense. It is, therefore, important that students know how to fall and develop a good kinesthetic sense. This must precede practicing the advanced techniques.

SUPERVISION

An instructor will significantly reduce the possibility of injury by carefully supervising each participant during the self-defense class. This means that the entire class will be in view and established practice procedures will be adhered to at all times. Strict control is critical for this activity because the skills that are being learned are designed to disable an antagonist. It is therefore necessary to enforce practice procedures that provide safety for members of the class, both when executing a skill and when simulating the attack.

Aggressiveness must be controlled when practicing dangerous tactics. The instructor needs to be in a position to observe all groups as they practice.

Appropriate instructor supervision requires the following:

1. An instructor must be in the activity area at all times when students are present.

2. An activity area that provides an unobstructed view of all participants is important.

3. The instructor must be aware of each student throughout the class.

4. The instructor should be with students who are trying difficult skills for the first time.

5. The instructor should be knowledgeable in all the skills that are being taught and insure that proper progressions are being followed.

6. Students should be taught how to assist their partners when practicing skills. Student understanding of the intricacies and dangers of the skills will increase overall class safety and assist the instructor in carrying out supervisory responsibilities.

7. It is important that the instructor knows the capabilities of each student in the class and adjusts class require-

ments to the psychological and motor readiness of the students.

8. Students must be comfortable with the instructor and be willing to seek assistance when needed.

9. The instructional area must be capable of being secured when class is not in session.

10. Students should be permitted to practice self-defense techniques only in properly matted areas.

11. Detailed lesson plans should be prepared and followed during each class period.

12. Potential dangers, both in the environmental setting for the class and in the class presentation, should be eliminated as part of the class planning process.

SELECTION AND CONDUCT OF THE ACTIVITY

Careful planning needs to be done in the selection of skills that will be incorporated into a self-defense unit. Self-defense tactics are designed for protection from a violent action and to thwart an attacker; they are not governed by rules designed for safe participation. It is particularly important, therefore, that the activity be conducted using specialized safety procedures. This poses an interesting dichotomy. Skills are selected because of their potential to disable an attacker, and yet the teaching procedure must be designed to provide extra protection to make the learning process safe.

It needs to be further emphasized that the student's attitude toward this unit is critical. The student must accept the fact that self-defense tactics are to be used for protection from imminent danger to oneself or someone else. The student must treat the skills in a serious fashion before they can be practiced safely. Many self-defense skills can never be practiced with full force. They are practiced in a simulated fashion and used with full intensity only in the event that the student is in a situation where personal safety or life is threatened.

The self-defense skill that is being learned will dictate the safety procedure that should be followed. There are certain guidelines that apply at all times and others that are specific to specialized tactics such as delivering a blow or throwing an attacker.

GENERAL

1. Each session should begin with warm-ups. Many self-defense tactics require explosive action and sudden movements. Warm-up is important to prevent muscle pulls and ready the body for strenuous activity.

2. Students must be physically capable of handling the rigors of executing self-defense techniques. A physical fitness unit is a good preliminary step to starting a self-defense class.

3. Incorporate physical fitness into your self-defense unit so the students will have strength, flexibility, and muscle suppleness to minimize the possibility of injury.

4. Competency in basic tumbling skills is a prerequisite to learning falling and throwing techniques. Students should, at a minimum, be able to do forward, backward, shoulder and forward dive rolls.

5. Tapping is the universal signal to stop. This signal must be respected by all members of the class and the hold broken immediately if a participant taps the mat, partner, or herself/himself.

6. Establish safety rules and make sure the rules are understood and followed.

7. Emphasis should not be on trying to prove that moves work, but rather on learning the techniques.

8. Proper progression is important. Start with basic skills and use these as the basis for more advanced techniques.

9. Regularly review basic skills to develop a firm foundation for the more difficult self-defense tactics.

10. Demand that students follow instruction consistently. Horseplay cannot be condoned.

11. The only techniques that should include contact with a partner are those

which do not involve inherent risk of injury.

12. Practice in a large area on surfaces having at least the resiliency of a wrestling mat.

13. The instructor should be able to demonstrate each skill that is being taught. It is important that the instructor know the dangers of each skill and be able to effectively impart this information to the students.

14. Work slowly when learning techniques. The skill must be learned before movements can be controlled during practice. Speed should be increased only as control is developed.

15. Never force a student to attempt a skill. Be sure the student has the necessary background before moving to new skills.

16. Do not permit the wearing of jewelry or other assessories during a self-defense class.

17. Comfortable physical education clothing that does not have buckles, snaps, or other items that can cause injury should be worn. Sneakers are the recommended footwear.

18. Safety and emergency procedures must be established and understood by the students. There should be access to a telephone and emergency numbers should be posted.

FALLING

1. Be sure that the students know how to do forward, backward, shoulder, and forward dive rolls before teaching falls.

2. Practice on thick mats to protect from injury.

3. Develop proper form by practicing each fall slowly. Speed up as the proper technique is learned. Learn the correct procedures to minimize impact when landing on the mat.

4. Follow proper progression when learning to fall.

5. Start falling from a low position (kneeling or squatting) and gradually increase the distance until the fall can be executed from a standing position.

BLOWS

1. Do not allow physical contact with a partner. This includes hand and foot blows.

2. Use padded dummies and other safe substitute targets such as playground balls when practicing blows.

3. Use imaginary opponents when using full force.

4. Make extensive use of simulation drills when practicing the various blows.

5. Emphasize the destructive nature of the blows that are being learned and the importance of treating dangerous techniques with respect.

6. Remember: never try to prove that a disabling blow works. Emphasize learning correct techniques for maximum effect.

HOLDS

1. Never allow students to apply full force to a hold.

2. Do not allow the use of fast or jerky motions on an unsuspecting partner.

3. Be sure the partner is aware of the hold and knows how to react to prevent injury.

4. Instruct the class members to always go with the leverage when a hold is being applied.

5. Stop immediately when one partner taps to indicate pain.

THROWS

1. Students should be thrown only after they have learned falling techniques and are able to fall correctly.

2. Simulate the throws many times before using a partner. Learn proper throwing techniques thoroughly.

3. Partners should be of a weight that the student can safely control when learning a throw.

4. Gradually increase the size of opponents as a student's skill increases.

5. Control skills are exceptionally important when making throws. Participants must be able to control their partner's body when throwing her/him to

the mat. Throws should be executed gently and never with full force.

6. Instruct students as to when they should release their grip to prevent a partner from falling incorrectly.

7. Gradually increase the pace of the throws.

8. Make certain that there is a minimum of 75 square feet per pair of students when practicing throws. Other students must stay away from this area when throws are being practiced.

ENVIRONMENTAL CONDITIONS

Safe surroundings are important for every physical education activity. The vigorous action that takes place in a self-defense class mandates an environment that will protect each student to the highest reasonable degree.

PHYSICAL SURROUNDINGS

1. An unobstructed matted area is needed. It is recommended that the mat have the resiliency of at least a wrestling mat.

2. The size of the class will determine the mat size that is needed. For some activities, such as throws, it might be necessary to rotate groups to provide appropriate safety parameters.

3. Ten foot circles, such as those painted on some practice wrestling mats, are ideal to use to keep satisfactory space between groups when practicing.

4. Wrestling rooms which have padded walls make good locations for teaching self-defense classes.

5. It is best to have one complete mat with the different sections taped together. Do not have small individual mats placed on the floor.

6. Any obstructions in the self-defense practice area should be matted.

7. Extra mats, including those of 6" and 8" in thickness, should be available when practicing falls and throws.

8. The mat area must be cleaned regularly.

EQUIPMENT

1. Partially deflated volleyballs and playground balls with target areas marked on them should be available for practicing various blows.

2. Punching bags, hand pads, blocking shields, tackling dummies, pillows and rolled sleeping bags are examples of equipment that should be available for students to use when practicing.

3. Small exercise mats should be provided so they can be rolled and used when practicing blows and throws.

4. Rules of conduct and safety and emergency procedures should be clearly posted in the practice area.

CONCLUSION

Self-defense techniques are valuable skills for students to learn. Even though the emphasis of this class is different from other physical education classes which key on sport, exercise and/or rhythms, the course makes a significant contribution to each student's education by developing self confidence and preparing them to handle dangerous situations. It is very important, however, that the safety guidelines that are covered in this chapter be followed so this physical education experience will be safe as well as beneficial.

REFERENCE

Tillman, K. G. (1983). Self-defense. In N. J. Dougherty (Ed.), *Physical education and sport for the secondary school student* (pp. 201–220). Reston, VA: The American Alliance for Health, Physical Education, Recreation and Dance.

CHAPTER 15

Soccer

JOHN FELLENBAUM
McCaskey High School
Lancaster, PA

photo by Jim Kirby

Called the world's most popular sport, soccer, as we know it, is not as foreign to the Americas as one might think. Written reports from Boston during the 1600s refer to soccer, and actually ban it from being played in the streets due to the injuries incurred by the participants. As the years progressed, soccer went through various modifications tending towards the more violent forms of rugby and American football. These setbacks were eventually overcome with President Theodore Roosevelt's White House conference aimed at curbing the American form of violent rugby-football, and with increasing contact with Europeans and other peoples of the world. Soccer has slowly and steadily made its way into the ranks of a national sport. Today, the soccer rebirth in the United States is phenomenal. Youths from coast to coast are playing this relatively simple team sport and parents are enjoying the advantages of watching their children engage in a sport which is healthy for their bodies and relatively gentle on their pocketbooks.

Unfortunately, when you have a game where little equipment is used and successful play depends primarily on body stamina, injuries will happen. Following is a list of common soccer injuries, the body parts most often affected, and suggestions for their prevention.

COMMON SOCCER INJURIES

Abrasions—scraping of the skin.
  A. Area most affected
    1. All parts of the body especially the legs
  B. Prevention
    1. Use safe and well-maintained equipment
    2. Avoid unsafe playing areas
    3. Avoid dangerous play

Contusions—bruising of the skin and underlying tissue.
  A. Area most affected
    1. All parts especially the quadriceps

  B. Prevention
    1. Avoid dangerous collisions

Blisters
  A. Area most affected
    1. Feet
  B. Prevention
    1. Conditioning of feet
    2. Properly fitting shoes
    3. Wearing two pair of socks
    4. Tape over the tender areas
    5. Use lubricant on friction area
    6. Use powder to reduce moisture

Strain—damage to tendon or muscle caused by overuse or overstress
  A. Area most affected
    1. Lower extremities, especially the gastrocnemius muscle, Achilles tendon, and patellar tendon
  B. Prevention
    1. Adequate fitness training
    2. Sufficient warm-up
    3. Restrictive taping

Sprain—stretching or tearing of ligament beyond its normal limits.
  A. Area most affected
    1. Ankle and knee areas
  B. Prevention
    1. Adequate fitness training
    2. Sufficient warm-up
    3. Restrictive taping
    4. Use of braces
    5. Avoid dangerous situations

Heat Exhaustion—rapid, weak pulse, lightheadedness, faintness, profuse sweating, disorientation.
  A. Prevention
    1. Adequate fitness training
    2. Regular water breaks every 15 to 20 minutes
    3. Plenty of water before play begins
    4. Don't play in excessive heat and humidity

As in any sport, soccer does have its injuries, but many can be minimized by proper attention to safety standards set by the instructor.

SUPERVISION

A. Proper attention should be given to the health status of the students—have them complete a health form.

1. Be aware of present physical problems such as fractures, sprains, strains, etc.

2. Be aware of health history, e.g. diabetes, allergies, asthma, etc.

B. Medical equipment should be available at all times.

1. First aid kits should be available including telephone numbers of the police, ambulance, rescue squad, etc.

C. If an injury occurs—the teacher should provide first aid only.

1. First aid training should be a must

2. Never diagnose unless qualified

3. Never permit the student to play through pain. Let pain be the guide—pain is nature's way of telling us something is wrong and to continue playing would only aggravate the situation.

D. Never allow a student who has had a serious illness or injury to rejoin class without a written note from the doctor.

E. Record the nature, circumstances, time, date, treatment, and follow-up of all injuries.

F. Never allow students to be without supervision while in the gymnasium or on the field.

G. No climbing or hanging from the nets or goal posts should be allowed.

H. Encourage good sportsmanship within the classroom structure. Stress the development of student self-control during competition.

I. Officiate games or instruct others to officiate as fairly as possible with safety of the students in mind.

J. Adapt the rules to the age and skill level of the students.

K. Constantly stress the rules of soccer with the realization that safety is promoted through rules.

L. Consider the weather and its effect on the field in the decision to go outside or remain inside. A wet field can be extremely slippery and lead to unnecessary injuries.

LESSON PLANS

A. Since soccer is aerobic in nature, begin each lesson with warm-up activities and conclude with a cool-down.

1. Warm-up—(slow stretching exercises *no* ballistic type). A thorough warm-up stretches all parts of the body to prepare for activity, stimulates the body systems, and diminishes the chance of injury.

2. Cool-down—exercises that gradually slow activity after intense exertion speed recovery time for the body and return the circulatory system to pre-exercise state.

B. Be aware of the conditioning and fitness level of your students. Soccer is an endurance sport. Consider having a fitness and conditioning unit before the soccer unit. Incorporate fitness and conditioning into your soccer unit lesson plans. Develop strength, endurance, and flexibility in the areas most vulnerable to injury.

C. Stress the proper progression of skills, to include:

1. Fundamental technique—Learn and practice skills with little or no movement around the field.

2. Match related skills—Perform learned skills with movement.

3. Match conditions—Perform learned skills in a game situation.

D. Proper instruction of skills is a must. Explain the skills; demonstrate the skills; and make sure everyone understands the skills.

E. Analyze the drills and teaching methods used with students' safety utmost in mind.

F. Provide ways and methods of practicing skills that are fun and motivating. This insures proper learning of skills and better body and ball control.

G. Provide ample feedback to the students regarding their technique. Allow sufficient practice time to improve skills.

H. The maximum number of students per team should be kept as close to the

TABLE I
Recommended Ball Sizes

Age	Ball Size	Circumference	Weight
Players under 6 yrs.	#3	23"–24"	8 to 10 ounces
Players 6 yrs. to 11 yrs.	#4	25"–26"	11 to 13 ounces
Players 12 yrs. and over	#5	27"–28"	14 to 16 ounces

rules (11) as possible allowing for less confusion and injury during play. The United States Youth Soccer Association recommends smaller team numbers for younger players. Instead of 11 vs. 11, play 6 vs. 6 or 7 vs. 7.

A teacher's responsibility for safety extends beyond the actual lesson or play to involve the equipment and environment in which the instruction takes place.

EQUIPMENT

A. *Shirts.*
1. Shirts or scrimmage vests should be of different colors for each team. This prevents confusion and helps prevent collisions.
B. *Shoes.*
1. Sneakers should be used for indoor play.
2. The following alternatives apply when playing outdoors: sneakers; all purpose athletic shoes; soccer shoes with molded cleats. All of the above are soft types of shoes to keep injuries to a minimum. Cleated shoes are ideal because they provide better traction and less slipping.
C. *Shinguards.*
1. Shinguards are a must for classroom competition. They provide safety by decreasing injuries in the shin area.
2. Shinguards come in several sizes and should be sized to fit the students.
D. *Goalie Uniform.*
1. Suggest wearing a long-sleeved and long-legged outfit (sweat suit) of a different color than the team shirt. A long-sleeved and long-legged outfit will protect the goalie from abrasions and contusions while diving for the ball. The different color shirt will help other players recognize the goalie.
E. *Soccer Ball.*
1. The ball should be sized to fit the age of the students for better ball control. It should be inflated to the recommended pressure for proper ball control and less injury to the body when heading and collecting.
2. Use smaller lighter balls for younger players. Table 1 gives recommendations for ball sizes for the various age groups.
3. The ball may be constructed of a variety of materials. For outdoor use, a leather or rubber coated ball (less expensive and more durable) is recommended. Indoors, an indoor soccer ball, nerf ball or slightly deflated outdoor soccer ball or volleyball is appropriate.

FIELD

A. *Size.*
1. For players under 12 years of age, the use of a smaller field with smaller dimensions is highly recommended.
B. *Playing Area.*
1. The grounds should be free of holes, ruts, glass, sticks, stones, etc.
2. The goalposts should be free of hooks and protrusions and should

be secure. There should be no loose bolts or connections.

3. A reasonable "buffer zone" of unobstructed space should be maintained around the playing field.

4. Daily inspection of the area before classes begin will protect students from unnecessary injury due to unsafe playing fields.

CONCLUSION

Prudent and reasonable care in following the safety rules outlined in the previous pages will help to prevent injuries in the soccer program. This is important not only for the safety of the students, but for the protection of the instructor against liability. Planning for safety is a prerequisite to any soccer program.

REFERENCES

Chyzowych, W. (1979). *The official soccer book of the United States Soccer Federation.* Chicago, New York, and San Francisco: Rand McNally.

Cramer. D. (1970). *United States Soccer Football Association coaches manual.* New York: United States Soccer Federation.

Fecht. G. (1979) *The complete parents' guide to soccer.* Santa Monica, CA: Goodyear.

Fellenbaum, J. (1983). Soccer. In N. J. Dougherty (Ed.). *Physical education and sport for the secondary school student* (pp. 235–249). Reston, VA: The American Alliance for Health, Physical Education, Recreation and Dance.

United States Olympic Committee Sports Medicine Council. (1985, January). *The medical aspects of soccer.* National Soccer Coaches Association of America and United States Soccer Federation.

Woog, D. (1986). "Prudent coaches keep game on field and out of court." *Soccer America,* July 31, 1986, p. 11.

CHAPTER 16

Softball

DIANE BONANNO

Rutgers University
New Brunswick, NJ

PATRICIA PETERS
and SONIA REGALADO

East Brunswick High School
East Brunswick, NJ

S oftball is truly one our our great national pastimes. In addition to the organized leagues sponsored by school systems and recreation departments, there are literally hundreds of thousands of "pick-up" games played each year. Indeed, beach parties, family picnics, company outings, and school field days are all fertile ground for a "couple of innings of ball."

Widespread participation in this sport, though, has its advantages and disadvantages in terms of safety. Active league play has resulted in numerous changes to rules, equipment, and playing field conditions which have contributed immeasurably to insuring the safety and well being of the player. Unfortunately, very few of these improvements have filtered down to the "pick-up" game or in some cases the physical education class or intramural league. In these instances, familiarity with the sport seems to be our worst enemy in regard to safety.

Familiarity with softball appears to breed carelessness. While we insist on having gloves and catcher's masks worn at the varsity game on Friday afternoon, we sometimes find it a nuisance to require the same gear for players in our class on Friday morning. Why? Is one set of students at less risk than the other? The answer is obviously no. The only thing that is different is our attitude.

In our minds, the game played by the varsity is fraught with risk. Anything can happen when playing another team on another field. We view the games played in our classes, however, quite differently. What can happen? we ask ourselves. It's only a game for fun—it's only a "pick-up" game among friends. Are all the precautions necessary between friends?

Yes, all the precautions are necessary—even among friends. Accidents can happen at anytime. Our only defense is to be prepared. If we take safety lightly in our classes or during intramurals, we are doing our students a disservice in two ways. First, we place them at greater risk than need be, which speaks for itself. Second, and not as obvious, is that we instill in them a careless attitude about safety, which can be just as debilitating as asking them to catch without a mask.

Safety is everyone's responsibility, at all times. Whether we're coaching a sport, teaching a class, or playing a "pick-up" game of softball, taking precautions is part of the game.

SUPERVISION

Supervision refers to the ability of the teacher or coach to monitor the activity that is occuring. Following are guidelines which should be kept in mind when planning for effective instructor supervision.

THE QUALITY AND QUANTITY OF SUPERVISION NEEDED

A. Instruction in softball should only be provided by individuals who are knowledgeable in:

1. *The rules* of the sport, especially as it is played by the age group they are supervising.
2. *The mechanics* of the skills especially those which place a player at greater risk, such as sliding.
3. *The teaching techniques* which are used to provide safe instruction.
4. *The teaching progressions* for each skill, especially as they apply to the age and ability level of the players.
5. *The potential hazards* inherent in the sport.
6. *The care and maintenance* of equipment.
7. *First aid and emergency procedures.*

B. As a general rule, the ratio of students to teacher should be smaller when the students are beginners or when new and potentially hazardous skills, such as sliding or batting, are being taught. In these instances the teacher/coach can improve the teacher/ student ratio by:

1. Dividing the group into small units, where each unit is given an

assignment which can be safely self-directed. This should allow the teacher/coach to move from unit to unit to introduce the new skill under conditions which permit better supervision.

2. Teaching students to provide feedback on a skill. Students who are chosen for this task must be trained and tested by the instructor to be sure they have a thorough knowledge of the subject matter. Providing the student assistant with written material is also helpful.

ORGANIZATION AND CONTROL

A. Instructors should station themselves at the area of highest risk. As a general rule, a high-risk area can be defined as one in which a new skill is being learned, a highly complex skill is being learned or practiced, or one in which a group of novices or poorly skilled players is practicing.

B. Be sure student assistants or managers are well instructed in the duties you expect them to perform. Two words of caution: student assistants should be reviewed periodically for effectiveness; and they should never be asked to assume responsibilities for high risk areas.

C. Softball fields provide wide open areas. Instructors should be sure that the activities they are conducting are placed in such a way that:

1. They can see all players at all times.

2. They can get from one activity to the next with minimal time lost if there is an emergency or if specific discipline is required.

D. Instructors should move from activity to activity in such a way as to ensure full view of the group at all times. Generally this means moving along the perimeter of the field.

E. Students should always be aware of the location of the instructor. If the area in which the activity is being conducted is large, the instructor may decide to:

1. Wear something that is brightly colored or distinctive so that he/ she can be spotted easily.

2. Rotate the group through his/ her location.

3. Announce a change of position before moving.

F. Bats, balls, or other equipment which may create an attractive nuisance for a child/player should not be left out if an instructor is not available to provide supervision.

G. Policies should be developed concerning potentially hazardous activities, e.g., sliding, baserunning, and catching. The policy should take into consideration:

1. The ability of the player.

2. The instruction provided.

3. The type of playing area provided.

4. The quality and quantity of supervision provided.

5. The type of softball game being played (e.g. fast pitch, slow pitch, 16-inch softball).

H. Safety rules that reflect the type of softball being played should be compiled and presented to the group at the beginning of the unit and reviewed periodically throughout the season. Following are general rules which apply to all situations and should be included on any list.

GENERAL SAFETY RULES FOR SOFTBALL

A. Don't throw the bat. Drop it after hitting the ball.

B. Check the area before swinging the bat. Be sure no one is near you.

C. Don't use the bat to hit stones or other objects. The bat should be used to hit the ball only.

D. When throwing to warm up, be sure you are throwing in the same direction as everyone else. Check to be sure no one could be hit by an overthrow.

E. Don't stand on the bag when playing a force out. Use the side or corner of the bag for the tag.

F. Don't fake a tag on a player.

G. Remember that the fielder has the right of way in the baseline when fielding the ball.

H. When playing offense, stay well back from the playing field. If there is a fenced-in dugout, be sure to stay there until your turn at bat comes. Stay alert for foul balls that may be hit toward the bench.

I. Never leave equipment lying in either fair or foul territory.

J. Call for the ball—avoid collisions.

PLANNING

A. Detailed lesson plans should be written for every instructional period or workout session.

B. Plans should include, but not be limited to:

1. Specific objectives which explain the purpose of the session and what the instructor hopes to accomplish.

2. Detailed explanations of the activities that have been selected to achieve the objectives.

3. Diagrams which illustrate the managerial aspects of the drills being taught or the organization of the group.

4. Notations of any special safety considerations for the skills being taught.

5. Provisions for warmup activities and review of prerequisite skills.

C. Lesson plans for rainy days should be prepared in advance. They should correspond to the activities being taught in the unit or outline an activity which must be performed in lieu of the skills being taught in the unit due to limitations on space, equipment, etc. If a substitute activity is planned for a rainy day, the most important consideration is that the students can safely perform the activity at their present level of ability or conditioning.

D. Be sure planning reflects an understanding of the learner's level of ability and the limitations that might be placed on learning due to lack of equipment or facilities.

E. Taken collectively, the lesson plans should reflect sound progressions for skill development.

SELECTION AND CONDUCT OF THE ACTIVITY

Conduct of the activity refers to the proper selection of an activity or teaching method based on the size, age, ability level, and experience of the player. Following are several points which should be considered when searching for the most effective course of action in presenting or reviewing material with your students.

READINESS

One of the first areas one should consider in the selection and conduct of an activity is whether a player is likely to succeed (ready) when trying a new skill.

A. Never force a player to attempt a skill if he/she is afraid or expresses unusual insecurity. This caution extends to previously learned skills as well as new ones.

B. Never force a player to assume a position on the field for which they have never had instruction or for which they express fear or uncertainty.

C. Never allow an individual to play at a level for which they have insufficient skill. If a level of play requires that a player be able to slide for safety purposes do not allow an individual to play if they cannot slide.

D. Stress self-control. Teach students to follow the rules and assume responsibility for their own safety. Teach them to check their equipment before they use it and to survey the playing field before they begin play. Have them remind each other of good playing habits (i.e. dropping the bat). Make everyone safety conscious.

E. Prepare the students for emergencies. Explain the potential hazards of the game and the methods for avoiding injury. Outline what should be done if an emergency occurs.

F. Never engage the group in game play unless they are ready. Be sure you know what they are capable of doing safely. If you feel it important to play the game early in the instructional period, modify the rules and equipment so that the game conforms to the skill and ability of the players. Following are some suggestions for modifying the game.

1. Modify Equipment. Use a ball that is bigger, brighter in color, or softer. Use a longer or shorter bat, or one that is lighter in weight.
2. Modify Rules. Allow for:
- no balls and strikes
- one pitch or 3 pitches per batter
- pitcher from own team
- fewer bases
- hit ball off tee—no pitcher
- eliminate infield positions
- eliminate outfield positions
- no batting

G. Be sure the players are physically ready to play the game. Stress conditioning in the early stages of the season especially for the arm and shoulder girdle.

H. Stress the need for warming up before practice or play. Teach the players a specific routine for warming up and explain the possible injuries that could result from inadequate warmup activity.

SKILL PROGRESSION

Progressions are one of the most important ways of ensuring safety in any sport. A proper progression minimizes the likelihood of injury during the instructional phase and prepares the player for injury-free ball during the execution phase. Following are suggested progressions for several of the basic skills in softball.

A. *Throwing.* Throwing progressions should always begin with a light weight ball that is easy for a player to grip. As the player becomes more skilled, a larger heavier ball may be substituted. Recognize, however, that a regulation ball may never be appropriate for some players. Before a regulation ball is substituted, consideration should be given to the age, size, and ability level of the player as well as the availability of gloves.

To ensure safety, throwing drills should always be set up so that (a) there is ample distance between throwing pairs/groups, (b) each pair is throwing in the same direction, and (c) throwing pairs never overlap.

THROWING PROGRESSIONS

1. Demonstrate proper mechanics of overhead throw.
2. Have players practice mechanics of the throw without the ball.
3. Throw short distances practicing mechanics.
4. Throw short distances practicing accuracy.
5. Increase distance, concentrating on accuracy and mechanics.
6. Practice running to the ball, fielding, and throwing.
7. Throw from different positions on the field starting with infield positions and progressing to outfield positions.

B. *Catching.* Catching progressions should always begin with a light weight ball that is large enough for the player to track easily. When working with very young players, it is a good idea to work with a ball that is brightly colored. As the catching ability of the player improves, a regulation ball can be substituted safely.

Note the precautions that apply to the placement of a throwing drill apply to catching as well. In addition, care should be taken to locate the catching drill on level ground. Grounders that take an irregular bounce are difficult and dangerous to field. Level ground will make it safer and easier for a player to catch the ball. It also minimizes the possibility of injury due to falling.

CATCHING PROGRESSIONS

1. Demonstrate mechanics of catching.
2. Have players toss ball to themselves and catch.
3. Have players throw ball to a wall and catch it on a rebound. Throws should be varied so that practice is gained catching balls that rebound at various heights and speeds.
4. Have players toss and catch with each other. Practice should

be gained:

- catching ball of varying heights
- catching balls thrown to the left and right of the midline
- moving to the ball
- moving backward
- moving laterally
- catching and throwing immediately to a target

5. Have players field balls hit off a bat.

C. *Batting.* Batting should be practiced in a designated area that is large enough to allow the batter to pull the ball left or right or hit a foul without interfering with another drill or game. Each player involved in the batting drill should be assigned a specific task and positioned on the field in such a way as to eliminate the possibility of being struck by the bat. This is particularly true of the players who are catching the balls thrown in from the field. They must be stationed in an area where they can perform their job without worrying about being struck by the bat or a line drive off the bat. When providing instruction during the early stages of learning be sure to use a light weight bat and ball to practice. This procedure should be followed as much to protect the fielders, who may not be highly skilled catchers, as to make it easier for the batter to perfect his/her skill. Another precaution which should be considered is using a light weight or "soft" ball (i.e., mush or cloth ball) when a batter is facing a live pitcher. This adaptation is suggested because of the dubious talent most young pitchers exhibit when trying to pitch the ball directly across the plate. If a ball strays from its intended path it is less likely to cause the batter injury if it is light weight or soft. During "live" pitching sessions don't forget to insist that the catcher wear a mask. Live batting practice has all of the elements of a real game, and it requires all of the same precautions.

BATTING PROGRESSIONS

1. Demonstrate the mechanics of the swing.
2. Using a light weight bat, have the learner practice swinging without a ball. Be sure the batters have ample room in which to execute the drill. Allow for the possibility of the bat flying off on the follow through.

3. Practice batting off a tee. Have the batters place their own ball on the tee. This will help to eliminate the possibility of a player being accidentally hit by a practice swing as he/she goes to place the ball on the tee for the batter.

4. Practice batting with the coach or instructor pitching. Care should be taken in this drill to place the ball into play slowly so that the fielders have time to recover. The tendency is to concentrate on the batter, pitching the ball as soon as the stance is regained. This can create a dangerous situation for the players in the field. As they are concentrating on fielding one ball, another is launched into the air. It would be very easy in this instance for a player to be hit by an unseen ball or for two players to collide because they were paying attention to two different situations.

5. Practice batting with another player pitching. Start this drill with a light weight ball. Remember that batting ability develops at a much faster pace that pitching. This can lead to two problems: first, the novice pitcher may inadvertently strike the batter with the ball; and second, the batter may hit a line drive back to the pitcher who, because of inexperience, is not ready to catch the ball. The effect of both of these situations can be reduced, as mentioned previously, by the use of a light weight ball and a modified pitch.

6. Practice batting with a pitcher who is throwing medium speed.

D. *Baserunning.* There are two primary areas of concern connected with baserunning drills. The first is the condition of the field where the runners are practicing. It should be free of holes, uneven surfaces, or any equipment or debris which may cause injury. It should also provide enough traction for the runners to accelerate safely without slipping and ample room for them to decelerate without fear of crashing into a wall, a fence, or some other unmoveable object.

The second condition focuses on the physical readiness of the players. Baserunning drills can be extremely tiring. As such they can be debilitating. Tired players don't worry about technique—they just want to get through a drill to save face. When the point of fatigue is reached, the likelihood of injury increases due to lack of concentration and inability to make the body perform correctly. To minimize the effect of fatigue, the instructor/coach should treat baserunning as a conditioning drill in the early stages of the unit or season. The number of times a runner is asked to perform should be based on physical condition, not on mastery of technique. As time progresses and the player's physical condition improves, more emphasis can be placed on proper form, with less regard to the number of times the player is asked to round the bases.

The following steps should be performed at a moderate speed while technique is being learned. As technique improves, maximum speed and acceleration should be the goal.

BASERUNNING PROGRESSIONS

1. Practice sprinting to check form.
2. Practice running straight through the base.
3. Practice swinging, dropping the bat, running through base.
4. Practice rounding bases.
5. Practice swing and running for double, triple, homerun.
6. Practice picking up coach's signal, before leaving the base, as approach to base is made.

Sliding. Sliding is a technique for advanced players who have the skill and ability to execute it properly. It is not a skill that should be taught to an entire physical education class. It is a skill, however, that should be taught, reviewed, and conscientiously practiced with varsity players who may need to execute the skill to avoid injury. Even in a varsity situation, though, it should be recognized that there will be players who are afraid to slide. The coach has only two choices with these individuals: either never ask them to slide, or if he/she feels it is a crucial skill at their level of play, cut the individual from the team. A player who is afraid must *never* be required to slide. It is a request that most surely will increase the chances of injury for the player.

A progression on sliding is not included in this section. Rather, several precautions are listed which should be considered when teaching the skill to advanced players.

SLIDING PRECAUTIONS

1. Perform learning stages of skill in sand pit or on a very grassy surface.
2. Have performers learn the skill in sneakers before using cleats.
3. Use loose or throw down bases until the skill is perfected.
4. Do not have have a baseman present until the skill is perfected.
5. Break the skill into manageable parts when teaching.

ENVIRONMENTAL CONDITIONS

When planning for safety in softball, the instructor must consider two major aspects of the environment in which the unit will be conducted. They are field preparation and layout and equipment maintenance. (Where specifications are given, refer to the National Federation of High School Association Rulebook on Softball.)

FIELD LAYOUT

The following guidelines are written for a regulation softball field. It is clearly understood, however, that most of the softball being played today, outside of structured league play, is being played on makeshift fields. Where applicable, a standard is modified to address this situation.

A. *Infield.* The infield shall be a skinned surface, free of rocks, grass, weeds, potholes, or foreign debris. If a skinned infield is not available, the area should be checked for irregular surfaces or holes.

B. *Markings.* All markings on the field including foul lines, batter's box, etc., shall be marked with a material which is not injurious to the eyes or skin. Materials such as lime are prohibited.

C. *Outfield.* The outfield shall extend unobstructed at least 200 feet from homeplate for male and female fast pitch, 250 feet for female slow pitch and 275 feet for male slow pitch. It should be free of all rocks, holes, and debris.

D. *Orientation.* Where possible, the field should be positioned so that a line running from home plate through second base points in an East-Northeast direction.

E. *Warning Track.* If a field is bounded by a fence, the fence shall be at least eight feet high. To warn the fielder of his or her approach to the fence, there shall be a track of a different surface than the outfield grass.

F. *Dugouts.* Where dugouts are not provided, an area shall be designated for player seating at least 25 feet out from the foul line.

G. *Backstops.* Backstops should be positioned not less than 25 feet behind home plate. If backstops are not in use, no one shall be allowed to sit or stand behind the catcher.

EQUIPMENT

Following is a safety checklist for equipment. The list in no way implies that every piece of equipment is required in order to conduct a safe program. The type of equipment needed will be dictated by the game played and the age and ability level of the players. The list does, however, represent a set of conditions which should be present if the equipment is used. (Technical specifications such as weight, length, etc. of specific pieces of equipment when used reflects the rules governing High School Federation ball at the time of this writing.)

A. *The Bat.*

1. The bat should be round and a one-piece construction of hardwood, metal, or plastic. Bats of two-piece construction, in which the barrel and the handle are separate units, are unsafe and should not be used.

2. The proper weight and length of a bat will vary will the age and ability level of the player. At its maximum, the bat should not exceed 34 inches in length. Fungo bats should not be used in regulation play.

3. The bat should have a safety grip made of a rough surfaced material. Smooth surfaced grips made of plastic tape are unsafe. Grips should be checked for tears and slippage. Damaged grips should be replaced immediately. If the repair cannot be made at once, the bat should be removed from play.

4. Wooden bats should be checked for cracks and splinters. Bats with cracks and splinters are unsafe and should be removed.

5. Every bat should have a safety knob at the end. If a bat is missing the knob or if the knob is damaged, the bat should be replaced.

6. Donut rings are not recommended for use on softball bats. Do not allow them to be used at any time.

B. *The Ball.*

1. The proper size and weight of the ball will depend on the game being played and the age and ability level of the players. It will also depend on whether gloves are available for all the players and whether the game is being played indoors or out. Be sure to use the ball for the purpose for which it was intended. If you decide to use a ball in a situation where it is not normally used, be sure you have

sound educational justification for doing so.

2. Balls should be checked regularly to be sure they meet specifications. Those that are misshaped, have torn seams, or are water logged should be discarded.

C. *Gloves.*

1. The decision to use gloves will depend on the type of game being played. Anytime a regulation size and weight softball (6¼–7 ounces in weight, 11⅞–12⅛ inches in circumference) is used, gloves should be worn for protection.

2. Be sure that the gloves that are issued are appropriate for the position.

3. Check laces to be sure they are not broken or worn. Worn or broken laces should be repaired immediately or the glove should be removed from play.

4. Work the gloves to be sure they are supple. Gloves that are stiff do not afford the player sufficient control.

5. Be sure gloves are properly fitted for the size of the player's hand.

D. *Headgear.* Headgear is required for use in all varsity situations that are governed by the National Federation of State High School Associations. According to the rules "It is mandatory for each batter, runner, and the catcher to wear a head protector. The head protector shall be a type which has safety features equal to or greater than those provided by the full plastic cap with padding on the inside. The head protector worn by each batter and each runner shall have extended ear flaps which cover both ears and temples. . . ." In a class situation, where students do not wear ball caps, sanitary precautions preclude the use of headgear. Measures to protect the batter, runner, and catcher in this situation should occur to include rule modification if necessary.

E. *Catcher's Equipment.* In addition to headgear, the catcher in a varsity situa-

tion may be required to wear some or all of the following equipment. Again, the exact choices will differ depending on the game played, the rules that are being enforced, and the ball and bat being used.

1. Mask. If the catcher wears a head protector be sure the mask is compatible with the protector. Check straps to be sure they adjust for tight fit. Have masks of varying sizes or adjustable pads to ensure a snug fit around face. Have the catcher check mask to be sure visibility is not impeded. Check the wire frame for dents or openings that may give upon impact with ball. Under no circumstances should a catcher be allowed to take a position immediately behind a batter without a catcher's mask.

2. Chest Protector. Secure appropriate protectors for each sex. Do not allow players to alter equipment in any way. Check the straps for wear and tear. Be sure protector provides snug fit without restricting movement in any way.

3. Shin Guards. Be sure guards are capable of covering lower thigh, knee, shin, instep, and ankles. Straps should be adjusted for a tight fit. Be sure buckles fit on the outside of the leg once the buckles are tightened and in place.

F. *Bases and Home plate.*

1. Peg Down Bases. Use two pegs and straps to anchor each base. Be sure anchor pegs are placed away from baserunner's sliding path. Permanently anchored bases are inappropriate for use in situations where players who lack high level sliding skills are allowed to slide.

2. Homeplate. Edges should be flat and even with the infield playing surface. If the plate has protruding pegs on its top surface, it should be replaced. Homeplate should be made of a smooth surfaced material.

CONCLUSION

Softball refers to many different games, each of which has its own special concerns in terms of safety. The best advice, when conducting any one of the softball-type games, is that the coach/instructor should consider every aspect of the activity from a high risk point of view and then initiate the precautions necessary to eliminate the likelihood of an accident.

REFERENCE

Sisley, B. L. (1983). Softball. In N.J. Dougherty (Ed.), *Physical education and sport for the secondary school student* (pp. 251–264). Reston, VA: The American Alliance for Health, Physical Education, Recreation and Dance.

CHAPTER 17

Swimming

RALPH JOHNSON

Indiana University
Indiana, PA

In the past thirty years a significant number of public and private schools have added a swimming pool to their physical plant or included them in the construction of new facilities. Its value is incalculable when considering the many activities and benefits a swimming pool makes possible. A comprehensive aquatic program in the hands of a professionally trained aquatic director can provide instruction, recreation, competition, rehabilitation, therapy, and fitness activities for everyone in the school and community. The swimming pool adds a measure of safety to the community, furnishes an outlet for teenage energies, offers the possibility to earn college athletic scholarships, and provides social activity for the disabled. It is a source of family activity and entertainment. The simple skill of learning to swim often opens the door to a vast world of fun and excitement.

Unfortunately, hazards such as unsafe design, careless maintenance, or improper supervision and instruction cause accidents leading to significant consequences for the victim and the school district. The National Electronic Injury Surveillance System (NEISS) estimates that swimming pools are annually responsible for over 140,000 accidents which require hospitalization. Primary concern in these statistics should be focused on the more than 13,000 serious diving accidents and the more than 1000 drownings which occur each year. While only approximately 4% of the spinal cord injuries and drownings occur in school swimming pools, one serious accident is too many. One death or permanent disability can ruin a program, destroy a career, and create a lifetime of guilt.

Concern for student and patron safety is a serious matter for all school district employees, from the pool custodial staff to the superintendent. To assist school officials in understanding the broad spectrum of their potential liability, the following general risk assessment is provided.

GENERAL RISK ASSESSMENT

1. Are you aware of what aquatic activities are considered to be high risk?
   ____ YES ____ NO

2. Does your school district employ a trained professional as an aquatic director to supervise and coordinate programs and activities and to be responsible for remedial and preventive maintenance?
   ____ YES ____NO

3. Has the aquatic director taken courses in aquatic facility management, pool chemistry and maintenance, aquatic program administration, and aquatic liability and hazard/risk reduction?
   ____ YES ____NO

4. Are all teachers and coaches assigned to the aquatic program currently certified in lifeguard training, standard first aid, CPR (Basic Life Support), and as swimming instructors by a nationally recognized agency such as the Red Cross or YMCA?
   ____ YES ____NO

5. Do your teachers, coaches, and supervisors possess current certifications from a recognized agency providing instruction in the activity to which they are assigned?
   ____ YES ____NO

6. Does the school district provide funding for continuing education or credit bearing certification courses to update or retrain the aquatic director?
   ____ YES ____NO

7. Are maintenance workers provided with funding to attend pool operator and equipment maintenance workshops?
   ____ YES ____NO

8. Have aquatic facility and program safety policies been established, including the development of a pool operations and procedure manual?
   ____ YES ____NO

9. Is there an ongoing program for updating aquatic policies and procedures?
   ____ YES ____NO

10. Does the school administration and aquatic staff have an understanding of the legal implications resulting from an accident in the school district's pool?
    ____ YES ____NO

11. Do your teachers and coaches provide a safety orientation for students at the outset of every school program and are students aware of their responsibilities for their own safety and the safety of others?
    ____ YES ____NO

12. Are you familiar with the skills and activities that teachers and coaches are conducting in terms of their risk to students?
    ____ YES ____NO

13. Has every precaution been taken with high risk activities to prevent the occurrence of an accident?
    ____ YES ____NO

GENERAL RISK ASSESSMENT—Continued

14. Is there a standard form and system for reporting aquatic accidents in your school district?
_____ YES _____NO

15. Are emergency and accident management procedures written and rehearsed to assure a prompt, organized response to an accident?
_____ YES _____NO

16. Have emergency and accident management procedures been reviewed by your attorney, school doctor, and local paramedics or hospital officials?
_____ YES _____NO

17. Are emergency and accident management drills conducted at least twice a month, one of those times during peak facility use?
_____ YES _____NO

18. Is current safety literature available to your teachers and coaches?
_____ YES _____NO

19. Are all accidents carefully investigated and reviewed, with the proper authorities and corrective action taken?
_____ YES _____NO

20. Are safety checks of facilities and equipment made by aquatic staff members weekly, with the report or check sheet filed in the appropriate office?
_____ YES _____NO

21. Is a hazard identification conducted by an outside professional or consultant at least once every three years?
_____ YES _____NO

22. Prior to being put into use, is all new equipment inspected for defects or deficiencies which could lead to an accident?
_____ YES _____NO

23. Are in-service training safety workshops conducted by the aquatic staff on a regular basis?
_____ YES _____NO

24. Are you familiar with all local, county, state, and professional safety and health standards which may affect the operation of your program?
_____ YES _____NO

25. When building a new facility or rehabilitating an old facility, is a professional aquatic consultant retained for the duration of the project to assure that all aspects of safety are accounted for?
_____ YES _____NO

26. When building a new pool or rehabilitating an old one, is the school's aquatic staff involved in the design and implementation process?
_____ YES _____NO

27. Is worn out safety, instructional, competitive, fitness, and recreational equipment replaced or repaired as needed?
_____ YES _____NO

28. Is the aquatic staff involved in the procurement of safe, high quality equipment?
_____ YES _____NO

GENERAL RISK ASSESSMENT—Continued

29. Have written safety rules regarding equipment and activities been conveyed to all teachers, coaches, and program leaders?
    ____ YES ____NO

30. Are all your students covered by accident insurance?
    ____ YES ____NO

31. Are your teachers, coaches, and supervisors covered by liability insurance?
    ____ YES ____NO

32. Are participants in competitive and high risk programs required to provide evidence of a physical examination with participant approval granted by the certifying physician?
    ____ YES ____NO

33. Are participants in competitive and high risk activities required to provide an agreement to participate or an informed consent document signed by a parent or guardian if the participant is of minority age?
    ____ YES ____NO

34. Are safety rules specific to the use of diving boards, slides, scuba gear, and flotation devices established in writing in your pool operations manual and conveyed to program participants verbally and/or in writing?
    ____ YES ____NO

35. Do your teachers and coaches carefully inspect equipment each day before use in order to assure its safe use?
    ____ YES ____NO

36. Is your pool currently equipped with essential first aid, life support, and lifeguarding equipment?
    ____ YES ____NO

The following scale is provided to help evaluate your general risk level.

General Risk Assessment

Number of NO's checked	Risk Level
2	Relatively Safe
4	Marginally Safe
5	Unsafe
7	High Risk
8 or more	Pull the Plug!

Understanding the major hazards and preparing effective strategies for accidents in the aquatic environment are related to four areas of concern: design, maintenance, supervision, and instruction.

DESIGN

NEW POOLS

Accident prevention begins with the architect or engineer. The pool designer should be selected on the basis of having successfully designed many pools during his/her career. Be sure that the design meets or exceeds all current criteria established by the following:

1. State Health Department.
2. County and City Health Department.
3. Professional Standards:
   • Council for National Cooperation in Aquatics
   • American Public Health Association
   • AAHPERD
4. Federal Government (Department of Health and Human Services).
5. Competitive Aquatic Sport Groups:
   • National Collegiate Athletic Association
   • U.S. Swimming
   • U.S. Diving
   • National Federation of State High Schools
6. Aquatic Safety Agencies:
   • American Red Cross
   • YMCA of the USA

When the architect's plans are submitted for approval, a comparison of design standards and guidelines should be made with publications issued by the aforementioned groups. Often design manuals used by architectural firms are not up-to-date with competitive, governmental, and safety agencies. Be sure that the plans are submitted to the state health department for approval.

In addition to hiring an experienced architect, it is wise to retain an aquatic expert, experienced and skilled in design safety, to review pool drawings and recommend necessary changes.

OLDER POOLS

Two hazards are evident with older pools (those designed and built in the late 40's and in the 50's and 60's). First, some design features once thought to be safe, such as hopper or spoon shaped bottoms and safety ledges, have proven over the years to be the direct cause of many serious accidents. Hopper and spoon shaped bottoms are deceptive and dangerous for divers who enter the water from a springboard into what appears to be 12 feet of water, only to discover that the pool is 12 feet deep in a very small area directly in front of the board.

The second design problem is related to technology. Diving from starting blocks 30 inches above the deck into water 3½ feet deep has always been dangerous. With the advent of the racing dive known as the "pike", "shoot", or "scoop" start, competitive swimmers are being exposed to unreasonable risks and are breaking their necks. High performance competitive type diving boards are enhancing the performance of varsity divers, but unfortunately, recreational divers are using them as well. Many older pools are not compatible with "high tech" diving boards, yet coaches and teachers are demanding state-of-the-art equipment without considering its effect on diving safety. Depth of water and the amount of deep water in the landing area is sometimes overlooked in the excitement of purchasing a new diving board.

The following checklist provides a quick reference in helping to identify some of the common design hazards found in both new and older pools.

DESIGN SAFETY CHECKLIST

Area	Item	Pass	Deficient	Fail
1. Pool Entrance:	Doors at shallow end	------	-------------	-----
	Locks are functional	------	-------------	-----
2. Pool Deck:	Non-slip	------	-------------	-----
	Slope-good drainage	------	-------------	-----
	Depth Markers 4"–6" high	------	-------------	-----
	Depth Markers on vertical wall	------	-------------	-----
	Depth Markers on deck	------	-------------	-----
	Depth Markers in Feet and Meters	------	-------------	-----
	No obstructions	------	-------------	-----
3. Pool Walls: (underwater)	Smooth surface	------	-------------	-----
	No obstructions	------	-------------	-----
4. Pool Bottom:	Smooth surface	------	-------------	-----
	Marked for depth perception	------	-------------	-----
	Marked at breakpoint	------	-------------	-----
	Drain grates screwed in	------	-------------	-----
	Safety ledge	------	-------------	-----
	Hopper/spoon shaped	------	-------------	-----
5. Ladders:	Attached securely	------	-------------	-----
	Non-slip steps	------	-------------	-----
	Edged in contrasting color	------	-------------	-----
6. Lifeguard Chair:	5–6 feet high	------	-------------	-----
	Positioned at pool edge	------	-------------	-----
	Safe seat and steps	------	-------------	-----
7. Starting Blocks:	Located at deep end	------	-------------	-----
	Non-slip surface	------	-------------	-----
	Anchored securely	------	-------------	-----
	Non-slip steps	------	-------------	-----
8. Diving Boards:	Anchored securely	------	-------------	-----
	Non-slip surface	------	-------------	-----
	Mount anchored	------	-------------	-----
	Non-slip steps	------	-------------	-----
	Double handrails	------	-------------	-----
9. Diving Area:	12 ft. deep—1 meter	------	-------------	-----
	13 ft. deep—3 meter	------	-------------	-----
	Depth extends forward 20 ft. from front edge of board	------	-------------	-----
	Depth extends 8 ft. on either side of board	------	-------------	-----
	Depth extends under board back to wall	------	-------------	-----
10. Lighting:	Deck (100 ft. candles)	------	-------------	-----
	Water surface (100 ft. candles)	------	-------------	-----
	Underwater (100 lamp lumens/sq. foot of pool surface)	------	-------------	-----

MAINTENANCE

Safety is directly related to good maintenance practices as well as compliance with local and state regulations. Copies of pool regulations should be obtained from local and state health departments. They should be kept on file and reviewed frequently. Some states require that a copy of their regula-

tions be posted in the pool area for the public to see. Failure to comply with these regulations can lead to conditions causing accidents, and makes the school district liable either through negligence or by direct violation of the law. Regulations common to all states pertaining to pool operation include the items listed below. Does your school swimming pool meet the following state regulations?

COMMON STATE REGULATIONS

Regulations	Pass	Fail
1. Copy of regulations on file	——	——
2. Current pool permit on file	——	——
3. Electrical inspection up to date	——	——
4. Proper safety equipment	——	——
5. Pool operations report maintained and submitted to health department when required	——	——
6. Bacteriological analysis conducted weekly	——	——
7. Chlorine and pH tests conducted as required	——	——
8. Water turnover rate maintained (8 hrs.)	——	——
9. Gas masks available and in working condition	——	——
10. Water clarity maintained as required by law (usually 6 inch black disc visible on bottom from anywhere on deck around deep end)	——	——
11. Water level maintained above gutter or skimmer	——	——
12. Test kit available with fresh chemicals	——	——
13. Capable manager in charge of pool	——	——
14. A certified lifeguard on duty for all classes and activities	——	——
15. Hazards reported and eliminated	——	——
16. Depth markings—proper size and location	——	——

The custodial staff can reduce the risk of all aquatic programs through good water quality, proper care of the deck area, pool equipment and safe handling of the many types of chemicals common to pool operations. Maintenance contributes to pool safety and risk reduction in three ways: 1) daily operations;

2) remedial practices; and 3) preventive techniques.

Daily operations consist of routine maintenance such as testing the water chemistry and adjusting appropriately, cleaning filters when necessary, cleaning the deck, starting blocks and diving board surfaces, adjusting the water level, vacuuming the pool, and maintaining correct water, air temperature, and humidity levels. Good daily practice includes proper storage of all types of equipment, maintaining above water and underwater lighting, and checking safety equipment. One of the most frequent causes of diving and drowning accidents is cloudy water which is directly related to filtration and water chemistry. Filters should be cleaned and maintained at a turnover rate of 5–8 hours. Water clarity and swimmer comfort are easily maintained if the pool environment is maintained as follows.

HOW DOES YOUR POOL RATE?

Item	Pass	Fail
1. Air Temperature: 3 degrees higher than water temp.	___	___
2. Humidity: 60–70%	___	___
3. Clarity: .1–.2 JTU (Jackson Turbidity Units)	___	___
4. Filtration: 5–8 hour turnover	___	___
5. Water level: over the gutter (pool not in use)	___	___
6. Vacuuming: every 1–2 days	___	___
7. Decks: sanitized 2–3 times a week	___	___
8. Langlier Saturation Index: between −.3 and +.3	___	___
9. Free Chlorine: 1.0–1.5	___	___
10. Chloramines: less than .3 ppm	___	___
11. pH: 7.4–7.6	___	___
12. Total Alkalinity: 100–150 ppm	___	___
13. Calcium Hardness: 100–300 ppm	___	___
14. Total Dissolved Solids: less than 800 ppm	___	___

Routine daily maintenance should be recorded in a daily pool log which is acccessible to custodial and aquatic staff. The log should contain information such as:

1. Who opened the pool and time opened.

2. Name of lifeguard for each class/activity.

3. Environmental factors—chemical levels, Langlier Saturation Index, humidity, air and water temperature.

4. Filter operation.

5. Chemicals added.

6. Vacuuming.

7. Miscellaneous maintenance.

8. Who closed pool, who witnessed the securing of the pool and time closed.

Remedial practices consist of making repairs as soon as notified if the condition can lead to an accident. A remedial maintenance form should be completed by the staff member who identifies the condition. The form should be completed and forwarded to the maintenance or housekeeping staff with a copy forwarded to the administration and one retained by the aquatic director. Such a form should include the following information.

Remedial Maintenance Form

Part I—Identification of Condition

1. Hazardous equipment or condition: _____ _____ _____
                                                       Time   Date

2. Maintenance/housekeeping notified: _____ _____ _____
                                                      Time   Date

3. Administration notified: _____ _____ _____
                                                 Time   Date

4. Reported by _____

5. Action Recommended_____

   _____

6. Action taken to prevent injury _____

   _____ _____ _____
                                        Time   Date

Part II—Action Steps

1. Received by Maintenance/Housekeeping_____ _____ _____
                                                      Time   Date

2. Condition verified by_____ _____ _____
                                                      Time   Date

3. Action steps taken   1. _____ _____ _____
                                                   Time   Date

                         2. _____ _____ _____
                                                   Time   Date

                         3. _____ _____ _____
                                                   Time   Date

4. Action steps completed 1. _____ _____ _____
                                                   Time   Date

                         2. _____ _____ _____
                                                   Time   Date

                         3. _____ _____ _____
                                                   Time   Date

5. Verified complete_____ _____ _____
                      Aquatic Director   Time   Date

Preventive maintenance is an ongoing process which involves continuing education and actually seeking out potential hazards. Continuing education includes course work in pool chemistry/maintenance, aquatic facility management, and aquatic liability. For example, has your pool custodian completed a pool operations course offered by:

1. Your state health or environmental resources department?
2. YMCA (P.O.O.L.) Pool Operator on Location?
3. National Recreation and Parks Association Pool Operators Course?
4. AAHPERD Aquatic Council Pool Chemistry/Filtration Course?

Annual maintenance also helps eliminate potential hazards. Questions regarding annual maintenance involve cleaning and inspection. Does your maintenance staff annually:

1. Drain the pool (if possible)?
2. Clean sand filter surface or the Diatomaceous Earth Elements?
3. Clean chemical feeders and containers?
4. Inspect the bottom and drain covers?

A weekly safety inspection is also a part of preventive maintenance which is often overlooked or considered too time consuming. A simple weekly check sheet should be completed and kept on file. The following equipment and areas must be carefully inspected:

1. Walkways
2. Fences
3. Doors/locks
4. Pool Office
5. Locker Rooms
6. Signs/exits
7. Shower Room
8. Drying Room
9. Rest Rooms
10. Pool Entrance
11. Deck
12. Safety Equipment
13. Fixed Equipment
14. First Aid
15. Filter Room
16. Chlorine Room
17. Chemical Room
18. Chemical Containers
19. Storage Room
20. First Aid Room

SUPERVISION AND INSTRUCTION

Supervision and instruction are safety factors which combine with safe design and proper maintenance to provide the lowest possible risk in school aquatic programs. Supervision is simply defined as being in charge of others as they participate in aquatic activities. The supervisor can be the aquatic director overseeing the daily operation of the pool, or the teacher overseeing students in a swimming class.

Supervision may be classified as general and specific. General supervision means that school aquatic professionals have responsibilities which extend to the equipment rooms, shower room, drying room, and locker rooms, as well as the pool. For aquatic coaches, general supervision responsibility extends to the bus, restaurants, other schools, and the weight room in addition to other athletic equipment and facilities used by the team. Specific supervision encompasses the pool, equipment, conduct of the activity, and care of the individual participants.

Swimming and aquatic activities have long been recognized by the profession and the courts as hazardous, requiring close supervision and careful instruction. Unlike basketball, tennis, and other land activities, recreational swimming requires constant supervision (a lifeguard). The elements of safe aquatic supervision include personnel, the environment, safety equipment, an organization and control system, record keeping, and insurance.

Personnel employed by the school are significant factors in providing the school district with safe instruction. Of primary concern in the supervisory process is the aquatic director. A professional aquatic director should possess the following qualifications:

1. BS in Education: emphasis or major in Aquatic Administration.

2. Three to five years teaching/aquatic facility administration experience.

3. Certification as YMCA or Red Cross Swimming Instructor, Lifeguard Training, CPR, Standard First Aid, Swimming Pool Operator, and Aquatic Facilities Management.

4. Experience as participant or coaching aquatic sports (swimming, diving, water polo, synchronized swimming).

5. Knowledge of (basic or instructor level certifications preferred) a variety of aquatic activities such as springboard diving, scuba, synchronized swimming, adapted aquatics, aquatic fitness, and pre-school swimming.

6. A recognition certificate by the Aquatic Council of AAHPERD as a teacher or Master Teacher in any of the 16 subject areas.

Another professional concern is for the faculty who teach courses in the aquatic curriculum. Their qualifications should include:

1. BS in Education: Emphasis as an Aquatic Specialist.

2. Certification as a YMCA or Red Cross Swimming Instructor.

3. Certification as an instructor by YMCA or Red Cross in the aquatic specialty areas that the teacher will be responsible for in the school curriculum.

4. Certification in lifeguard training, CPR and Standard First Aid.

5. Recognition certificate by the Aquatic Council of AAHPERD as "Teacher of" or "Master Teacher of" in the aquatic specialty areas being taught in the school curriculum.

Lifeguards are a recognized standard of care and no school swimming program should function without a lifeguard on duty for every class and activity. This has been a standard identified by the American Red Cross since the publication of their Swimming and Aquatic Safety test in 1981. It has been proven time and again that the teacher cannot adequately provide instruction while working simultaneously in the capacity of a lifeguard. Many school districts have employed an adult who resides in the community to provide lifeguard services for their classes. Lifeguards must not be assigned instructional duties—their responsibility is entirely focused on the observation and supervision of the students in the pool area. Lifeguard qualifications include current certification in:

1. YMCA or Red Cross Lifeguard Training.

2. CPR—Basic Life Support Course.

3. First Aid—Standard or Multimedia Course.

The environment is a key element in the safe conduct of school swimming classes. The environmental factors listed below are necessary for the safe conduct of swimming classes:

1. Lighting—100 foot candles of illumination at the surface.

2. Clear water—.1–.2 Jackson Turbidity Units.

3. Signs—emergency exits, entrances to locker rooms.

4. Pool rules—enforced and posted in pool areas and locker rooms clearly describing expected behavior in a positive manner.

5. Air temperature—3 degrees F above the water temperature.

6. Bottom markings—lane indicators in the swimming area or crosses on bottom 6 feet out in front of each diving board. These markings serve as a point of reference for divers, enhancing depth perception and visual activity.

7. Walking surfaces (deck, starting blocks, diving boards)—clean and non-slip.

8. Obstructions—no obstructions or equipment left out on the deck. Underwater obstructions such as ladders, safety ledges, hopper bottoms, drains, hydrostatic relief valves must be painted with contrasting colors.

9. Telephone—with a list of emergency phone numbers.

Appropriate safety equipment must be available to provide for rescue and first aid. Fundamental equipment includes:

1. First aid kit—developed for aquatic purposes, checked and re-supplied weekly.

2. Backboards—minimum of 2 designed according to Emergency Medical

Services (EMS) specifications.

3. Reaching poles—at least one on all four sides of the pool.

4. Rescue tubes or rescue cans—at least two, as it is always good to have flotation equipment available for a variety of rescues.

5. Blankets—(minimum of 2) helpful for shock.

6. Gas mask—(SCBA) Self Contained Breathing Apparatus is necessary in pools which use chlorine gas, bromine, calcium, or lithium hypochlorite.

7. Miscellaneous equipment—O_2 inhalator and splints depending on ambulance response time.

The conduct of a safe swimming class is also contingent upon organization and an effective control system. This control system has a minimum of eight components:

1. Lesson plan—written and kept on file.

2. Course syllabus—identifies activities which will be taught and specific information on how the class will be conducted.

3. Oral orientation—covers the syllabus in detail to rule out lack of communication with those students who might not read the syllabus.

4. Emergency/accident management procedures—written and rehearsed, planned responses to each situation which could possibly occur in the facility or program. The following list includes the minimal considerations:

   a. *Emergencies* (no injury at this stage).
   - power failure
   - fire
   - C_{12} gas leak
   - tornado
   - securing or closing the pool

   b. *Accidents*.
   - drowning/near drowning
   - spinal cord injury
   - severe bleeding
   - trauma—wounds, broken bones
   - seizures

5. Communication—in the event of an emergency, accident or other situation where it is important to get the attention of the class, a whistle or an air horn is necessary. An emergency alarm switch in the pool which sounds in the administration or nurses office may be helpful as well.

6. Active supervision—the teacher must stay close, especially in high risk activities such as diving, springboard diving, scuba and water polo. At no time should the teacher or lifeguard leave the class or pool area while an activity is in progress.

7. Record keeping—retain all lesson plans, incident and accident reports, student skill test results, maintenance requests, staff meeting minutes, in-service training logs, and personnel evaluations.

8. Insurance—students should be encouraged to purchase accident insurance. Teachers and aquatic directors would be wise to obtain a minimum of $1,000,000 of professional liability insurance.

Safe, quality instruction is comprised of several key elements. The important elements of safe instruction include lesson plans, participant readiness, teacher qualifications, identification of high risk activities, and the conduct of the activity. The following list contains important concerns for the safety conscious teacher

1. Lesson plans—daily lesson plans should be developed in accordance with texts and standards developed by the YMCA of the USA and American Red Cross.

2. Participant readiness—to determine motoric readiness students should be screened with a swim test to determine if their skill level justifies involvement in the class. A procedure should also be developed regarding student health and medical excuses which will determine when they can go back in the water after a period of illness. Psychological readiness is also a concern. Some students come to class with learned or perceived fears about drowning. Coercion, embarassment, or force should never be used as a means of gaining participation, especially in high risk aquatic activities.

3. Aquatic Activities which have high risk potential:

a. Diving—from pool side or starting blocks into less than 5 feet of water.

b. Springboard diving.

c. Skin and scuba diving.

d. Beginner and advanced beginner classes.

e. Water polo.

f. Adapted aquatic classes and activities.

4. Personal teacher qualifications:

a. Teachers must be certified in swimming and other specialty activities they will be teaching.

b. Continued certification must be maintained.

c. Teachers must update when national agencies such as Red Cross and YMCA change their courses and standards.

d. Updating in aquatics also includes attending the variety of workshops and courses offered by:

- colleges and universities
- Aquatic Council of AAHPERD
- CNCA—Council for National Cooperation in Aquatics
- NRPA—National Recreation and Parks Association
- state and county health departments

The actual conduct of the aquatic activity is the final step in assuring a safe aquatic experience for all students. Conduct of an activity involves:

1. The lesson plan. Of particular importance are:

a. Psychomotor objectives—they must be realistic for the swimmer's skill level, justifiable and consistent with YMCA and Red Cross standards.

b. Relate all class activities directly to planned objectives.

c. Provide clear verbal descriptions of skills, a demonstration or film of the skill and a great deal of closely supervised practice.

d. Include written safety considerations into each plan.

e. Do not deviate from the plan.

2. A course syllabus. A handout should be provided which identifies course requirements and performance standards. A statement should also be made requesting students to identify medical conditions such as hypoglycemia, diabetes, seizures, allergies which might affect their safety while swimming and diving.

3. Checking safety, instructional and fixed equipment. Items used for rescue or participation should be checked daily and fixed equipment (i.e. ladders, diving mounts and boards) checked weekly.

4. Emergency/Accident Management Procedures. During the first day of class, several students should be identified to participate in an organized response to a class emergency. These students can assist by clearing the pool, keeping other students away from an accident victim and securing assistance from other school officials.

5. Teacher attitude. The teacher must be a good role model. Pushing students into the pool and clowning on the diving board are examples of unacceptable behavior.

6. Teacher/Student Ratio. Acceptable ratios have been identified by professionals and aquatic agencies.

a. Beginner/Advanced beginner: 1 teacher for 15 students.

b. Intermediate/Advanced courses: 1 teacher for 22 students.

Teachers should not be expected to instruct a class with diverse swimming ability without teacher aides (properly certified) or other teachers assigned. In addition, a lifeguard must always be assigned to each class or activity being conducted in the pool.

7. Class Orientation. Students must be informed during the first class meeting and reminded frequently of class protocol such as:

a. staying out of the water until being told to enter by the teacher.

b. chewing gum not permitted during class.

c. warning about drugs and alcohol.

d. obeying the rules of the pool.

e. identifying other expected behaviors.

8. Warnings. Clearly identify high risk activities such as diving into shallow water and tell the students what the consequences are i.e., quadriplegia. Identify and warn about the proper use of equipment such as starting blocks and springboards.

9. Aquatic equipment. Be sure to use equipment as it was intended to be used by the manufacturer.

COMMON NEGLIGENCE IN SCHOOL AQUATIC PROGRAMS

Listed below are the common causes of liability cases identified by attorneys, expert witnesses, and professionals over the past 20 years. They are:

1. Improper location or absence of a lifeguard.

2. Improper location or absence of the teacher or coach.

3. Unacceptable teacher/student ratios.

4. Large classes (more than 25 students) with diverse skill levels (beginner to advanced level) under the direction and supervision of one teacher.

5. Improper instructional techniques.

6. Failure to use lead up skills or acceptable progression.

7. Failure to warn and identify the consequences of student behavior.

8. Equipment failure.

9. Inadequacy of instruction (teacher unqualified or uncertified).

10. Expired aquatic certifications (failure to re-certify) and false certifications.

Aquatic teachers should know that all accidents cannot be prevented. However, reasonable attempts made in conjunction with the guidelines provided in this chapter will provide an excellent defense. Caring and professionalism *does* count.

REFERENCES

Fairbanks, A. R. (1983). Swimming. In N. J. Dougherty (Ed.), *Physical education and sport for the secondary school student* (pp. 267–287). Reston, VA: The American Alliance for Health, Physical Education, Recreation, and Dance.

CHAPTER 18

Track and Field

LeROY T. WALKER
North Carolina Central University
Durham, NC

There are many approaches to the development of a safe environment in track and field. The literature is replete with specific recommendations which are essential to provide a safe environment for individual activities. There is, however, less discussion about the *total* environment in track and field—a sport in which multiple events are the core of competition.

Of equal significance to the provision of a safe environment in track and field is a basic understanding of the multiple events. Therefore, safety in track and field is tied to demonstrated knowledge of the coach or teacher.

It is generally agreed that knowledgeable and sensitive leaders can produce motivation to achievement, enjoyment, self-fulfillment, and improved skills if the athletic experience is conducted in a safe environment. Safety in track and field demands attention to the performance of the specific events. However, to guarantee the overall safety in multi-event competition, other factors must be considered.

The following general safety rules must be adhered to by the leaders and participants alike.

1. In view of the fact that many activities are conducted at the same time, it is imperative to look around before walking onto the track to avoid walking into the path of a runner or hurdler.

2. Before walking into the throwing area, look to see that the throwing circles are not occupied.

3. If jumpers are on the runway, do not walk into the path of a jumper.

4. If a participant is preparing to throw, look first to see that the area is clear.

5. Do not throw implements back toward the throwing circles.

6. If walking during a recovery phase of a workout, move either to the outside lane or completely off the track.

7. Do not walk between hurdles if a hurdler is approaching.

8. Do not leave implements on the track or on the field which may trip a performer.

There are a number of additional factors which must be observed in safety in track and field. Among them are

- equipment safety
- selection of clothing
- running surfaces
- training format

Equipment safety. The quality and quantity of equipment (and supplies) available for instruction influence the safety factor in track and field.

Clothing. Track and field athletes participate in a variety of weather conditions including heat, cold, and rain. It is also necessary to wear support gear in some events. Participants should avoid support garments that restrict movement.

It is important to avoid wearing rubberized or plastic clothing. Increased sweating does not cause permanent weight loss. The rubberized or plastic clothing does not allow body sweat to evaporate. Excessive dehydration and salt loss may eventually lead to heat stroke and heat exhaustion.

A variety of shoes are required to service participants in the multiple events of track and field. Shoes for running are of different construction than those intended for field events. Since the athletes are of varying body build, the shoes must be pliable, properly fitted, provide for excellent support, and fit firmly but not too tight.

Running surface. It is a "safety must" to avoid constant work on hard synthetic surfaces which lead to foot and leg problems. However, the surface itself may not create as much a problem for the athlete as improper foot strike. The coach must be aware of the proper foot strike for various events and train the athlete appropriately.

TRAINING FORMAT

A series of factors must be considered in developing safety control in track and field. Among the factors are mode, frequency, duration, and intensity.

Mode. It is always best to utilize conditioning or pre-conditioning activities prior to competition. The selection of activity may vary but should focus on cardio-vascular endurance (walking, jogging, running).

Frequency. This factor is important but less critical than duration and intensity. In developing a margin of safety, the coach must develop a training regimen which creates and exercises habit.

Duration. Research reveals that a safe approach to duration is to modify the length of performance according to the maturational level of the athlete. In general, 20–30 minutes of intense training per activity category provides the greatest return for the time invested.

Intensity. In viewing a safe approach to training, it is recommended that the athlete generally works at 60–80% capacity.

BASIC SAFETY LAWS

Safety in track and field demands that several basic laws be followed to guarantee a margin of safety in training.

Flexibility training is critical to safe participation and demands adherence to the following principles.

1. Specificity—flexibility training must focus on joint action and the demands of the event, e.g., running vs. throwing or jumping.

2. Overloads—gains in flexibility take place when the participant achieves the limit of existing range regularly, thus allowing new limits to be set.

3. Reversibility—improvement in flexibility will be lost if regular work is not maintained.

In the attempt to achieve greater safety in training, several pitfalls must be avoided.

1. Insufficient warm-up. Training with weights without warm-up causes many injuries.

2. Over training. This occurs when the body is being worked so vigorously that it does not have time to repair itself.

3. Hard training sessions before a competition.

4. Weight training too often.

5. Increasing body weight without an appropriate increase in strength.

6. Increasing bulk to the point of restricting movement.

SAFETY IN TRAINING FOR SPECIFIC EVENTS

Sprints. It is imperative to develop a balance between strength-building exercise and high repetition movements for greater endurance and improvement in coordination. Speed enhancement in sprinting can be safely pursued by developing both coordination and strength.

Hurdles. The hurdles event demands very serious attention to safety considerations because of the dangers inherent in the event. There must be a verification of the technical preparation of the hurdlers, their coordination, boldness, and rhythm.

To avoid injury caused by faulty hurdle clearance, the hurdlers must have the necessary physical and psychological preparation. Critical to the safety of the participants are: basic training for muscle efficiency stamina and flexibility; belief in the ability to undertake stride conversion in the intermediate hurdles race; and development of the ability to use alternate legs in the intermediate hurdles in an emergency.

Distance running. The primary safety feature in training for distance running requires that the coach recommend physical activity with muscle groups other than the fatigued group. There must also be training variations to avoid boredom. It is desirable to develop a sane training regimen which will stabilize the aerobic capacity of the distance runner. Long distance runners usually develop aerobic capacity to a maximal limit through sustained training. Quality work increase would tend to enhance a safe stabilization. Safety in training for distance running demands:

- discipline which permits and encourages vigorous practice
- development of a good balance between natural speed and endurance
- that the athlete progress through several years of hard work
- that the athlete develop the physio-

logical and psychological capacity to endure pain and fatigue

The javelin. The leader must develop a program of training for strength and flexibility to avoid injury to knees, groin, trunk, sides, lower back, and shoulders. Safety considerations are significant because throwing the javelin is an unnatural movement due to the separation of the hip and shoulder axis and the delayed arm thrust for delivery with elbow ahead of the delivery hand.

PSYCHOLOGICAL AND PHYSIOLOGICAL CONSIDERATIONS

Safety in track and field is significantly influenced by the psychological and physiological dimensions of training. These factors are most clearly manifested in five areas:

- the running program during the summer months
- the nature and extent of any weight-training program
- the nature and extent of any off-season competition in other sports
- the nature and extent of any injuries that may have been sustained during the summer, or which may have lingered from the previous season
- the event or events for which the athlete will train

The athlete must have a complete understanding of the facts concerning proper care of the body. It is important to use an objective approach to health facts for the well-conditioned body, rather than a long list of training rules which are almost impossible to implement. While there are some fundamental health facts which have a definite influence on the performance of an athlete, most of the "training rule" lists include items which are basically psychological. To break one of the published rules often would have little effect upon the performance of the athlete, but it may have serious social and emotional implications. Goals for the athlete should be high and he/she

should be dedicated to the Spartan simplicities.

PSYCHOLOGICAL CONSIDERATIONS

The athlete is not only the sum of his physical qualities but also an intricate combination of psychological conditions. However great his/her speed or strength, these may be rendered useless if there is not an effective combining of the physical and psychological qualities at the most appropriate moment.

One of the fundamental principles is that psychological conditions change and have varying effects upon the track and field performer.

"Psyching" is a term frequently used by athletes. It refers both to the performer's influence on the opponent and the ability to prepare for competition. "Psyching" takes many forms. It varies from simply ignoring an opponent and exuding confidence in the preliminary warm-up to dropping hints which start an opponent thinking negatively and running for second. A great performance has tremendous "psyching" influence. Psychological effects vary according to strength and length, and they are difficult to explain or predict.

An important point for the athlete to understand is that psychological states may be useful or undesirable. Useful states include interest, readiness, self-confidence, enthusiasm, and perseverance.

Practice sessions should be organized to keep interest and enthusiasm high. A shorter practice session in which motivation and concentration levels are high is much more effective than a longer, loosely organized, and boring session.

The ability to sustain an intense workload is diminished if the athlete has lost the zest for practice. Too frequently, this condition is brought on by an hour and a half workout extended to three hours. Should it be necessary to work over an extended period of time, vary the program, change the work pace— put a little "spice" in the session.

PHYSIOLOGICAL CONSIDERATIONS

The athlete's training in track and field is largely a self-determined responsibility. While the coach may direct practice routine, the athlete is responsible for diet, sleep, and rest.

There are a wide variety of training patterns which the athlete can choose to achieve a physiological base. An understanding of the effects of activity on the human body is absolutely essential in planning the individual workout. Athletes respond differently to weight training or other systems. Select the plan which is best for the individual. Slavish imitation may prove detrimental. Following are some general principles for training.

1. Perform exercises correctly in terms of the results desired. If an exercise cannot be performed correctly for the desired repetitions (usually a minimum of eight), reduce the amount of weight.

2. Increase repetitions each workout until 10 to 12 can be performed. Five to ten pounds should be added to the load when repetitions can be easily handled and performed with less than full effort.

3. Rest 2 to 3 minutes between exercises.

4. Schedule weight training workouts with three factors in mind:
- alternate days for more effective workouts
- space exercises during the workout
- train but do not strain

Perform the exercises in a proper sequence. Shift the demands on muscle groups during workouts. This is accomplished by changing emphasis. Exercise the legs and the back, then the chest and arms. The workouts may vary from 30 minutes to 2 hours, given proper organization.

Muscular strength and endurance increases when exercises are repeated against increased resistance. The following principles should be remembered:

1. Progressively increase the total load.

2. Progressively increase the total time given to a load.

3. Progressively increase the repetitions against a constant and known resistance.

4. Progressively increase the speed of the performance.

5. Increasing the body weight without an increase in strength is bad. Always continue strength-building exercises in combination with weight control measures.

6. Exercising before proper warm-up has been completed is risky.

7. Continuing intense weight-training immediately prior to competition is not desirable. It is essential to allow muscle fibers to repair and recover from soreness.

Every athlete may not have access to a training center. They can, however, improvise their own bar weights to use at home in the basement or back yard. Use of free weights can be of great value in developing the body.

CONCLUSION

Safety in track and field is an ongoing process. It demands attention not only to the individual events, but to the sport as a whole. A safe track and field program depends on the knowledge and experience of the teacher or coach. By following the guidelines set forth in this chapter, he or she can work toward providing the safest possible environment for students.

REFERENCES

Walker, L.T. and D'Annolfo, S. (1983). Track and Field. In N.J. Dougherty (Ed.). *Physical education and sport for the secondary school student* (pp. 321–343). Reston, VA: The American Alliance for Health, Physical Education, Recreation and Dance.

CHAPTER 19

Tumbling

DIANE BONANNO
Rutgers University
New Brunswick, NJ

There was a time when it was standard practice to ask performers to execute their floor exercise routines and tumbling runs on bare wooden floors. We cringe today thinking about the injury that could have resulted from such a request, and undoubtedly look askance at the physical educator or coach who made those demands. We have to ask ourselves, however, if our smugness is well founded. Granted, we may not be making the same blatant mistakes that our predecessors did when they taught this activity, but are we certain that we have considered the element of participant risk from every perspective before we ask our students to become involved?

Logic leads us to believe that tumbling is a high risk activity because participants who engage in the sport often find themselves moving through space in ways that are unfamiliar to them. In truth, when we examine the accidents that occur in this activity, we find that the element of risk is more closely associated with instructor performance, gymnasium conditions, and performer readiness than it is with the dangers inherent in any one specific skill. This is an important observation for it helps us to recognize that the risks in tumbling are usually a function of judgment, a factor that is well within our ability to control, rather than a function of the activity itself. It also helps us to realize that sound judgment is our best defense in cases of liability.

Given two instructors with equal knowledge of the mechanics of tumbling, the one who also possesses information on the potential hazards of the sport has a better chance of conducting an accident-free program. The reason is simple: if you are cognizant of the potential hazards, you can design strategies to avoid them. In the case of tumbling, as in all sports, your risk management strategies should concentrate on the supervision you provide, the environment you create, and the degree to which you prepare your students to participate in the activity.

SUPERVISION

Both general and specific supervision are important in every activity that is taught in the gymnasium. In the case of tumbling, however, the need to form deliberate patterns of teacher behavior are of greater concern than in other activities because tumbling generates a greater variety of individual responses. Placement of mats, student groupings, and the ability of each individual in the class to work independently are just a few of the elements that must be considered to ensure that the teacher's view of the class is not obstructed while giving individual attention to those who need it.

Following is a checklist that should be used when planning strategies to ensure adequate instructor supervision. It includes guidelines for determining the quality and quantity of the supervision needed, the type of organization and control that is necessary, and the planning that must be done to avoid potential hazards.

THE QUALITY AND QUANTITY OF SUPERVISION NEEDED

1. Supervision should only be provided by qualified instructors who have a thorough knowledge of:
- the mechanics of the sport
- appropriate horizontal and vertical skill progressions
- the most up-to-date teaching techniques
- spotting techniques and the use of spotting equipment
- the care and maintenance of matting and safety equipment
- the principles of gymnasium layout
- first aid and emergency procedures
- general student characteristics (physiological, motorical, and emotional)
- individual student readiness

2. Where possible, supervision should be provided by those who possess gymnastics safety certification or the equivalent achieved through in-house training programs.

3. Students should never perform without the aid of a spotter. Where appropriate, individuals in the class can be used to improve the performer/spotter ratio, but it should be remembered that students who assume spotting responsibilities are part of the supervision provided by the teacher. They should, therefore, be specifically trained in proper spotting techniques and safety principles and periodically evaluated on their ability to perform effectively in this capacity.

ORGANIZATION AND CONTROL

1. The tumbling area must never be left unattended while an activity is in progress even if it is for only a few moments. A qualified instructor must be stationed in the area at all times. Note: being in the equipment room, even though it is adjacent to the gymnasium, does not qualify as being present on the floor where the activity is being conducted.

2. The instructor should have the entire tumbling area in view at all times. Even though assistance (direct supervision) is being given to a specific student, the instructor is not relieved of the responsibility of having everyone else in the class within view (general supervision). In other words, physical presence does not constitute supervision, knowledgeable and alert presence constitutes supervision.

3. The instructor should be in the area where the greatest need for assistance is anticipated. If a new skill is being taught to a small group within the class or if an individual is attempting a particularly difficult skill for his or her ability level, the instructor should be present to provide help.

4. Students should always have direct access to the instructor. They should know where to find him or her immediately and they should be taught to seek assistance whenever they are attempting something new or difficult.

5. Students should never have direct access to the tumbling area; it should be locked whenever it is unsupervised.

6. Mats should not be left open or placed in an area where unsupervised students can gain access to them. The prudent person should assume that if mats are accessible and/or open they will be viewed as an invitation to participate.

7. Policies should be developed that explain the department's position on gymnasium security and the steps that are to be taken to ensure that an unsupervised area is never left open to the public. The procedures that emanate from this policy should include:
- an explanation of who is responsible for opening and securing the area
- the exact manner in which the area should be opened and secured
- the times at which the area is to be opened and secured
- the placement/condition of the equipment when the gymnasium is secured

8. Rules of conduct and safety should be posted in several places throughout the gymnasium to serve as a constant reminder of the behavior that is expected. Care should be taken to use words that the participants can understand. The tone, although nonthreatening, should convey to the participant the serious intent of the message. At the very minimum the rules should include the following points regarding supervision:
- without exception, no one is allowed in the tumbling area unless an instructor is present
- tumbling practice may not begin without the express permission of the instructor
- a new skill may not be attempted without the express permission of the instructor
- all tumbling skills must be performed on a mat with the assistance of a qualified spotter
- only teacher approved spotters may be used

9. The safety rules should be reviewed with the students on a regular basis and time should be taken to explain why they are necessary and the type of injury that can result if they are

ignored. As a general rule, the younger the student, the more frequently the instructor needs to present a formal reminder to the entire class.

PLANNING

1. Detailed lesson plans should be prepared for each instructional period. They should demonstrate, without a doubt, that the instructor has considered every aspect of the lesson and that he/she has made every effort to eliminate any potential hazards.

2. The lesson plan should explain the instructor's efforts to provide a well supervised activity. At the very least, it should include information on:

- mat placement and how it relates to the instructor's ability to provide specific supervision while maintaining general supervision
- placement of qualified spotters and their responsibilities as the secondary line of supervision
- the efforts that are taken to make the students cognizant of the safety rules and the conduct of behavior that is expected of them
- an explanation of the efforts that are made by the instructor to make him or herself readily available to the students
- the steps that are taken to ensure the security of the gymnasium and equipment when they are not in use during a supervised class

CONDUCT OF THE ACTIVITY

Conduct of the activity refers to the selection and development of a program as it relates to the age, ability levels and readiness of the students, the type of instruction offered, the measures that are taken to ensure an individual's safety, and the warnings that are given so that the individual understands the inherent dangers of the skill they are about to try. Following are the guidelines which should be considered when planning for a tumbling unit.

PARTICIPANT READINESS

Participant readiness is a very useful concept in tumbling, especially as it relates to liability and risk management. Generally "readiness" refers to the performer's potential for success when attempting a new skill or activity. If the performer demonstrates the requisite elements necessary to perform a skill, we say that his potential for success is much higher than his potential for failure and that he is "ready" to move on in the progression. Level of readiness, therefore, can help us determine what is safe and what is hazardous for each individual in the class.

When we use the word readiness, more often than not, we are referring to the participant's level of motor ability. If the participants have the requisite movement vocabulary to perform a skill we are usually satisfied with their level of readiness and allow them to progress to the next level of difficulty. While this perspective is universally accepted, it presents problems in regard to tumbling and liability.

The unique aspects of tumbling require a carefully planned approach to safety. Tumbling is one of the few activities in which the individual has little, if any, previous experience. This, in conjunction with the fact that tumbling requires the student to move through space in ways that cannot be related to familiar activities, alerts us to other forms of readiness that must be tested before a student can be allowed to move on in the skill progression. In addition to ensuring motoric readiness, we must also ensure an appropriate level of psychological and physical readiness.

Attempting a new activity generates a certain amount of excitement, but it also generates a certain amount of fear which must be dealt with if we are to ensure our students' safety. Fear of failure, fear of the unknown, and a lack of understanding about what may happen to us when we plunge head first into an activity for which we are unprepared are all elements of psychological readiness that must be addressed as our students advance through a tumbling progression.

The issue of physical readiness, on the other hand, relates to the performer's ability to successfully complete a skill based on his/her physical condition. Physical readiness includes two components: (1) the performer's present condition in terms of physical disabilities, muscular strength and endurance, flexibility, postural alignment, and body composition; and (2) the performer's physical status just prior to performance based on a warm up routine.

Following are several points which must be considered when trying to determine or improve a student's level of readiness.

MOTORIC READINESS

1. Stress body awareness activities throughout the tumbling unit.
2. Check to be sure that the student can perform fundamental movements requisite for tumbling.
3. Teach the students to use proper landing techniques.
4. Help the performers to be more aware of what they are feeling when they are executing a skill.

PSYCHOLOGICAL READINESS

1. Never require a student to do a skill that he/she is afraid to do. Work with the student to overcome his/her fears, but never force a student to perform by making threats or suggesting that the student is acting foolishly.
2. Do not put extra pressure on a student to perform by making the accomplishment of a particular skill requisite to receiving a passing grade. Find an alternative method for grading a student's performance. Prepare a list of skills that move horizontally as well as vertically and grade the student on the number of skills attempted. For example, list at least ten variations of the forward roll and the same number of variations for each of the other skills which appear at the simpler end of the skill progression. Base your grade not on the number of skills accomplished in the vertical progression but on the number accomplished overall.

3. Stress self control. Teach the students to be responsible for their own safety and well-being. Have them learn and practice good safety habits. Teaching the students to be in control will help them reduce their fear and any reckless behavior that may result in injury. For their safety and the safety of those around them, have them learn and practice the safety rules. A written handout, which you review with them at the start of the unit, is probably the best means of conveying this information. If you decide to exercise this option, remember to use language that the student can clearly understand. Figure 1 is a sample of a safety handout which can be given to secondary school students participating in a tumbling unit.

4. Keep variety in your lessons. If you provide variety and excitement in your lessons your students will be less likely to try to create variety and excitement on their own.

5. Provide a positive working environment for your students. Demonstrate patience and appreciation for their efforts. Don't indirectly push your students to try skills beyond their means because you only give praise to those who are extremely talented or those who attempt the difficult skills. Be positive about everyone's efforts regardless of how small their accomplishments may be.

6. Prepare your students for emergencies. Much of the anxiety and dread we experience during an emergency is due to our feeling of helplessness in the situation. The actions of those around us appear to be chaotic because we do not have a clear understanding of what is to be done. Preparing our students for emergencies in gymnastics will help us to do three things: (1) alleviate the sense of helplessness that is pervasive; (2) ensure the proper kind of help from our students when we need it; and (3) discuss the possible injuries that can result from an accident in tumbling and what we can do to avoid them.

For Your Safety

Maintaining personal safety in gymnastics is *your* responsibility. To minimize accidents and protect yourself from injury, conduct your own personal safety check at the beginning of every practice session using the outline given below.

Before Performing: Check Your Clothing

☐ Remove all jewelry, including rings and earrings.

☐ Be sure your hair is worn so that it does not block your vision or the vision of your spotter.

☐ Be sure to wear the appropriate footwear. Heavy sneakers or shoes can be extremely dangerous to you and your spotter.

☐ Never chew gum or have anything in your mouth while you are performing.

☐ Wear clothing that is comfortable, but not baggy. Baggy clothing can impede the ability of the spotter to assist you.

☐ Be sure that your clothing is free of buckles, buttons, rivets, or zippers.

☐ If eyeglasses must be worn, be sure they are secured to your head.

Before Performing: Check the Area

☐ Be sure the area is sufficiently matted for the skill you are going to perform. As a general rule, the less familiar you are with the skill and/or the more difficult the skill, the more matting you should have.

☐ Check the matting to be sure that it is not slippery and that it is free of faults such as rips or gashes.

☐ If using more than one mat, be sure that they are securely fastened together.

☐ Check the landing surface to be sure that it can absorb the weight of a landing or fall.

☐ Be sure you place your tumbling strip or individual mat in such a way as to permit ample space for traffic or spotter movement.

☐ Be sure that mats are located a sufficient distance from walls or other apparatus.

☐ Check the area to be sure it is free of small equipment such as balls or ropes that can cause you to trip.

☐ Be sure the pathway you have chosen for your tumbling run does not interfere with someone else's pathway.

☐ When you are not performing, be sure to yield the right-of-way to those who are.

Fig. 1. Student safety checklist.

Before Performing: Screen Your Spotters and Yourself

☐ Do not attempt a skill with a student spotter unless your instructor has given you permission to do so.

☐ Be sure to use two spotters at all times unless two spotters will interfere with the free flow of the movement.

☐ Be sure you have a thorough understanding of the skill before you make your first attempt.

☐ Determine whether you are in the proper physical condition to safely execute the skill. Be sure your body is well conditioned in regard to strength, flexibility, and muscular and cardiovascular endurance.

☐ Do not attempt a skill which requires a level of fitness beyond your present physical ability.

☐ Be sure you understand the proper progression.

☐ Be sure your spotters know what skill you would like to try and that he/she knows how to spot it.

☐ Be sure you know the problems you may encounter when attempting this skill.

☐ Be sure that the spotters are strong enough to spot a person of your size and ability level.

☐ Be sure you trust your spotters and that your spotters are confident in spotting you.

☐ Attempt new skills at the beginning of the workout session before you become fatigued.

At the Time of Performance: Check Yourself

☐ Be sure to warm up sufficiently so that your muscles and joints are ready for the demands you are about to make on them.

☐ Stop and rest when you or your spotter are tired. Your body cannot perform as well when you are tired and you may cause yourself serious injury.

☐ Follow the progression step by step just as the instructor has outlined.

☐ Only attempt skills in which you have received instruction. Instructions given to another individual do not apply to you.

☐ Perform at your level and not above. Do not try something because of a dare or because someone else says that it is easy. Know your limitations and abide by them.

☐ Always use a spotter.

☐ Follow a skill through to its completion; never change your mind in the middle of a movement. You can seriously injure yourself or your spotter if you do.

☐ Be sure your spotter knows exactly when you intend to begin. Have a signal that you have arranged between the two of you so that there is no doubt in anyone's mind that you are ready to begin.

Fig. 1 continued.

7. Generate an attitude of respect and understanding in your gym. Teach your students, through your example, to have respect and understanding for one another. Teach them to step in and assist; help them to be aware of other people and their needs.

PHYSICAL READINESS

1. Before the tumbling unit begins, review the students' medical reports with the school nurse or the athletic trainer. Be familiar with any condition a student may have that could negatively influence their performance in tumbling or that could be aggravated by the activity.

2. Conduct a physical screening program before the tumbling unit begins. Determine a level of performance that should be met on each test to ensure a proper level of conditioning for each participant. The screening program should include tests that measure strength and muscular endurance of the arms, abdomen, and legs, tests for flexibility of the shoulder girdle, legs, and lower back, a posture screening to determine defects or misalignments that may be aggravated or cause injury, and a test for body composition or a simple weigh-in. Check points should be set for each test that will help the teacher identify students who will be at risk without a special program.

3. Discuss the physical limitations found in the medical record review and the physical screening with the participant and if necessary with the parent or guardian. During the meeting discuss the physical limitation and the relationship it has to the success/risk in tumbling.

4. Do not allow a student to resume practice after an injury or serious illness unless you have written permission from a doctor or other qualified expert.

5. Prepare an individualized program for anyone you have identified as having special needs. The program should have a fitness component as well as a listing of approved skills which can be ameliorated through conditioning.

6. Keep accurate records of all students' progress. Especially document the progress of those for whom you have prepared special programs.

7. Design a basic warm up routine which is required at the start of every tumbling session. Teach the students the warm up routine you have designed. If you do not intend to perform the routine as a group, post the program on the wall in several areas of the gym and explain the importance of its careful and consistent application.

8. Do not combine the warm up routine with a training program. Conduct the warm up routine in the beginning of the workout session and the training program at the end. The warm up routine should be composed primarily of stretching and flexibility activities. Light jogging and skipping should be used to raise the temperature of the body, not to improve cardiovascular fitness. Work to improve any component of fitness should be left until the end of the session.

CURRICULUM AND LESSON PLAN DEVELOPMENT

CURRICULUM

1. The tumbling unit should be outlined in a curriculum guide that is especially designed for the age and general ability level of the students enrolled in the class.

2. The curriculum objectives should reflect an understanding of gymnastics and the general ability level of the participants.

3. The activities that appear in the unit should be directly related to the achievement of the objectives.

4. The activities should be screened to ascertain whether:
- they constitute the most appropriate means of achieving the objective
- they are appropriate for the intended age group
- the teaching staff is capable of delivering the activity
- there is a record of injury connected with the delivery of this activity

- they are recommended by experts in the field
- they fit appropriately in the skill progression

5. The activities should be organized in a proper progression. The progression should:
- move vertically as well as horizontally, that is to say the skill should be presented with many variations so that the performer does not feel pushed to move on in the vertical progression until he or she has sufficiently mastered the skill. Skills can be varied by changing the starting position, changing the finish/landing, putting the skill in a sequence, or changing the position of the arms or legs during movement.
- contain many leadup activities for each skill. The leadup activities should familiarize the performer with the basic components of the skill before they ever attempt the full movement.
- contain body awareness activities
- contain spatial awareness activities
- contain combinations of skills which can be performed safely by those who have mastered the requisite movements

6. The tumbling unit should contain sound justification for its inclusion in the overall curriculum.

7. The tumbling curriculum should contain a series of units that demonstrates expected skill development from grade to grade.

8. The curriculum should outline the appropriate teaching techniques.

9. You should not deviate from the curriculum guide. If you decide to do so, however, you should state this in your lesson plan citing the educational principles you used to reach your decision.

LESSON PLANS

1. Specific lesson plans should be prepared for every lesson you teach.

2. Your lesson plan should include:
- the objectives for the lesson
- the activities that were used to achieve the objectives
- a detailed description of the teaching methods that were used to deliver the activity

3. Taken collectively, your lesson plans should demonstrate the progress of your class in the tumbling unit.

4. Lesson plans should be kept on file in an accessible location such as a central office.

THE STUDENT SPOTTER

1. Train student spotters in the recommended techniques.

2. Give them ample practice with people who can perform the skill before you ask them to spot someone who is just learning.

3. Evaluate them periodically to ascertain their effectiveness.

4. Only ask them to work with someone they can handle. Never ask them to assist someone who outweighs them or is too tall for them to spot safely.

5. Screen the performer they are about spot to be sure the performer is ready to attempt the skill and that he or she demonstrates reasonable potential for success.

6. Never ask them to spot a performer who is attempting a moderately difficult skill unless you have worked with the performer and you are sure he or she only needs slight assistance.

7. Never ask them to spot a performer who is attempting a difficult skill no matter how talented the performer is.

8. Give them frequent breaks to reduce their level of fatigue.

9. Give them every available advantage in terms of matting. Never ask the spotter to assist unless there is ample matting.

10. Only ask them to spot performers who are executing skills from a stationary position. Never ask them to spot someone who is on the run.

THE TEACHER AS SPOTTER

1. Do not substitute spotting for good fundamentals. Do not put a student through a skill unless they are physically, motorically, and emotionally ready.

2. Thoroughly understand the mechanics of the skill before you attempt to spot it.

3. Become familiar with all the things that can go wrong during the execution of a skill so that you are prepared for any emergency.

4. Review the components of the skill with the performers before they begin any attempt. This will allow you to give feedback as well as to reinforce the important aspects of the skill.

5. Explain the mechanics of your spotting technique to the performer so that he or she knows what you are going to do.

6. Try a new spot (one you are just learning) on a performer who has mastered the skill. This should preferably be done in the presence of a qualified instructor who can assist you if necessary.

7. Spot only those students you can easily assist. Never spot someone who is too heavy or too large for your physical capability.

8. Stay close to the performer and provide continuous assistance throughout the execution of the skill. As the performer becomes more accomplished, avoid excessive spotting which may impede the natural rhythm of the movement.

9. Become aware of each performer's idiosyncratic behavior. Prepare for the worst thing they may do.

10. Do not give in to a performer who wishes to try a skill, but who is not ready for the challenge.

11. Use spotting techniques that employ biomechanical principles that assist you in the lift and protect the performer's vital areas (spine and neck).

12. Establish a signal between the performer and you which eliminates any surprise as to the exact time an attempt will take place.

13. Never leave a performer posed to execute a skill and turn to talk to someone else.

14. Never lose contact with the rest of the group while you are spotting a specific person. Between attempts, take time to supervise the area.

15. Never lose your concentration. Complete the entire spot before moving on to correct a situation in another part of the gym.

SAFETY EQUIPMENT

1. Use safety equipment (safety belt, overhead belt, and traveling overhead belt) that best suits the circumstances. The decision should be based on:
- the ability of the gymnast
- the ability of the spotter
- the difficulty of the skill being learned

2. If safety equipment is to be used, you should practice with it on a regular basis so that you can work the equipment efficiently and do not present a hazard to the performer.

3. Only qualified instructors should use overhead safety equipment.

4. Safety equipment should not be used unless it is inspected for safety just before use.

5. You should be familiar with the potential problems associated with using an overhead safety belt so that you are prepared for any emergency.

ENVIRONMENTAL CONDITIONS

In addition to providing effective supervision, appropriate activities, and proper teaching techniques, you have a responsibility to provide a safe environment and well maintained and up-to-date equipment. Following are guidelines you should use to ensure a safe environment for your students.

GENERAL CONSIDERATIONS

1. The tumbling area must never be left open or unsupervised.

2. Tumbling equipment should never be left out in a multi-purpose area. The mats should be secured in an equipment closet. If an equipment room is not available, the mats should be secured in some manner so that they cannot be used by unsupervised students.

3. Warning signs should be posted throughout the area reminding the students of the safety rules, especially those which forbid any type of activity

without the assistance of a qualified instructor.

4. Students should not be allowed to move equipment unless they have been taught how to do it properly. This will protect the students against injury and the equipment from damage through mishandling.

5. Spectators, including students with medical excuses should not be allowed in the tumbling area. A place should be set aside for nonparticipants that keeps them out of the path of the performers.

6. Where safety specifications have been established by a national association or a manufacturer, be sure your facility and equipment meet or exceed the minimum standards.

7. Develop an inspection policy which stipulates:
- the regularity (yearly, monthly, weekly, or daily) with which the equipment and the facility should be inspected
- the specific personnel or outside organization that is responsible for the inspection
- the items to be inspected and the conditions that are considered acceptable
- the records to be kept and the place of filing
- the procedures used to determine whether an item is to be replaced or repaired

8. Be sure the floors are cleaned daily and if need be, between classes, to be sure that chalk, dust, and other slippery material has been removed.

THE TUMBLING AREA

1. The tumbling area should be large enough to accommodate the number of students who will be participating.
2. The area should be free of any pillars or posts.
3. The walls should be free of any protruding parts.
4. The area should be physically separated from all other activities, especially those that require the use of balls. A partition of some sort should be used (i.e. ceiling to floor netting, ceiling to floor moving door). Cones and other such markings are not acceptable unless the opposing activity is compatible (dance is an example of a compatible activity).

5. The area should be easily accessible to emergency first aid personnel.

6. A phone or some other means of communications with emergency personnel should be available on site. If direct communication is not available, a plan which is known to all instructors, should be devised which will ensure the fastest method of obtaining help.

7. The area should not contain windows that are at eye level. Windows, if any, should be located high in the room.

8. Any windows in the area should be masked in some way so that the light that enters is muted. Bright light may interrupt the vision of the performers and cause them to break their concentration or loose their line of sight.

PHYSICAL LAYOUT

1. Place mats in a pattern so that you can maintain a clear line of sight with every group.
2. Be sure that ample space (6–10 feet) is left between each mat to accommodate the traffic flow.
3. Place mats in such a way that you can specify the exact direction in which everyone should tumble.
4. Keep mats at least six feet from walls.
5. Keep mats away from doors including equipment room doors even if the room is not normally used during the class period.
6. Many safe organizational patterns are possible. Figure 2 illustrates two possible configurations.

MATTING

1. Use mats only for the purposes for which they were intended. Information on recommended use can be obtained from the manufacturer and the national bodies governing the sport of gymnastics.

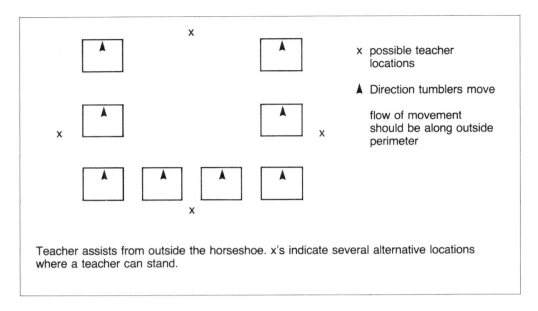

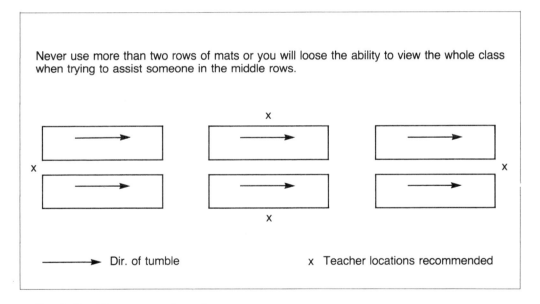

Fig. 2. Tumbling area configurations.

2. Remember that mats are not a substitute for good progressions and competent professional spotting.

3. The amount and kind of matting required will depend on:
• the skill being performed—the more difficult the skill, the more matting required

• the ability level of the performer—the lower the ability, or the less experienced the performer, the more matting required
• the landing required by the performer and the stability under foot required by the spotter
• the age of the performer

- the resiliency of the mat due to age and use

4. Check mats daily for: rips and gashes; worn surfaces; cleanliness; deterioration of cushioning material; resiliency and absorption; and quality of connecting surfaces (e.g. velcro fasteners). Remove mats that require even minimal repair.

5. Be sure all mats have a warning label attached. Extra warning labels can be obtained from the manufacturer to replace worn or lost notices.

6. A two-inch base mat is recommended for basic class work.

7. A landing mat is recommended for teaching difficult skills.

PARTICIPANT WARNING

It is the instructor's duty to notify the participants and if necessary the participants' families of the possible risks in tumbling. A warning in the form of signs that illustrate what can happen to the participant if safety rules are ignored, a personal letter which explains the hazards that are involved with the sport, or a written test which evaluates the student's knowledge of the safety rules and the possible consequences of unsafe practices all provide notice to the participant of the possible hazards in the activity. The decision to use one or all of them will depend on the age and experience of the performers.

SAFETY—AN ONGOING PROCESS

Tumbling can be a safe and exhilarating experience for students if the teacher takes control of the activity and makes it such. Implementing the recommendations made in this chapter will be a positive first step in minimizing the risks associated with the activity. Once the standards are met, however, one should not become complacent. Risk management requires constant vigilance and persistance if we are to constantly ensure the safety of our students.

CHAPTER 20

Volleyball

BARBARA L. VIERA

University of Delaware
Newark, DE

Volleyball is an activity which is relatively safe when played at all levels of ability and by different age groups. For this reason it is a popular activity for backyard barbeques, picnics, parties, and any occasion when people get together to socialize and have a good time. The main reason that this activity tends to be safe is that it is truly a non-contact sport. The two opposing teams are separated by the net and thus there is usually little or no body contact between opponents. If, however, the game is played by two highly competitive teams, there can be contact above and below the net between spikers and blockers. During games played by less skilled players, the danger of injury is greater because players lack effective body control and often fall into the net and over the center line into their opponent's side of the court. Because players are confined to a small area and the game demands constant jumping and movement on the court, it is not surprising that an occasional injury does occur when one player runs into or falls on top of another. These injuries are usually minor. The two body areas which are most susceptible to such injuries are the ankles and the fingers. It is, nevertheless, extremely important to the safety and success of the game that the players maintain a high level of communication on the court. Every time players know that they are going to play the ball it is essential that they call for it to notify their teammates of their intention. Good communication can eliminate many of the more common errors which cause collisions and can, therefore, reduce the potential for injury.

When discussing volleyball safety there are four major areas that need to be addressed: the teaching of proper technique for the performance of the skill; the selection of proper teaching strategies; the proper set up and use of correct and adequate equipment; and the use of proper clothing and protective equipment by the players. Because the repeated use of a body part in an inefficient position can cause muscle pulls, strains, or sprains, players using improper technique are often injured. Teachers must be able to select the correct teaching strategy for the level and strength of their students. A teacher who hits a ball at a student who is incapable of receiving it at the given intensity puts that student in a dangerous situation. The equipment must be up to standard and safely set up. Perfectly good equipment can become very dangerous if it is improperly installed. Finally, students need to prepare themselves for a game by making sure that they are not wearing anything that will be a hazard on the court, and by wearing any necessary protective equipment.

SUPERVISION

When teaching volleyball, there are several things which should be considered in order to make the class as safe as possible. The ideal situation would be one in which there is at least one volleyball available for every student in the class and at least one court for every twelve to fifteen students. Students will learn more quickly if they have the opportunity to handle the ball as often as possible. Unfortunately, however, the ideal situation is rarely found in the everyday teaching environment. When faced with a group of students working in a small enclosed area, there must be some control over how and where the students move. The following is a list of suggestions for making the class fun and safe.

1. In the initial class sessions when basic ball handling is being learned, do not set up the nets. They are not needed and could be an obstruction to free movement.

2. When running drills involving two or more players, make sure that all groups are moving parallel to each other and far enough from each other that there is no danger of collision.

3. The teacher must be in a position in the gymnasium where all students are within view and must be aware of

any extraneous activity which could cause an accident.

4. When the teacher uses a piece of equipment as an instructional aid, it must be used so that it is not a hazard to the students. An example of this is the use of a chair or box for the teacher to stand on when spiking or serving the ball to the students. It must be far enough away from the net so that there is no danger that the blockers will come down on the chair and suffer an injury.

5. In teacher led drills, the goal is to extend the students toward their potential. At the same time, however, it is essential that the teacher know the capabilities of each student so that none are forced to participate beyond their capabilities.

6. When the activity of the day is volleyball, that is the only activity which should be allowed. If the balls are available at the beginning of class for students to use in warming up, they should not be allowed to shoot at the basketball hoop or play variations of bombardment.

7. No student with an injury should be allowed to participate. This is particularly true of finger and ankle injuries.

8. Students should not be allowed to begin their warmup unless the teacher is present in the gymnasium.

9. At the end of class all the volleyballs should be collected and put away until the teacher is ready to begin the next class.

10. Students should practice their drills on the court so that they gain an appreciation of the size of the playing area. Developing an awareness of the players around them helps students build the ability to react appropriately in a game setting.

11. When running drills that involve both spikers and blockers, it is essential that the teacher make the students aware of the danger of balls rolling under the feet of the jumping players. Players who are serving in the role of retrievers for a drill should be told where to return the balls and how to get them there. Players should also be

taught to react to a given signal during drills in case the ball does roll under the feet or toward the feet of jumping players. A simple "NO" spoken with an authoritative voice should be warning enough so that players do not jump until the area is safe.

12. When more than one adjoining court is being used at the same time, it is essential that a rule be established which prohibits players from entering an adjoining court to play the ball. As soon as the ball enters an adjoining court it should be whistled dead by the official or teacher.

SELECTION AND CONDUCT OF THE ACTIVITY

Many injuries occur in volleyball because the student attempts to perform a skill without the proper technique. Students must be taught the proper beginning position and method of execution of each of the basic skills in volleyball. It is also extremely important that the teacher uses the proper terminology in the teaching of the skills. Often a student uses the incorrect technique because they have misunderstood or misinterpreted the teacher's explanation. A good example of this is the expression, "hit the ball with the finger tips," used when teaching the overhand pass in volleyball. In this skill the ball is contacted with the upper two joints of the fingers and not the finger tips. If players attempt to hit the ball with the finger tips they are likely to jam their fingers. Following is a list of considerations for teaching the basic skills of volleyball. Understanding and implementing them will help to insure that the students learn proper technique and therefore play a safe game.

1. Make sure that the correct terminology is used so that students thoroughly understand what is expected of them.

2. Teach the students the skills they need to gain good body control. This is particularly important in three areas:

a. Teaching spikers how to stop forward momentum into the net. The planting of the heels before take-off is essential.

b. Teaching blockers how to move to join a teammate for a double block without knocking that player over. It is the middle blocker's responsibility to move to the outside blocker and not to the ball.

c. In defensive techniques in which the player hits the floor to save a ball, the player must be skilled in the proper method of falling. It is important that when falling the player learns to land on the body parts that have sufficient muscular padding and not on parts that are boney such as the knees, elbows or hips.

3. When teaching the block and spike, make sure that students learn to land on both feet simultaneously. Landing on only one foot puts extra strain on that foot. If the player comes down on one foot and lands on a teammate's or opponent's foot, it is very likely that a serious sprain will result.

4. When teaching the spike in volleyball, make sure that the students hit the ball with a fully extended arm. Hitting the ball with a bent arm makes the player depend heavily on the rotator cuff muscles for attaining power. This added strain on the rotator cuff can cause tendonitis. On the other hand, when hitting with an extended arm you use the powerful muscles of the shoulder and back (Johns, 1977).

5. When teaching the dive or sprawl, make sure the players flex their knees and arch their backs. Failure to do these things causes the player to jam the toes into the floor causing bruised joints, especially of the big toe (Johns 1977).

6. Make sure students condition their ankles.

7. If a student has weak ankles, they should be taped before each class and competition.

ENVIRONMENTAL CONDITIONS

The equipment used in volleyball is relatively simple. It consists of a net, standards for holding up the net, and volleyballs. If the competition is at a high level, the net also needs to be equipped with antennae. These should be attached to the net near the sideline, the exact location depending on the set of rules governing the competition. During competitive volleyball it is also essential to have an official's stand. The United States Volleyball Association, the National Association for Girls and Women in Sport, and the National Federation of State High School Associations all publish rules and each set includes specific regulations pertaining to the safety of participants. Following is a list of considerations for the teacher when setting up the gymnasium either for a class or for a competition.

1. The best standards are usually fairly heavy and must be handled with care when setting them up. Some standards include a base and will stand on their own as long as there is no tension placed on the net before they are firmly attached to the floor. If a slight tension is placed on the net, however, the standards will fall over very easily. When the teacher uses student assistants to set up, they must be aware of this danger. It is possible for a standard to fall over and hit a student and the resultant injury could be very serious. Teachers should make sure that the standards are held upright by someone until they are attached to the floor. This will eliminate the chance of an accident.

2. The standards must be placed at least three feet from the sideline.

3. Round standards are less hazardous to the players than any other type.

4. Standards which fit into a sleeve in the floor are safer than those with a base which requires guide wires. Support wires are very dangerous to a player who is moving to play a ball and is unaware of their location. If guide wires must be used, the heavy chain type are

better than the wire cable type, and any type must be covered with a soft, flexible material. The National Federation of State High School Associations requires that this material be at least ½" thick and that must be applied to a height of 5½ feet (True, 1986–87).

5. The standards, referee's stand, and all the tensioning devices should also be covered by soft, flexible material. The National Federation of State High School Associations recommends this material be at least ½" thick (True, 1986-87).

6. The cranks which are used to place tension on the net should be removable if at all possible. If they are not, the type which fold back so that they are not sticking out would be the next best. If neither of these types are available, the tensioning mechanism must be completely covered with soft flexible material (Smith, 1986).

7. The antennae must be securely fastened to the net. Each antenna has a device to attach it to the net. Once attached, a piece of white athletic tape should be wrapped around the attachment for added security and also to protect the player from being hurt on the antenna. If, during a competition, an antenna becomes dislodged, the competition should be halted immediately until it can be reattached. A loose antenna could cause a serious eye injury.

8. The wire cable which extends through the net should have a plastic covering on it. This prevents the wire from splintering and causing injury when anyone touches it as they try to set up the net. The cable at the bottom of the net should be rope, as rope is less likely to cause injury to a player who accidently runs into it.

9. Due to the high degree of tension placed on the nets to get the correct height, a great deal of stress is also placed on the floor plates used with standards that have a base. Often when these standards are improperly attached, or if no guide wires are used when they are needed, the floor plates

begin to raise up from the floor. These plates can become a hazard to unsuspecting athletes when the standards are not in place.

10. If wire supports are used for the standards, it is recommended that in addition to covering them, strips of material be hung from the wire to alert players of their presence (Smith, 1986).

11. A clear area should surround the court. The United States Volleyball Association recommends that this clear space be at least three meters for an outdoor court and at least two meters for an indoor court (Smith, 1986).

12. The surface of the court must be smooth and should not be abrasive in any way.

13. If an outdoor court becomes soft or slippery, the game should be stopped immediately (Smith, 1986).

14. Any off-court areas where hazards exist should be declared nonplayable. Players should not be allowed to enter nonplayable areas for the purpose of playing the ball. Players should be made aware of this and during play the ball should be whistled dead as soon as it goes into such an area.

15. For beginners, the air pressure in the ball should be kept at the lower end of the acceptable range. Unfortunately, most teachers have a tendency to make the ball pressure too high which causes the ball to hurt the student's forearms and even cause some bruising.

16. During competition, the floor often gets wet after a player falls while making a good defensive effort. It is essential that the competition be halted until the floor can be toweled dry. The wet surface is extremely slippery and very dangerous.

17. Certain items worn by players can help protect them from injury. There are also several items which can be a hazard to the wearer or to other participants in the game. Following are suggestions for a player's personal equipment that help to prevent injury.

   a. Long sleeved shirts help to protect the arms and elbows from floor burns, particularly when the player is forced to hit the floor during a defensive maneuver (Johns, 1977).

b. Knee pads are highly recommended at all levels of play. They protect the knees from floor burns and bruises. Many players are not as inhibited about hitting the floor when they wear knee pads and thus have better defensive skills.

c. All three sets of rules prohibit the use of jewelry and certain other articles during play. Generally, rings, bracelets, dangling earrings, and necklaces long enough to clear the chin must be removed. Although post earrings are allowed, it is recommended that these also be removed as they can get caught in the net or on another player's clothing and cause damage to the ear (Smith, 1986).

d. The wearing of a hard cast is not allowed on any part of the body. Hard splints or other protective devices are not allowed to be worn on any body part waist high or above. Soft bandages of any type are allowed (Smith, 1986).

e. Protective type braces for the lower extremities are allowed as long as there are no exposed metal parts that may be a hazard to other players (Smith, 1986).

f. Prosthetic limbs may be worn under certain conditions. They may have to be approved by the governing body of the rules being used. It would be wise to check in advance and get the approval in writing so that there will be no problem with the officials on the day of a competition. These devices should be covered with padding and should not endanger the other participants in any way.

g. Anything worn on the head should be soft and pliable. Hats are not allowed but sweat bands, barrettes, and bandanas used as sweat bands are all allowed as long as they are being used to secure the hair and not just for adornment. Braided hair with beads must not be allowed to swing freely in a hazardous manner (Smith, 1986; True, 1986–87).

h. All players should wear appropriate footwear.

i. Eyeglasses should have unbreakable lenses and should be firmly attached to the head.

j. It is strongly recommended that gum chewing not be allowed during participation.

REFERENCES

Johns, D. (1977). Care and prevention of common injuries in competitive volleyball. *Volleyball Technical Journal, 4,* (1), 46–50.

National Association for Girls and Women in Sport. (1986). *Volleyball Guide.* Reston, VA: American Alliance for Health, Physical Education, Recreation, and Dance.

Smith, R. E. (Ed.). (1986). *United States Volleyball Association Official Guide.* Colorado Springs, CO: United States Volleyball Association.

Tomasi, L. (1979). Injury prevention and treatment. In B. Bertucci (Ed.), *Championship volleyball by the experts* (pp. 245–259). West Point, NY; Leisure Press.

True, S. S. (1986–87). *Official high school volleyball rules.* Kansas City, MO: National Federation of State High School Associations.

Viera, Barbara L. (1983). Volleyball. In N. J. Dougherty (Ed.), *Physical education and sport for the secondary school student* (pp. 345–363). Reston, VA: The American Alliance for Health, Physical Education, Recreation and Dance.

CHAPTER 21

Wrestling

DOUGLAS PARKER

Springfield College
Springfield, MA

photo by Jim Kirby

Wrestling is an exciting activity for students of all ages. Facilities and equipment are much improved compared to past years and interscholastic wrestling is ranked among the top five sports in numbers of participants and teams. However, considering the dual combative nature of the activity, it is obvious that safety factors must be a high priority with physical education teachers.

In some parts of the country, elementary school students are familiar with wrestling. Many of them have seen interscholastic matches and some have older brothers who are on wrestling teams. Unfortunately, however, the only kind of wrestling that many other elementary school students have seen is the fake "rassling" seen on television. It is very important, therefore, that students be informed never to use techniques that would endanger their opponent's life or limb. The Federation of State High School Associations' film *The Winning Edge: Wrestling by the Rules* is immensely valuable is reinforcing this concept. It is a one reel film, 18 minutes in length, and is available from the federation's Kansas City, Missouri office. This film should be viewed by all students prior to the start of a wrestling unit.

To present a high quality wrestling instructional program, it is advisable to start dual combative activities at the third grade level. By this time, the students have experienced self-testing activities and are psychologically ready to test themselves against others. If safety measures are stated emphatically by the teacher, the students will be aware of and establish patterns of behavior which will show concern for the safety of others. It is not uncommon for some students who have not experienced simple dual combatives at eight or nine years of age to be apprehensive about participating in actual wrestling when they are older. Simple combative activities, therefore, such as chicken fighting, foot push, hand wrestling, hop and pull, chest wrestling, and arm lock wrestling will provide for the needs and interests of students. This type of activity will also help students develop the balance necessary for actual wrestling.

The teacher should refer to the current *Official high school wrestling rules* (National Federation of State High School Associations,) for illegal holds and illustrations of these holds. The rule book also includes potentially dangerous holds. Some techniques and holds, although legal, may be dangerous if not executed properly. The instructor must guide the student in the defensive position as well as the person performing the technique. Some positions are uncomfortable and may be frightening to a beginning wrestling student. The front cradle hold is an example of this situation. Some students may feel they will have trouble breathing when held in this position and their opponent's body weight is on them. The teacher should be aware of this, and help the students understand the holds and their reactions to them.

The most potentially serious injury in any activity involves the spinal cord. The physical education teacher presenting a wrestling unit must be aware of those techniques, holds, and body positions that have the potential for injury to the spinal cord. The teacher must present wrestling techniques and activities with special emphasis on this safety aspect, especially with regard to the area of the cervical vertebrae. The teacher should instruct the students to stop any wrestling activity whenever a student's head is in a vulnerable position or injury to the spinal cord may result. Signals should be developed whereby the teacher or an opponent can signal for an immediate release of a potentially dangerous hold. The teacher should introduce all dual combative lead-up activities and actual wrestling lessons with the following neck strengthening activities:

- neck bridging
- resisting half Nelson
- resisting quarter Nelson
- resisting three-quarter Nelson
- combination sit-up and neck resistance exercise

To further emphasize safety measures and also encourage the problem-solving method of learning, the teacher should have the students experience isolated "tasks" or "situation wrestling." Situation wrestling is defined as a trial in which one student will attempt an offensive technique and the other a defensive technique. Examples include the turnover, breakdown, and go-behind.

When the teacher "shows and tells" technique, safety factors should be thoroughly explained. To help with safety measures as well as accelerate the learning process, the teacher should have at least one assistant. The assistant may be a co-teacher, student teacher from a local college or a skilled senior student. Instructional emphasis should be on precise techniques and drills to perfect techniques. Under no circumstances should the teacher's methods emphasize brute strength and aggressiveness. There is no place for a "macho" attitude in the instructional program.

Progressions must be considered by a teacher when presenting wrestling instruction. When young people learn to walk they experience falling, and learn how to fall and adjust to falling without injury. However, since falling techniques are rarely used after early childhood, students must re-learn falling skills. Under no circumstances should a person fall with the fingers pointing backward. This position locks the elbow joint and a dislocation may occur. Falling to the mat safely should be part of every lesson's warm-up period. The teacher should not start the wrestling unit with takedowns, even though the official match starts with the wrestlers in a neutral standing position. For the purpose of safety, takedowns and counters for takedowns should be taught last, after basic techniques and falling skills have been well learned and practiced. When teaching "takedown throw" techniques, especially those involving high amplitude, dummies should be used initially. "Live" throws should only be permitted on an individual permission basis, after the technique has been perfected using a wrestling dummy. The teaching order should be as follows:

1. Falling techniques.
2. Getting out of pinning combinations.
3. Reversing from the defensive position.
4. Breaking the opponent down from a position on hands and knees.
5. Applying pinning techniques.
6. Escaping from the defensive position.
7. Takedowns from neutral position on the knees or at least one knee down.
8. Takedowns from standing.
9. Counters for takedowns.

Because of the complexity of wrestling skills and the potential for injury, it is essential that safety be of the utmost concern to all. Following are concepts that are essential to the safe conduct of a high-quality instructional wrestling program.

THE INSTRUCTOR

1. Presents the important rules of wrestling and assists students in gaining an understanding of potentially dangerous positions and techniques which should be used with caution.
2. Gives beginning students lead-up activities which are appropriate to their ability levels and which relate to some aspects of wrestling.
3. Has interscholastic or collegiate wrestling experience.
4. Has an assistant or student teacher who was a high school or college wrestler.
5. Took a wrestling course in college.
6. Has a working knowledge of basic wrestling techniques and the ability to present them in logical progression.
7. Has an understanding of exercise techniques which will prepare students for wrestling.
8. Presents dual activities or combative games that will not only stimulate students' interest but help them develop balance and other qualities of motor movement necessary for wrestling.
9. Exhibits concern for cleanliness and safety.

STUDENTS

1. Suitable clothing is t-shirt, shorts, and warm-up pants. Loose fitting clothing should not be worn. Belts, buckles, zippers, snaps, etc. are not allowed.

2. Rings, watches, bracelets, necklaces, earrings, and other forms of jewelry may not be worn.

3. Fingernails must be trimmed beyond the ends of the fingers.

4. Hair should be cut short.

5. Clean socks should be worn. Shoes should be taken off and left around the edge of the mat. The soles of shoes carry bacteria, as well as dirt. Sneakers with heavy soles may also cause injury.

6. The students should be weighed and their actual weights recorded. Names and weights should be posted. Students should not be matched up with more than a 10 lb. difference in weight.

7. Students should be prohibited from wrestling when recovering from illnesses or injuries.

8. It is recommended that the teacher do skinfold tests on the students to determine their lean body weight. Skinfold calipers are inexpensive and the procedure is simple.

9. Students should be paired or partners selected based on weight, age, and physical development. Lean body weights are more important than actual weights.

10. Students must recognize their responsibility for their partners' safety as well as their own.

11. Students should be aware of other students' place on the mat as well as their own.

12. Students will be required to officiate matches and supervise classmates. They should be prepared to stop students physically using a "hands on" method and also catch them and command "stop" if they are in danger of going out of bounds.

MATS

1. The wrestling unit should be conducted on a plastic cellular foam mat at least one inch thick. Thicker mats provide more safety. Old packed-down hair and felt mats are not suitable in physical education classes today. Tying these mats together and using a plastic cover is not an acceptable safety practice.

2. The mats should be washed daily with a concentrate that cleans, disinfects, and deodorizes. The product should also serve as a fungicide and virucide.

3. Sections of mats should be securely taped together. If the mats are put down daily, two inches of tape is satisfactory, providing that it is applied well. Three inches or four inches of tape is recommended if the mats are used for several days or weeks.

4. The temperature of mats should be between 60 and 70 degrees. A mat at 40 degrees is hard, rigid, and has a "boardy" surface. It will not absorb as much shock. A mat at 90 degrees is soft and has a greater tendency to "bottom out."

5. It is advisable to recondition foam mats every five years. If the vinyl coating peels off a mat, the exposed foam core has less ability to provide safety.

6. Foam mats should be turned over periodically so both sides receive equal use.

7. Each pair of students should have 100 square feet of mat space on which to practice. Specific areas can be marked off by tape temporarily or by permanent 10-foot painted circles. The typical 40' × 40' wrestling mat has nine, 10' diameter circles on the practice side. The students should be instructed to confine their wrestlng activity to the area inside the circle. Space between circles is a "buffer zone" for safety.

8. If the wrestling unit is taught in a room with walls close to the mats, the walls should be padded up to a minimum of five feet. Posts, radiators, and

similar protrusions must be padded with mat material.

EQUIPMENT

The teacher should have knee pads, elbow pads, earguards, and face masks in the equipment room and available for students.

An effective and safe teaching method for teachers is to assign three students to a group. One student will be assisting with instruction, leading technique drills, starting and stopping situations, and officiating matches. Obviously, a student cannot assume the responsibility of the teacher, but if properly instructed and supervised, he/she can make the learning environment considerably safer. The students will rotate roles from offense to defense to official. When preparing and writing lesson plans, the teacher should include statements that relate to safety measures. While accidents and injuries may occur, the teacher who emphasizes safety and makes the students aware of potentially dangerous situations will have fewer injuries and accidents as well as a more successful wrestling unit.

CONCLUSION

Many students will enjoy wrestling because of their interest and developmental need for this type of activity. The enjoyment the student receives will relate directly to the teacher's personality, knowledge, wrestling talent, class discipline, experience, and emphasis of safety factors.

REFERENCES

Hess, I. (1983). Wrestling. In N.J. Dougherty (Ed.), *Physical education and sport for the secondary school student* (pp. 383–396). Reston, VA: The American Alliance for Health, Physical Education, Recreation and Dance.

Official high school wrestling rules. Kansas City, MO: National Federation of State High School Associations.

The winning edge: Wrestling by the rules. [Film]. Kansas City, MO: National Federation of State High School Associations.